Unpuzzling Your Past

A Basic Guide to Genealogy

Second Edition

EMILY ANNE CROOM

BETTERWAY PUBLICATIONS, INC.

WHITE HALL, VIRGINIA

Published by Betterway Publications, Inc.
P.O. Box 219
Crozet, VA 22932

Cover design and photograph by Susan Riley
Typography by Typecasting

Library of Congress Cataloging-in-Publication Data

Croom, Emily Anne
    Unpuzzling your past.

    Bibliography: p.
    Includes index.
    1. United States — Genealogy — Handbooks,
manuals, etc.   I. Title.
CS47.C76   1989   929.1   88–34971
ISBN 1-55870-111-7

Printed in the United States of America
0 9 8 7 6 5 4

Table of Contents

Foreword

Friends often have said, "I'd like to work on my family tree, but I wouldn't know where to begin." Or, as they head for a visit with elderly relatives and I advise them to ask lots of questions about their family history, they usually answer, "I wouldn't know what to ask." Or a young friend calls me on the telephone, "I've got a history assignment to do a family tree, and I don't know how to do it." Or I see a family eagerly enter the library 30 minutes before closing time and tell the librarian they want to "look up their family tree."

So, this book is the result of prodding by friends and relatives who wanted very basic information, the kind that is obvious to the experienced searcher or professional historian but not at all obvious to the novice.

Many books are available to help family historians with more advanced searches and the specialized problems of looking for Civil War or Revolutionary War ancestors, immigrant ancestors, or early settlers of the colonies. This book, however, is intended to help the family get started, by answering their most basic questions and by emphasizing the use of family sources, especially the living ones.

Relatively speaking, we have plenty of time to search for the distant past, but preserving the more recent past, the last 80 to 100 years, should take place while the best sources are available: the family members and friends who experienced those years, who knew the great- or great-great-grandparents, who can relate a treasury of family stories and describe the family homes and weddings and Christmas celebrations. I knew only one of my own great-grandparents, and it never occurred to me to sit down and talk with her—until it was too late.

Most families, extended to include cousins, have one or more elders who remember rather clearly events of the early twentieth century and who knew family members whose lives and the stories they told reached back to the mid-nineteenth century. No amount of library research can duplicate or replace what these people can tell us.

Even our own generation lived what many students consider rather ancient history. They find it hard to believe that life existed without television or air-conditioning, just as some of us wonder at "the way it was" before cars or electricity. Probably we ought to record, as part of our family history, our own reminiscences and reactions to what happened around us.

If it is to have meaning, family history cannot be separated from the nation's history and culture. Therefore, to give our family history perspective as well as interest, we must eventually try to put the family into the society and culture in which it lived and worked. This book is intended to help the beginner gather this kind of information, especially for the more recent past.

Finding the family is, of course, the first step. This process is called genealogy, a fascinating, rather addictive hobby which quite naturally begins at home. Like working a jigsaw puzzle, it can involve one person or the entire family. It will take some evaluating and testing to fit pieces together and will give you pleasure and satisfaction as more and more pieces fit into place. The rule-of-thumb "begin with what you know and go from there" is certainly appropriate to genealogy. I like to compare the process to putting together the easily recognized straight-edged pieces of a jigsaw puzzle first to form the frame and then trying the other pieces to find where they belong. In genealogy the straight-edged pieces are the most recent names, dates, and stories that we know or can find easily. Once those are recorded, we have some framework from which to look for more and in which to fit "missing pieces" as we find them. The middle of the puzzle is divided into families, some of which "fall into place" more quickly and easily than others. Working backward in time, or toward the middle of the puzzle, the family historian may complete some sections of the puzzle but never really finishes the whole...and never really wants it to be finished.

If you have wanted to work on your own family tree but never knew just what to do first, this book is for you. If you have done some searching but have not tapped the sources closest to you or in the ''ancestral'' hometowns, this book is for you, too. However you use it, enjoy yourself and have fun working your own special puzzle.

A special word of thanks to those who have pushed me hardest, encouraged me most, and asked lots of basic questions: my sister Judith King; my parents P.B. and Fletcher Croom; and my friends Charlotte Metcalf, Ruth Galey, Lorine Brinley, Ann and Steve Hudson. And a big thank-you to Mrs. Nettie Barnes, my former junior high school teacher, who introduced me to genealogy in the first place.

1

In the Beginning

Has anyone ever asked you where your "people" came from? Your parents? Your grandparents? Your immigrant ancestors? Can you answer?

Or try the question "Who were your great-grandparents?" That's the question that launched my search for family history. I was in the seventh grade. I thought I could answer easily because I had known one of my great-grandmothers. Well, I couldn't. With great confidence I started naming names. When I stopped at four, I was jolted into reality. "What do you mean I've got eight great-grandparents! I've only heard of four." Yes, I have two parents; yes, they each had two parents; yes, those each had two parents. Alas, I really did have eight great-grandparents, but my father's side of the family was one giant blank. Those people were hiding somewhere, and I had to find them.

I took to letter-writing. My dad knew only one older relative. So I wrote to that great-uncle in Tennessee. We corresponded until his death. From him I got a few answers, a few erroneous traditions, and a bunch of cousins. I was on my way! After several visits to Tennessee and a number of years, I feel that I know three of those four "missing persons." For example, Isaac was an asthmatic farmer with 13 kids; he created a few problems by not requiring them to go to school. Pitser was a Methodist farmer who owned a mill and got up at three in the morning to go to work. Mary Catherine hated housework; so she raised peacocks and lambs while her daughter kept house. The fourth? Well, her name was Ann Marie....

Thus, the search goes on. And it goes beyond these four. It reaches as far back as there are records available. It is like working a jigsaw puzzle. Once you have the outside edges put together, the challenge is to find and sort the inside pieces. Some are easy to put in place; some take fine discrimination and careful testing. Sometimes, no amount of searching can turn up evidence of people you know have lived. The puzzle never really gets finished, and you never really want it to.

How many of your great-grandparents can you name?

1. _____
2. _____
3. _____
4. _____
5. _____
6. _____
7. _____
8. _____

Things You Need

The tools for working this puzzle are simple and inexpensive. There are many ways to organize your work. There is no right or wrong way. The only requirement is consistent organization. Having tried several systems, I have found the following to be the most efficient and effective.

1. Three-ring, loose-leaf notebook binder and three-hole notebook paper. These are preferable to spiral notebooks because they allow easy additions of notes, clippings, letters, and photographs. A hole punch is a handy tool when you add these pages.

2. Three-hole dividers, one for each surname. As you gather more information, you can add dividers. Eventually you may divide into new notebooks. My Metcalf–Campbell book has these divisions:

    a. Metcalf–Texas, which covers the most recent four generations;

    b. Metcalf–Alabama, added when I discovered that they came from Alabama;

    c. Metcalf–Georgia, representing the earliest information yet gathered;

    d. Campbell–Texas, covering the wife's family;

    e. Campbell–Alabama, since the two families moved together to Texas from the same Alabama county;

    f. Godwin, a grandmother's maiden name.

As more information on the Godwin line surfaces,

I will divide that section of the notebook.

If you begin with your surname or maiden name, that name becomes a notebook. However, other surnames immediately enter the picture because each generation adds a wife-and-mother and her mother and her grandmother, and so on. You must decide for yourself whether to concentrate on only one line at a time. I could never do that.

In the days before computer-made indexes, I was reading the 1850 Tennessee census, hoping to find my last nameless great-grandparent with her husband and children. I was reading family by family the entire Madison County census looking for my Isaac Croom. Fortunately, the census-taker saved Isaac's part of the county for the latter part of his duties and enabled me to experience one of those electrifying moments of which every genealogist dreams. I came across a man named Sterling Orgain—not your common ordinary name, but the same name as one of my maternal ancestors that I had not been able to find anywhere. Glancing quickly down the list of children, I found my very own great-great-grandmother and the brothers and sisters my grandmother had told me about! No one had had any idea (at least any that proved correct) of their pre-Texas whereabouts; but here they were, in Madison County, Tennessee. So my search in Madison County *had* to include Crooms *and* Orgains.

Why divide the notebooks by state? Frequently families migrated in groups. Elliott Coleman moved from Virginia to Tennessee in 1845 because an aunt and some family friends had moved there and had written back glowing reports. He and a friend decided to try it; soon three of his younger brothers joined them, and a sister moved just across the border into Mississippi. My search for them was centered in that one county, where I found records on all four Coleman brothers. When they witnessed each other's deeds, acted as surety on each other's marriage bonds, bought dry goods from the same merchant, subscribed to the same newspaper, attended the same church and civic functions, conducted business in the same town, their descendants have reams of notes to copy. There is no point in copying each source two or three times and filing under each brother's name. Keeping it all together under "Coleman–Tennessee" gives a good *family* picture. Elliott was not an isolated individual but the oldest brother of a family group.

Elliott married a Patton girl from the next-door county, which was full of her relatives, and now mine, too. This marriage added the Patton section to the notebook. As I read the records of both counties, for Elliott and his in-laws, I made all my notes with a carbon copy, one for the Coleman section and one for the Patton section, if both names appeared in the same record. Otherwise, I kept each page of notes for one family only and marked in the top right-hand corner the surname under which the page was to be filed. (See Figure 1.)

Choose one or two of your surnames to begin with. Remember, you may already have at least eight to choose from, with your eight great-grandparents. Set up your notebook, and you are ready to begin one of the most fascinating, rewarding, never-ending, mystifying, and addictive hobbies available to humankind.

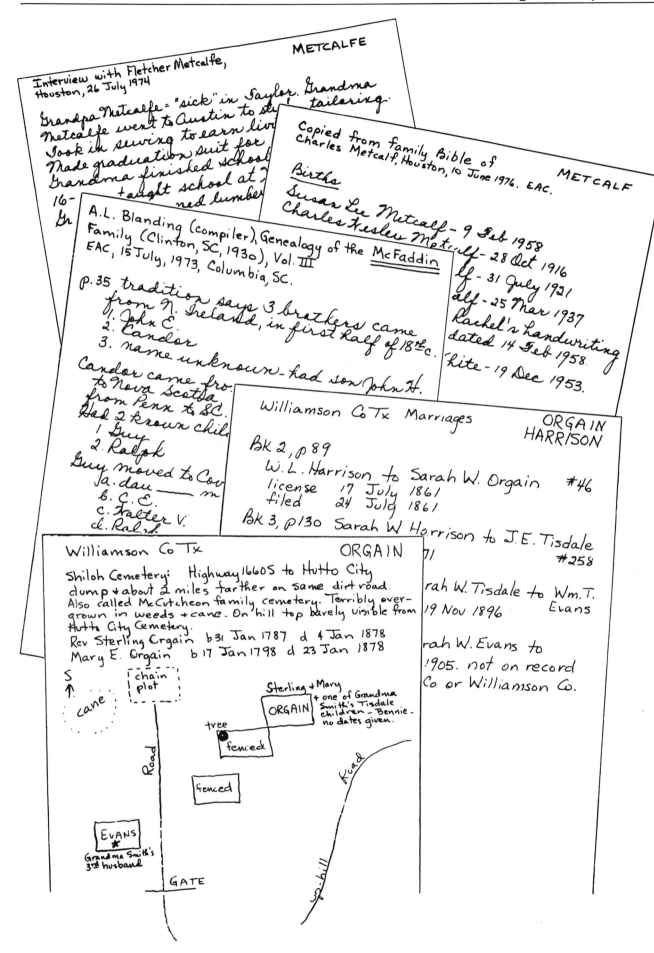

2
Strategies for Winning

Games have rules, and successful game players—like detectives—have strategies for winning. The genealogy jigsaw puzzle has a few of its own rules. The successful genealogist, being both game player and detective, develops and uses the strategies that get the best results. What are the special rules and strategies of this game?

Be scientific. Write down your sources of information: who told you or where you read it. This process is called documenting. In doing this, the historian has the same purpose as the scientist. Both are trying to prove something. People will ask, "How do you *know* Great-grandpa was from North Carolina? Papa always said he was from Alabama." What documents or sources can you point to that prove, or even suggest, his North Carolina origin?

To document your notes, title each page with a heading that contains the source–information. (See Figure 1.) For an interview, tell the name of the person you are interviewing, the location of the interview, and the date. When copying data from family Bibles or cemeteries, tell who copied the information, where it can be found if needed again, and the date. For published books, give the author, title, publisher, date of publication, volume and page numbers. The process is a simple one if you ask yourself, "Where can I find this exact information again if I need it?"

Be thorough. Approach your subject from several angles. Write down as much information as you can. Evaluate all your information. A good historian will try to learn who, what, when, where, how, why, and with what results. The family historian wants to know where and how just as much as who and when. Perhaps you talk with several people who knew your Great-grandmother Metcalfe. Each one may give you something different in your effort to "know" her. One talks about her church activities. Another remembers her sewing and knitting. Still another describes the house in Taylor that she lived in. One saved her favorite recipe. Your puzzle needs all of these parts to be complete.

Be resourceful. Investigate (eventually) all possible sources. The most reliable sources are the firsthand, or primary, sources. They are the first recordings of events or names or dates. Their informants were usually persons involved in the events: the father of a new baby gives the information for the birth certificate; the son of the deceased man fills out the death certificate; the bridesmaid in the wedding describes the event in her diary. Firsthand sources include such things as wills, deeds, tax lists, birth and death certificates, marriage licenses, old letters and diaries, church registers, original newspaper reports, census records, some Bible records, people who took part in the event you are investigating, and people who knew your ancestor personally.

Be cautious. We cannot believe everything that appears in print. Like the scientist and detective, we must not jump to conclusions. Genealogists must be ready to question what they are told and what they read. They must evaluate, guess, ask another way, and try out alternatives. Here is an example of this process.

We were trying to identify Uncle George's wife. Sister said that Uncle George's wife was Aunt Tella but could not remember her real name. A cousin said she called George's wife Aunt Stella. Hearing both nicknames, these two relatives remembered that Tella and Stella were both short for Costella, but neither could remember Aunt Tella / Stella's maiden name. The 1880 census shows her given name as Euphima, but no relative present had ever heard of anyone by that name. We asked whether George might have married twice, first to Euphima and then to Costella. No one remembered, and the county marriage records and the family Bible, both of which might have answered the question, were destroyed by fire years ago.

We continued down the list to other aunts and uncles and their spouses. Everyone agreed that Uncle Walter married Sally Campbell and Papa married Emma Campbell. Two Campbell girls? Were they sisters? Then it clicked. Mama always said she and

Aunt Tella were sisters. That made Aunt Tella a Campbell too. Three sisters married three brothers? Then we read the 1870 census of Mama's family, and Aunt Tella was there: E C or Euphima Costella Campbell. Then someone remembered, "Oh, yes, that *was* her name."

A new question had appeared in answering the original one: What about the third girl, Sally, who married Uncle Walter? The marriage record proves that she was a Campbell. Costella and Mama had a sister Sarah, or Sally; but if their sister Sally had married Walter, she would have been 25 years older than her husband. We asked again, "Were Aunt Sally and Mama related?" The response was non-committal. We approached it from a different angle: "Did you know any of Aunt Sally's relatives?" Answer: Aunt Sally's mother was called Aunt Cindy. Okay, part of the dilemma is solved. Mama's mother was Emily, not Cindy. So, Aunt Sally was not Mama's sister. The new question arising now was "What Campbell family *was* she part of?" Additional searching and asking may answer this question and raise still others.

Another caution for genealogists concerns copying. Handwritten or typed copies of originals can contain errors; so it is wisest to consult the original whenever possible. Microfilm and photocopies of an original preserve its accuracy. They are good substitutes when the original is not available.

Copied records are second-hand sources. They may contain valuable information, but human error is more likely in copying, especially when researchers read handwriting of a century or two ago. When you do your own copying, be as accurate at possible.

When I was searching for my great-grandfather Isaac's first marriage record, I found a typed copy of the marriage book in a library. Eagerly I copied the name of the bride as given: Elizabeth Steer. Months later, I had an opportunity to see the original marriage record and discovered that her name was not Steer. The name had been hyphenated in the original; and the copier had taken down only the first syllable, and that incorrectly. Her name was Sturdivant.

For accuracy and detail, it is helpful to photocopy records and photograph tombstones and houses if the information is likely to be questioned or is of major importance.

Be systematic. Keep all information about one family together. This practice makes your search and the use of your findings much easier. Organize your search before you go on an interview or to look at public records. Know what you are looking for. File your notes in the proper section of your notebook. As you see in Figure 1, your filing and note-keeping can be quick and easy if you write at the top of each page the surname or section to which the notes pertain.

Be considerate. One group of teenagers was conducting a survey and was eager to collect answers. A likely source of information walked into the room and they pounced on her like wild cats on prey. She was petrified and answered in a hesitant whisper. It was then necessary to discuss, again, the courtesies of interviewing. "We are conducting a survey for history class. Would you be willing to answer a question for us?" "My history class is interviewing people about their experiences during the depression of the 1930s. Would you be willing to share your experiences and impressions with me?" "I am tracing family history, and am trying to find out about the Campbell family who lived here before World War I. May I talk with you about them?" "Aunt Susan, I am trying to compile family history on Grandpa Smith's side of the family. Do you have an evening this week when I could come over and discuss it with you?"

In interviewing people, you will get more cooperation when you are on time, tactful, polite, to the point, and appreciative—and when you don't stay too long. Usually 45 minutes to an hour is long enough for such a visit. Repeated but shorter visits are usually more effective than one long, and therefore tiring, visit of several hours.

In libraries and public buildings, observe their particular rules as well as common courtesies. When you go into a county courthouse to look at public records, introduce yourself to the clerk and ask for permission to see, or for the location of, the particular documents you are interested in. It is helpful to explain that you are working on family history. You need not go into detail about your search; the employees are not usually research experts and are not being paid to listen to a visitor's family tales or history. If you have a question about using a particular document, ask for help. You may find it beneficial to ask the clerk to give you the name of a local historian or genealogist or society to contact in your search.

FIVE-GENERATION CHART #29

Compiled by _E.A.C._

Address _____

b = birth date & place
m = marriage date & place
d = death date & place

#1 on this chart
is the same as #_2_
on Chart #_27_.

1
Ferdinand E.
Coleman
b c1794
m 3 Jan 1822 Cumberland Co. Va.
d 3 Jan 1822
Cumberland Co Va
1867 Cumberland Co.
Spouse _Elizabeth_
a. Phillips
b. 31 Aug 1805
d. 24 Oct 1847
14 children.

2
Elliott E.
Coleman
b by 1764
m 23 Nov 1789 Cumberland Co,
d Va.
1822
Cumberland Co,
Va.
children:
1. Martin H.
2. Ferdinand E.
3. Mary E.
4. Elliott R.
5. Archer Allen
6. Creed O.
7. John Henry
8. Wm. Priddie
9. Martha
10. Susan E.

3
Elizabeth H.
Daniel
b c1773
Cumberland Co Va
d c1853
Cumberland Co Va

4
William
Coleman
b c1740 c-45
Goochland Co. Va.
m 7
d 1810-1811
Cumberland Co Va
4 Known children:
1. Elliott H.
2. Sarah
3. William Jr
4. Henry

5

6
William Daniel
b c1740
Cumberland Co Va
m 28 Mar 1763
Cumberland Co Va
d 1812
Cumberland Co
Va
7 children.

7
Martha "Patty"
Field Allen
b 25 Aug 1746
d 1774
by Dec 1820

8
Thomas Coleman
b c1710-1720

9
b
d
m

10
b
d

11
b
d

12
William Daniel
b c1710-14
m c1738-40
d 1775

13
Elizabeth (Watkins?)
c1738-40

14
Samuel Allen
b c1713
m 1737
d 1774

15
Martha Archer
b
d

16
Daniel Coleman
bc 1680-85 d.1769
(9children)

17
Daniel Coleman
bc 1680-85 d.1769
(9children)
Patience
d. July/Aug 1771

18
19
20
21
22
23
24 James Daniel
bc 1680
m 21 Jan 1704
d.1727
25 Margaret Vivion
d.1727
26
27
28
29
30 John Archer
31 Martha Field?

See Chart #

12

3
Charting Your Course

Several kinds of charts provide good worksheets for your family history puzzle. The first two represent the outside edges of your puzzle, the basic information that you gather on each person's life. This information is called vital statistics. It includes

when and where (county and state or location in foreign country) he was born
when, where, and whom he married
when and where he died
where he is buried (cemetery, city or county, state)

This information is identified by abbreviations on most charts to save space:

b—born
m—married
d—died

The five-generation chart (Form 1) shows you and your ancestors, or your "family tree." The chart shows each person as a child of his parents, a line coming from the union of two people. The chart is a handy reference for "who fits in where."

The five-generation chart shown in Figure 2 shows Ferdinand G. Coleman as #1. He was born about 1794. "c" stands for the Latin word *circa* which means *around* or *about*. He married Elizabeth A. Phillips on 3 January 1822. He died in 1867. All of these events took place in Cumberland County, Virginia.

Ferdinand's father, Elliott, is #2 on the chart. Elliott's birth date is not known, but has been estimated from available evidence, which can be listed or explained on the back of the chart. His wife (and Ferdinand's mother) is listed as #3. Her birth and death dates are approximated from available information and therefore are shown as "about 1773" and "about 1853."

Elliott's parents are numbers 4 and 5, although nothing is known of his mother or her family. William was Elliott's father; William's father is #8, Thomas, whose parents were Daniel and Patience, 16 and 17.

The blanks indicate that nothing is known, or has yet been gathered, about those people.

Notice that each mother in Figure 2 is listed by her maiden name, her name before she married. Elizabeth's mother, Patty, is shown by her nickname as well as by her given name. #13 is Elizabeth, and her maiden name is shown with a question mark to indicate that evidence points to Watkins as her maiden name or that some searchers feel that was her maiden name, although nothing has been proved at this time.

As more information is gathered and additional charts are needed to go farther back in time, write in the number of the next chart on which you can find that person. In Figure 2, Ferdinand's maternal line, through his great-great-grandfather John Archer, is continued on Chart 12. As you see, Ferdinand himself was a continuation of chart 27. Any person can be number 1 on such a chart.

On the five-generation chart, each column represents a generation. On your own chart, you will be the first generation, #1. Your parents are in the second column and are the second generation going back in time. Your four grandparents make up the third generation and third column; your eight great-grandparents are the fourth column. Your sixteen great-great-grandparents will occupy the fifth column. The father's name is listed first in each set of parents.

Begin your own chart with yourself as #1. Fill in the vital statistics which pertain to you. Your father is #2, and your mother is #3, shown by her maiden name. Fill in their vital statistics as well as you can using information you have at home that is known to be accurate. Your father's father will be #4; your father's mother, #5. Your mother's father will be #6; your mother's mother, #7. List their names and as much information as you have now. It may be helpful to list below #1, 2, 4, and 6 their children's names, as in Figure 2. File the chart in your notebook so that you can add information as you find it. Some family historians prefer to keep all their five-generation

FAMILY RECORD OF THE ___Elliott Glen Coleman___ FAMILY

Birth date ___1824___
Birth place ___Cumberland Co VA___
Death date ___3-17 Feb 1892___
Burial place ___Kyle - Hays Co. Tx___
    unmarked grave
Military service:

ELLIOTT GLEN COLEMAN II
Full name of husband

Birth date ___25 Feb. 1828/29___
Birth place ___SC. in or near Chester Co.___
Death date ___19 June 1901___
Burial place ___Zephyr, Brown Co. Tx___

MARGARET CATHERINE PATTON
Full name of wife with maiden name

Other spouses

Marriage date ___12 OCTOBER 1847___
Place ___FAYETTE Co, TENN.___ moved to Hardeman Co — Bolivar.

#	Sex	CHILDREN Full Name (all Coleman)	Birth Day	Birth Mo	Birth Year	Death Day	Death Mo	Death Year	Marriage to	Date
1	F	MARY ELIZA CATHERINE "	23	Sept	1848	7 Whiteville	Mar Tenn	1908	PITSER MILLER BLALOCK Bolivar Tenn.	30 Nov 1869
2	F	LUCY "			1850	be-	fore	1860	—	—
3	F	WILLIE "			1853-4	be	fore	1860	—	—
4	M	FERDINAND GLEN "			1855	31	Aug	1928	—	—
5	M	THOMAS PATTON "		by	1858				SALLIE M. JACKSON	14 July 1889
6	F	KATE EWING "	11	June	1859	16	Oct	1942	HENRY MONTGOMERY	29 Jan 1890
7	M	ELLIOTT GLEN III "			1862		c	1886	—	—
8	M	EDWARD M "			1865				MATTIE PENNINGTON	21 July 1887
9	F	LOUISA JANE HARDY "	16	Feb	1868	24	Mar	1917	GEORGE WASHINGTON ADAMS	29 Aug 1889
10	F	LILLIE "	15	Dec	1870	14	May	195_	JAMES THOMAS FISHER	SEPT 1889
11	M	EZEKIEL McNEAL "	5	Aug	1872	19	Aug	1955	ELLA MAE MINOR ARNOLD	13 Sep 1909
12	M	JAMES TURNER "	16	Oct	1875	24	Sept	193_	MARTHA ELLEN FISHER	5 Apr 1899
13										
14										
15										
16										
17										
18										

Husband (notes) To Tenn -1845. To Tx. 1872. CARPENTER. built Episcopal Church, Gonzales Tx + Methodist Church, Kyle Tx. FARMER too. Presbyterian.

Husband's Father ___FERDINAND GLEN COLEMAN___
Husband's Mother ___ELIZA PHILLIPS___ dau Peter Talbot Phillips and Elizabeth A. Allen.

Wife (notes) Presbyterian

Wife's Father ___THOMAS PATTON___
Wife's Mother ___CATHERINE EWING McFADDEN___ dau of Isaac McFadden of Chester Co SC. + Elizabeth Steele

charts together in a separate notebook. Others prefer to keep one in each notebook illustrating the families in that particular notebook.

Form 2, the family record chart, is very useful. It contains one family, a mother and father and their children. A sample is shown in Figure 3. The husband's full name and the wife's maiden name head the sheet. The *II* added to Elliott's name distinguishes him from his grandfather for whom he was named. Elliott's birth date is not known; so only the approximate year of his birth is given. His death date also is not known but has been narrowed down by existing evidence to be between 3 February and 17 February 1892. The sources used to estimate these dates can be listed on the back of the chart.

The wife's birth date is given one way on her tombstone and another way in the Bible record; so both years are listed: 1828/29. These differing sources can be listed and explained on the back of the chart. Because her exact birthplace has not been determined, the chart shows the approximate location, "in or near Chester County, SC," as suggested by available sources, also explained on the back.

Children numbers 2, 3, 4, and 7 never married, as shown by the dashed lines. A blank space with no marking would indicate that the marriage information is not yet determined.

The blank birth dates for several of the children mean that the exact dates are not known. If they are ever found, they can be added. The years have been estimated from census records and family letters. Nothing is known about children numbers 5 and 8 after they married; no death date can be guessed. Child number 7 died as a young man, about 1886, judging from available sources. These sources can be explained on the back of the chart.

Because so many seventeenth, eighteenth, and nineteenth century families were large, and other nineteenth and twentieth century families have been generally smaller, I have found it useful to have several sizes of family record charts. One has lines for 18 children and vital statistics, as in Figure 3. One has room for 8 children with more space to write in where they were born, married, and buried. The third (Figure 4) is for families of four or fewer children and provides space for additional information such as religion, occupation, politics, and education.

Begin your own family record charts with your childhood family: your parents as *Husband* and *Wife*,

you and your brothers and sisters as the *Children*. Fill in full names as they would appear on a birth certificate. Nicknames can go in parentheses; or you can underline the name a person goes by. For example, one little girl is called Bitsy, but her real name is Sarah Elizabeth. On the chart, she should be listed as Sarah Elizabeth (Bitsy). Cordelia Celeste was always called Delia. Her entry on the chart would be Cordelia Celeste.

Make a second family record chart for your father's family, with his parents at the top and their children, your aunts and uncles, listed below. Fill in another one for your mother's family the same way. You may even want to fill out one for your aunts and uncles and cousins since they too are part of the family history. I like to keep a family record chart for each generation of ancestors: one for each grandparent in his/her childhood family, one for each great-grandparent as a parent and as a child, etc.

If you keep these charts handy, you can readily add information to them. I like to keep the appropriate family record chart as the first page of each notebook section. In the case of the four Coleman brothers living in the same county, all four record charts would appear at the beginning of the Coleman-Tennessee notebook section. Other family record charts, on families for whom I have no notebooks, I file alphabetically in a single notebook.

Copies of your five-generation charts and family record charts can be sent to relatives when you are seeking information.

Dear Aunt Jane,
I am working on our family history and am trying to gather all the information I can on Grandma Smith's side of the family. I'm enclosing a family record chart with her children on it. I've filled in what I could; you see there is a lot I don't know. Would you please fill in whatever you can and return the chart to me? The second chart is one of Grandma Smith's childhood family. I could remember only 3 of the children, but I thought there were more. I'd appreciate any of that information that you can fill in, too. Thanks a million! I'll send you copies of whatever I can gather from other sources.

Love, Sarah

Dear Grandaddy,
I have decided to put together some family history, and certainly do need your help! I can get our three generations pretty complete from being part of them,

but I don't know anything before that. I'm enclosing a family-tree chart and would greatly appreciate your contribution to the information. Can you fill in the spaces for your parents and grandparents? By the way, did you know your grandparents? If you can fill in any of the other names, please share what you can, and return the chart to me. I'll be talking with you soon.   Love, Sarah

FAMILY RECORD OF THE *Thomas Moody Metcalfe* **FAMILY**

Birth date (twin) 17 Oct 1852 Birth place Owensboro, Shelby Co, Kty Death date 11 Dec 1930 Burial place Hutto, Williamson Co, Tx Religion Politics Democrat	*Thomas Moody Metcalfe* Full name of husband Occupation wood & coal yard Education
Birth date 7 April 1864 Birth place Bagdad, Williamson Co, Tx Death date 22 Sept 1956 Burial place Hutto, Williamson Co, Tx Religion Presbyterian Politics Democrat	"Mattie" *Martha Emma Harrison* Full name of wife with maiden name Occupation taught school, seamstress, ran rooming house. Education Sam Houston Normal, Huntsville Tx
Other spouses (his or hers): —	Marriage date 16 Oct 1884 Place Williamson Co, Tx

CHILDREN of this marriage

#	Full Name Nickname	Birth	Death	Marriage
1	Mary Otis Metcalfe Religion _____	25 Mar 1886 Hutto Williamson Co Tx Politics Democrat	1965 or 1966 Haskell Tx Occupation Piano teacher	11 June 1907 Taylor Tx Orville Ewing Patterson Education Cincinnati Conservatory
2	Hunter Orgain Metcalfe Religion Presbyterian	19 Oct 1887 Hutto Williamson Co Tx Politics Democrat	12 Jan 1968 Marfa Tx Occupation lawyer judge	2 Sept 1914 Georgetown Fletcher Elizabeth McKennon Education graduate - Southwestern Univ, Georgetown, Williamson Co Tx
3	Joseph Franklin Metcalfe Religion Presbyterian	1 Dec 1889 Hutto Williamson Co Tx Politics Democrat	28 Feb 1972 Elgin Tx Occupation banking; city employee	13 May 1914 Elgin Tx Ethel Louise Taylor Education business college
4	Thomas Moody Metcalfe Jr. Religion _____	2 Dec 1896 Williamson Co Tx Politics	11 Feb 1948 Hutto Tx Occupation WWI. US Navy; merchant marine	? ? Education high school

Husband's Father Joseph Metcalfe , Mother Mary Belle Allison
Wife's Father William Lucius Harrison , Mother Sarah F. Orgain

4

How to Begin the Puzzle:
The Outside Edges

The logical way to begin anything new is to start with what you know. In working a jigsaw puzzle, it is easy to begin with the outside edges because they are straight and easily identified. In genealogy this means to begin with yourself and work backward. The pedigree charts and family group sheets will show you how much you already know.

The best source to use in filling in the rest of the "straight edge" pieces of your family puzzle is the people in your family: your parents, your brothers and sisters, your grandparents, great-grandparents, and aunts and uncles. With their answers written down and filed in your notebook, you have a springboard from which to gather other information. If you are lucky enough to have grandparents and older relatives living, you have a gold mine at your fingertips. They generally love to talk, especially when you are interested enough to listen carefully and ask questions. Some of their stories may seem totally unrelated, but record, either in writing or on tape, as much as you can. You never know when you may need this information.

Say you decide to talk with your grandmother. You are armed with your charts, paper, pencil, and a list of questions. A logical place to begin is "Where were you born?" If your grandmother is like mine, she will answer quickly; but it took me five years of asking to find out *when*. Who were her parents? Who were her brothers and sisters? When did she and Grandaddy get married? Where? What was his full name? When and where was he born? Who were his parents? When did he die?

You can move in any of several directions next. You may decide to inquire about your aunts and uncles. Does she remember the birthdates of her children (your aunts and uncles)? Even a year filled in is better than nothing. Encourage her by letting her know that you appreciate any piece of information, even if it is incomplete. Whom did each one of the aunts and uncles marry? Does she remember when

they married? Together, can you list your cousins? Probably she has their addresses so that you can write to them directly to ask for any missing information.

Once Grandmother has shared her own life with you, ask her what she remembers of her parents, grandparents, or great-grandparents. Who were her brothers and sisters? When and where was each of them born? Whom did they marry? Are they still living? Get their addresses. Where and when did her parents marry? When and where were her parents born? When and where did her parents die? Where are they buried?

Did she know her own grandparents? What were their names? When and where were they born? When and where did they marry? When and where did they die? Who were their children? Who were their brothers and sisters? Who were their parents? Where are they buried? Where did they live?

If Grandmother cannot remember exact dates, use a general reference point to help both of you. Did he die before World War I? Was she born before you were? Did he get married when the family was still living in Palestine? Any piece of information may help you pinpoint the date you are seeking. For example, she may tell you about the house burning down. When was that? Well, she was about eight; so it was about 1908. Yes, Grandpa was still living with them then. So you conclude that her grandfather died after 1908. Cousin Mahala may remember that Grandpa died just before her wedding, which was in 1915. So you begin to narrow the gaps. Their grandpa died between 1908 and 1915.

Lists of brothers and sisters are not really vital statistics, but they are vital pieces of information to have. The only information we could ever get out of my grandfather was a partial list of his twelve brothers and sisters and his father's name. This was mighty little to go on, especially after we lost the slip of paper containing these names. But we remembered his father's name and one sister. When I got into the search, I found several men by his father's name but only one with a daughter named Theodocia. It was the sister's name that led us to the right family in our search.

Once you have picked your grandmother's brain, there are other people who can help you fill in the gaps. You can contact aunts and uncles, great-aunts and great-uncles, your parents' cousins, and older friends of the family. Ask them about the vital statistics of their own part of the family and about your direct ancestors to whom they too are related. Write down whatever they tell you, even if it is sketchy.

Sometimes you may find differences of opinion on names or dates. Two aunts give different death dates for Grandpa. Two cousins give different names for cousin Sarah's husband. Write both in your notes. At a later time, when you find out which name or date is correct, then mark out the incorrect answer. But in the meantime, you don't know which to keep and which to discard. Keep them both.

So far, you have been gathering pieces for your puzzle by talking and listening to the people around you. When you cannot talk with them in person, the next best method is to write to them. To increase their cooperation, make their job easy. In a letter, explain your project and ask for their help. Enclose a self-addressed stamped envelope and a page of typed or neatly printed questions with space left for their answers. They can simply fill in the blanks and return the page to you. Title the page with a heading like ''Questions from Susan Metcalf to Mrs. Wilmer Medders, 19 June 1975 — CAMPBELL family.'' When the page is returned, you know to file it under Campbell in your notebook. From the answers, add to your charts. I always reassure these correspondents that I appreciate any information they can give, however small, because it's more than I have now. After all, not everyone is a walking memory bank. It is better that they leave some blanks than make up something to fill in!

If you are seeking information on two different families, such as Campbell and White, send a separate question page on each family name. Each one will fit nicely into the notebook. Filing systematically can be just as important as gathering the information.

Regardless of any other information you seek, try first to gather this basic information from each relative you consult *for each generation* as you work back in time:

1. Names of parents; birth, marriage, death dates and places (vital statistics); their children's names and vital statistics; their brothers' and sisters' names and vital statistics.
2. Spouse(s) and children for each person.
3. Names of grandparents with any available vital statistics.
4. Names of great-grandparents with any available vital statistics.

Conducting and Tape Recording an Interview

As the interviewer, make a list of questions in advance, and give your informant either the questions or an idea of what you want to cover before you begin. Of course, you are not limited to these questions; ask any others that occur to you as the interview progresses. Make your questions short and to the point; ask one question at a time. The following attempt to be ''formal'' ended up being wordy, redundant, and confusing:

''Now, Aunt Ellie, I'd like to get a little background as to your birth and childhood, your full name at birth, when and where you were born, your parents' names, and something about your brothers and sisters, as to their names and whether they were older or younger than you if you can't remember their birthdates, some of your early education and childhood experiences, especially as they relate to what it was like to grow up on a farm.''

A much better attempt is to begin simply: ''Okay, Aunt Ellie, let's begin at your beginning. When and where were you born?'' She may give you all the rest of the information you might have asked for, without your having to ask. If she leaves something out, or if you get confused or lost, ask for clarification. You may have to ask other questions to help her with an answer or to keep her on track. It may be helpful to summarize periodically to make a graceful transition into a new subject, to stimulate any further memories, to return to the subject you want to pursue, or to be certain that you understand what she is really saying.

Word your questions so that they encourage more than *yes* or *no* answers. Try to elicit facts as well as feelings, reactions, and descriptions. Remember, the facts you seek are more than names and dates, although you often must begin with these; you also want to find out *how, why* or *why not,* and *with what results or effects.*

Experienced genealogists will agree that in order to be a good genealogist, one must also be a good historian. In order to make the most of your session, you must have done enough advance preparation to know what questions to ask, or what has no relationship to the topic or period under consideration, and to be able to converse with some degree of accuracy. Your interviewee may mention an event or person or tradition that is new to you or that you neglected to include in your outline of questions. Learn to be alert to catch such "jewels" when they are tossed your way; they may be more important in the long run than your prepared questions. Feel free to divert the conversation away from the paper to expand and develop these new topics.

How do you handle sensitive or controversial subjects? Very carefully. If they must be brought up because of their importance to the overall picture, hold these questions until you and your interviewee are comfortable talking and sharing with each other. The session is not a forum for expressing your own opinions or winning a convert to your view. All you need is your interviewee's statements, even if you disagree.

Be alert to the reaction of your interviewee to your bringing up this kind of subject. If he or she is willing to talk, you may get valuable information. If it seems to be an emotionally upsetting topic, be prepared to drop it for the time being. Every family has "closets" they prefer not to open for airing; we need to be sensitive to their wishes, even when our curiosity is aroused.

While your interviewee is speaking, be an attentive listener, one who pays attention and thinks ahead at the same time. Eye contact, enthusiasm, appropriate facial expressions, and natural reactions encourage and reassure your informant. If the interviewee seems to be getting tired, confused, or involved too deeply in a topic that you consider completely off the subject, you may be able to initiate a short break.

You may want to tape record your interview even though you are taking notes. Here are a few suggestions for having a successful taping session:

1. Use the best quality tape recorder you have available and a good quality tape. Usually a 60-minute tape (30 minutes per side) is suf-
ficient, although you would be safe to have an extra along. A battery-operated tape recorder may not be able to pull a longer tape with good results. Take extra batteries or use an AC/DC adapter and cord.

2. Assure your informant that it will be an informal visit; both of you need to relax and be comfortable. Tell him or her that you will gladly stop the tape at any time if he wants to say something "off the record" or if he gets tired. Create an atmosphere conducive to thinking and taping by turning off televisions or other noisy appliances and by sending pets and children elsewhere.

3. Place the microphone (or tape recorder if the microphone is built in) an equal distance between you and your interviewee so that both voices can be heard equally well. If the speaking voices differ much in natural volume, place the recorder closer to the softer voice. Place the tape recorder on a stationary object such as a table rather than in a lap to minimize noises made when someone shifts positions or rattles paper.

4. Test your equipment and voices before you begin, and listen to the sample to affirm that all is working and voices are being heard and understood. Label both sides of the tape before you begin.

5. Identify on tape each person involved in the session, the date and place of the interview. If more than two are present, it might be helpful to have each person introduce himself or herself, to put a voice with the name for easier identification in the future. Include yourself in these introductions.

6. You will get a better recording if each person who speaks remembers:
   a. to speak slowly and loudly enough to be clearly understood.
   b. that dropping one's voice (trailing off) at the ends of phrases will mean losing what is said. The longer the interview, the more the voices tend to drop in volume and clarity toward the end.
   c. that more than one person speaking at a time means a garbled, confused section of tape where no one is understood. When it is possible, it is advantageous to limit

the session to you and one interviewee.

7. It is helpful to spell aloud any proper names mentioned, especially those which may be unusual or misunderstood on tape. Beginning and final consonants are easy to lose on a tape. For example, is the name "Card" or "Carg"? "Paul" or "Carl"? "Bud" or "Pug" or "Pup"? This problem is complicated by voices which speak with regional or "foreign language" accents, which speak rapidly, or which trail off on the ends of words and phrases.

8. It is helpful to leave the tape visible in the tape recorder so that you can tell when the tape is running out. If you can, finish one topic before the side of the tape is completed, and begin the new side with a new topic.

9. Don't let the tape control the interview. Pauses for thinking or reflecting are often valuable to the conversation; you do not have to fill every moment of tape-time with sound.

10. Remember that many people, especially the elderly, are nervous around tape recorders and do not like to hear their own voices played back. Do what you can to allay these fears and, at the same time, to make yourself and the tape recorder less important than the interviewee and what he/she is saying.

11. Be sure that you and the interviewee have the same understanding about how the tape is to be used. If necessary, write out a "contract" for both to sign that explains the purpose and intended uses of the tape.

When the interview is completed, you will want to thank your interviewee, perhaps take pictures to commemorate the occasion, and leave the way open for another session at a later date.

If video taping equipment is available to you, you may want to record family gatherings and group interviews. Both video and audio tapes become valuable for their content and for the memories.

(SAMPLE INTERVIEW LETTER)

Emily Croom to Emily Blalock, 9 July 1973:

Dear Aunt Emily,

Here are a few more questions...please...

1. When grandpa Pitser Blalock married Emma Bishop, she had 2 daughters. What were their names?

    She had <u>three</u> daughters — Lucy Nell (who was married and living in Memphis when they married), Egene and Alberta.

2. I found Emma and Sim Bishop in the 1880 census with a 3-month-old son named Robert. Did he die young or move away? I had never heard of him before.

    Robert died before Emma married Pitser. I do not remember his age when he died but I did hear her speak of him and I know he died before he reached adulthood.

3. Do you have any idea what Emma's maiden name was?

    No, if I ever knew I have forgotten.

4. I found a county court order of 1867 binding 6 black children to Jesse Blalock. Do you have an idea of why this was done? It didn't say they were orphans.

    No, I do not know. I have never heard this story.

5. When did Emma Bishop Blalock die?

    I do not know the exact date of her death. I know that she was living when Lowe died in 1940. It seems to me that she died in the early or middle forties, though. However, we were not notified at the time of her death and heard it sometime later.

5

What's In a Name?

Names present special challenges to the genealogist. For example, your family name may be spelled several different ways in public documents. The census taker recorded what he heard, or thought he heard. The copier wrote down what he thought he read. A variety of spellings is often found for the same name and same family:

Metcalf – Metcalfe – Midcalf – Midkiff – Medcalf
Robinson – Robertson – Robberson – Robison
Allen – Alan – Allyn – Allan – Alline – Alin
Neale – Neil – Neill – Neal – Neele

One author reports 17 different spellings of Robertson and 21 variations of Sullivan in the 1790 census. [1]

Surnames may change over the years. A French immigrant named Pierre de la Chapelle may find his name Americanized to Peter Chapel. The German immigrant Johan Peter Muth became Peter Mood. Zimmerman may be translated to Carpenter; the French Le Blanc may become White.

Such changes can reflect the way the family pronounced their name or the attempt of a clerk to approximate what he heard and make it manageable for the English-speaking community. In this way, an Irishman named Sean Maurice could become John Morris; a Welshman named ap Howell might become Powell; and the German Koster has been altered to Custer.

Surnames, of course, do become given names. There are many examples, such as Allen, Keith, Glenn, Clyde, Davis, Lloyd, Elliott, Dudley, and Newton. Combining surnames has given these nineteenth century Southerners really interesting names: Green Bird, Bright Bird, Green Cash, Ransom Cash, Green Hill, Green Moss, Wiley Crook, and Valentine Cash.

Given names (Christian or first names) may be spelled in varieties of ways and Americanized just as surnames are. However, given names present the additional challenge of nicknames and abbreviations.

Female nicknames, by which the individuals were known to their contemporaries, are often found in place of ''real'' names in documents. Many good dictionaries can help you determine the given name from a nickname. Here are some common first names with their usual nicknames:

Mary	Mamie, Molly, Mollie, May, Maisie, Polly, Minnie, Moll
Margaret	Maggie, Peg, Peggy, Meg, Midge, Madge, Daisy, Maisie, Meta, Greta
Martha	Marty, Martie, Mattie, Patty, Patsy
Elizabeth	Beth, Eliza, Liz, Liza, Lizzie, Lisa, Lise, Elsie, Betty, Betsy, Bitsy, Bess, Bessie, Libby
Eleanor	Ella, Ellie, Nell, Nellie, Nelly, Nora
Sarah	Sallie, Sal, Sadie
Frances	Fran, Frankie, Fannie
Ann(e)	Annie, Nan, Nannie, Nina, Nancy
Katherine	Kathy, Kate, Katie, Kat, Katy, Kay, Kitty, Kit
Henry	Hank, Harry, Hal, Hen
Richard	Dick, Rick, Ricky, Rich, Richy
Robert	Rob, Bob, Robby, Bobby, Dobbin, Robin, Robbie
John	Johnny, Johnnie, Jack, Jackie, Jock
James	Jamie, Jim, Jimmy, Jem
Theodore/Theodorick	Ted, Tad, Teddy, Theo, The, Dode, Dory

Sometimes records give us nicknames of previous centuries which are less common today:

Sukie, Suchy	Susan
Tillie	Matilda, Mathilda
Effie, Effy	Euphemia
Tempy	Temperance
Millie	Amelia, Mildred, Millicent
Lettie	Letitia
Hettie	Esther, Henrietta, Hester

---

[1] J. N. Hook, *Family Names: How Our Surnames Came to America* (New York: Macmillan, 1982), 324.

Ollie	Olive, Olivia
Winnie	Winnefred
Hallie	probably Henrietta or Harriet

Of course, nicknames were, and are, used as complete given names. *Lucy* is often a "real name" instead of a nickname for Lucretia, Lucia, Lucille, or Lucinda. Stella was both a given name and a nickname for Costella and Estelle, just as Larry is often a given name rather than a shortened form of Lawrence today.

Some nicknames can substitute for more than one given name:

Patty	Patricia, Patience, Martha, Matilda
Lina, Lena	Eveline, Emeline, Carolina, Angelina, Selina, Selena, Helena, Paulina, Magdalena, and others
Bell(e)	Arabella, Anabelle, Isabel, Rosabel
Nora	Honora, Honoria, Leonora, Eleanor
Dora	Theodora, Eudora, Dorothy
Ed(die)	Edgar, Edmund, Edward, Edwin, Edwina
Nell	Ellen, Helen, Eleanor
Frankie	Frances, Francis, Franklin, Francine
Delia	Cordelia, Adelia, Ledelia, Adele
Sam(my)	Samuel, Samson, Samantha
Jenny	Jane, Virginia, Janet, Jeannette (Jennet), Jennifer
Allie	Alice, Aline, Alene, Aletha
Cindy	Lucinda, Cynthia

In documents copied by hand, male names are often abbreviated. These are some common examples:

Daniel	Danl	James	Jas
Samuel	Saml	Nathaniel	Nat^l
Jonathan	Jno	Christopher	X^r
Richard	Rich^d	Alexander	Alex^r
Thomas	Thos		

Naming practices vary from place to place and century to century, but certain consistencies have existed for nearly four centuries in the area we now call the United States. For example, children were, and still are, often named for grandparents and other relatives. Sometimes a middle or given name is a clue to the mother's maiden name or to a grandparent's name. These illustrations are taken from three different centuries. Hunter Orgain Metcalfe was named for his grandmother Sally Orgain. Benjamin Allen

Phillips was named for his grandfather Benjamin Allen; Samuel Black Brelsford, for his grandfather Samuel Black. Emily Cooper was named for her father's deceased first wife, Emily Blalock Cooper. Emily Cooper Blalock was named for the same deceased lady, in this case, her father's sister. On the other hand, Pitser Miller Blalock was named for a neighbor, not thought to be a relative; and his brother Edward Philpot Blalock was named for their father's foster brother. Then Thomas Blalock King was given one name from each grandfather.

One genealogist has suggested a pattern to naming practices of the eighteenth and early nineteenth centuries, especially in England and Wales, which may give you a clue in studying families of the American colonies and the United States. [2]

Eldest son—often named for the father's father.
Second son—often named for the mother's father.
Third son—often named for the father.
Fourth son—often named for the father's eldest brother.
Eldest daughter—often named for the mother's mother.
Second daughter—often named for the father's mother.
Third daughter—often named for the mother.
Fourth daughter—often named for the mother's eldest sister.

Of course, a daughter was, and still is, sometimes given a feminine form of her father's name: Josephine / Joseph, Georgianna / George, Pauline / Paul, Philippa / Philip, Willie / William, Jessie / Jesse, Charlotte / Charles, and even Drusilla / Drew. Almanzon Huston even named one of his daughters Almazona.

Every culture and era seems to have names whose origins are obscure. They may be nicknames, "made-up" names, combinations of other names, names of characters in literature, place names, sounds which pleased the parents, or simply an attempt to choose something different. When we genealogists find these names in records, sometimes they are a result of phonetic spelling. Some may be corruptions of other names or attempts to keep names in a family within

---

[2] Angus Baxter, *In Search of Your British and Irish Roots* (New York: William Morrow and Company, 1982), 47.

a particular pattern: names in alphabetical order, or names beginning with the same initials. These are some of the numerous such names found in this country from 1750 to the present: Benoba, Bivy, Callie, Devra, Dicy, Dovie, Floice, Fena, Hattie, Jincey, Kitsey, Lovie, Luvenia, Laney, Lottie, Levicy, Mittie, Nicey, Ora, Olan, Olean, Ottie, Ozora, Parilee, Parizade, Perlissa, Peariby (Pheribah, Pheriby, Fereby), Rebia, and Sinah.

In the United States, each era seems to have had its own pattern of names, in addition to the standard ones which have been used for centuries. The ''period'' names may be related to the attitudes, events, or personalities of the generation, even in subtle ways; or they may be simply ''fads'' which give way to new patterns after several decades.

Girls, and sometimes boys, of the latter seventeenth century and the eighteenth century, especially among New England Puritans, were named for virtues: Patience, Piety, Prudence, Amity, Obedience, Rejoice, Reason, Temperance, Truth, Grace, Charity, Civility, Mercy, Faith, Honour, Hope or Hopeful, Constant or Constance, and Pleasant. Another group of names perhaps suggested experiences of the parents: Desire, Sorrow, Mourning, Comfort, Anguish, and Seaborn. Some Southern men had the given names of Merit and Sterling, which could come from surnames as well as from valued traits.

In the late seventeenth century, Germans poured into Pennsylvania, bringing with them their custom of naming children with two given names. Some families even kept the first name the same for all the sons, for example, and varied only the middle name: Johann Peter, Johann Friedrich, Johann Sebastian, and Johann Georg. As these families and their descendants moved throughout the colonies, other ethnic groups picked up the double-naming custom; and by the mid-nineteenth century, the practice was widespread. As we have seen, the idea allowed parents to name children after grandparents and to perpetuate a surname from previous generations at the same time. Patty *Field* Allen, Hiram *Hawkins* Brelsford, Elliott *Glen* Coleman, George *Rogers* Clark, and many others carried surnames as their middle names and give genealogists at least a clue to another set of roots.

Especially between 1650 and 1860, many children received Biblical names, some of which, of course, are ''standard'' names which have been favorites for centuries. Common female names included Sarah, Eliza-beth, Rebecca, Susanna, Rachel, Martha, Mary, Priscilla, Ruth, Hannah (Anna, Anne), and Judith. Less well known Biblical names were also used: Jerusha, Keturah, Dorcas, Ascenath, Jemina, Zilpah, Phebe (Phoebe), and Orpah. Favorite male names from the Old Testament included Isaac, Jacob, Joseph, Benjamin, Levi, Jesse, David, Samuel, Daniel, Joshua, Moses, Elijah, Seth, Jeremiah, and Ezekiel. New Testament names, of course, included Matthew, Mark, Luke, John, Simon, Peter, James, Thomas, and Rufus.

United States children were, and are, also named in honor of famous Americans or prominent local personalities. In the early years of the Republic, some families showed their patriotic feelings by naming daughters or sons Liberty, Justice, or America. Other families, caught up in the westward movement, named daughters for their new or former states: Virginia, Carolina, Tennessee, Missouri, Louisiana, and Georgia.

These given names from the eighteenth and nineteenth centuries were not titles but actual first names: Major Croom, Admiral Croom, Squire Blalock, Pharoah Lee, Doctor Godwin, Lieutenant Campbell, and Patsy Empress Jones.

From the mid-eighteenth century to about the mid-nineteenth century, Europe, and therefore the United States, experienced a revival of classical architecture, language, and cultural influences, which seems to have carried over into naming practices. Of course, Latin and Greek had for centuries been part of the ''classical'' school curriculum. These are some of the Latin and Greek names and derivatives used during that classical revival period. Some, of course, are still used today and are considered quite usual; others were used for boys and girls alike.

Aurelius, Artemis, Artemesia, Caesar, Cassius, Cassia, Claudia, Clementine, Chloe, Fortunatus, Florian, Fabius, Fabian, Fabia, Guglielmo, Guglielmus, Horatio, Honoria, Hortense, Julius, Junius, Justin, Justina, Latinus, Lydia, Lucian, Lucius, Lucia, Marcellus, Marcus, Nonna, Ophelia, Octavius, Octavia, Pericles, Pompey, Primus, Parmenius, Phyllis, Philena, Portia, Penelope, Parmelia, Philadelphia, Quentin, Rhoda, Sylvanus, Sylvia, Stephanie, Sophia, Sibyl, Sophronica, Theophilus, Theodocia, Tessa, Urban(us), Valentine, Virginious, Virgil, Xene, Zeta, Zenobia, Zephyr.

Many nineteenth and early twentieth century daughters, especially in the South, received the names of flowers and gems: Violet, Pansy, Rose, Daisy, Lily, Ruby, Jewel, Pearl, and Opal. Interesting combinations have come from these names: Lillie White, Rosey Brown, and Pansy Violet Flower.

In the late nineteenth and early twentieth centuries, more children seemed to be named Maude, Malvina, Nora, Lillian, Louise, Edna, Thelma, Elvira, Verna, Gertrude, Gladys, Herbert, Marvin, Albert, Alvin, Ernest, Elmer, Grover, Maynard, Maurice, and Oscar than in previous or following generations. The mid-twentieth century, likewise, had a characteristic set of names which were not so common in earlier or later years: Carol, Linda, Barbara, Shirley, Joan, Janet, Gay(e), Diane, Jill, Joyce, Karen, Carolyn, Sharon, Larry, Dennis, Dean, Ron(ny), Hank, Jerry, Kenneth, Terry, and Carl. Finding popularity in the 1970s and 1980s has been a group of "multi-ethnic" names which have no relationship to the ethnic background of the family using them, and some of which are used equally for boys and girls: Meredith, Lindsey, Whitney, Jason, Jordan, Ashley, Megan, Michelle, Heather, Tiffany, Nicole, Kristen, Allison, Kendra, Ryan, Trey, Travis, Derek, Darin, Shawn/Sean, Ian, Eric, Kevin, Scott, Kendall, Robin, Jennifer, and Kimberley.

Through all these eras, certain "standard" names have continued in popularity: Robert, Richard, William, George, David, Thomas, James, John, Susan, Elizabeth, Emily, Mary, Catherine, Sarah, Anne, and Margaret.

Names can present special problems to the genealogist when several people of the same name appear in the same location at the same time. Their relationship, if any exists, cannot be assumed. Eighteenth century records bearing the name Daniel Coleman or James Shaw or William Black can baffle the researcher quickly. It is difficult to separate these men to determine just how many Daniels, Jameses, or Williams there were, and which records belonged to which man. The genealogist must be careful. We cannot assume the man is automatically our ancestor because the name is the same.

Estate names or other descriptive appellations sometimes help to identify men in the records. Peter Bland "of Jordan's Point" would distinguish this Peter from others. One James Turley drew an eye after his name to separate himself from other James Turleys in the area. He is referred to now, as perhaps he was then, as James One Eye. Perhaps this designation tells us something of his physical appearance.

Sometimes men added "Jr." or "Sr." after their names to distinguish themselves from their father or son or other relative of the same name. For example, three men named Isaac Croom lived in Madison County, Tennessee, during the mid-nineteenth century. The senior Isaac was the uncle of the other two. Of these nephews, one carried his middle initial, *N.*, and the other occasionally added "Jr." to his name. Isaac, Jr., was separating himself from his uncle Isaac rather than from his father, who was Charles.

Discrepancies and problems related to names and relationships cannot always be solved. However, you can form educated guesses. Use primary (first-hand) sources as often as possible and evaluate them thoroughly. Gather as much information as possible. Sort it and use only the most reliable. Support your guesses with facts.

6

Hand-Me-Downs:
Family Traditions

Oral tradition is the stories which have been passed down from generation to generation by word of mouth. This tradition is stronger in some families than in others, but genealogists can use whatever they find. Family stories sometimes grow with the age and imagination of the teller, but there is often much truth in them. Some of the details may get lost or altered, but the basic truths remain.

Many of these traditions tell of the origin of the family: four Mood brothers came to Pennsylvania from Germany; three McFadden brothers came from Ireland. The stories of origin often blur with age: "Mama used to tell me about a couple who eloped and came from Scotland." Somewhere, sometime, this couple may be identified. In the meantime, preserve the story. One important task of the family historian is to preserve this oral tradition by recording it on tape or on paper.

Similar traditions may involve when, or how, or why the family came. Traditions also give vital statistics: Grandpa was one of six boys and had six sisters — twelve children altogether. That was the oral tradition, and yet no one could name all twelve kids. By interviewing descendants, we finally listed ten names which we could prove with census and Bible records. That left two girls' names missing. After finding a distant cousin with a trunk of old letters, the family found a reference to "sister Luta sleeping in the crib" and another mention of "little Willie" recovering from the measles. Then cousin Bea remembered that she had heard about a little girl named Willie. Using the dates of the letters and the census records, we approximated the dates of the lives of these two little girls who died in early childhood. The oral tradition had proved true.

In some cases, these family traditions can be documented and proved correct. The missing details can sometimes be returned to the story through newspapers, letters, public records and interviews. They can become history as the facts are re-established.

However, much of the tradition must be accepted as just that when the records or people who know are not available. For example, the father of those twelve kids was one of fourteen children, eleven of whom have names in the records. Tradition says that three of the children were boys who died in infancy. Their names, if they were named, have not appeared in any records. The tradition is considered correct because several branches of the family have handed down the same story; but it probably cannot be proved.

Many families pass on stories of Civil War experiences: the slave who saved the family or the family home, the wife who ran the farm, the day church services were interrupted by the approach of the enemy, or the enemy who befriended the family. My Civil War ancestor Susan lived in Columbia, South Carolina, when General Sherman's army marched through and burned the city. Susan was among many who fled from their burning homes. She carried the baby and instructed her other two children, a toddler and a pre-schooler, to hold tight to her skirt. In her other arm, she hoped to carry a little bag of family silver, handmade by her father-in-law and his father who had been fine silversmiths. As her little troop struggled on foot toward the "insane asylum" to find refuge for the night, they were approached by a Yankee soldier, who asked if he could help her. She knew she had to give him either the baby or the silver because she could not manage both. She regretfully handed him the bag of silver and resigned herself to the loss of a valuable and meaningful family collection. However, the next morning, miraculously, the enemy soldier reappeared and returned to her the bag of silver! Throughout the years of great sectional bitterness which followed the war, Susan continually reminded her family that there was at least *one* honest Yankee in the world.

In almost every family there is some disaster which the family survived and still relates: the Drought, the Storm, the Flood, the Epidemic, or the Fire. One such story is preserved in several unrelated families: the Fire in which everything was lost except the piano! The move westward provided many experiences which were preserved in oral tradition: selling the family heirlooms because they could not be moved, trying to carry the piano in the wagon, Indian raids, or the loss of loved ones along the way. Moving from South Carolina to Texas was a lengthy, tiring process for Susan and her children, as they came to meet Papa. On the last leg of the journey, they traveled by stagecoach. At the last stop before their destination, the driver got quite drunk at the local tavern and apparently forgot about his passengers. Leaving him in the tavern, Susan herself (or was it her little son?) held the reins and let the horses take the coach on to their new hometown. The coach pulled up before the only building with a light burning — the tavern — but Susan was spared having to venture inside. A young man stepped up, introduced himself as Temple Houston (grandson of General Sam Houston), and said his family was expecting them, but had become worried because the stage was so late arriving.

Black families have unique traditions which sometimes include slave biographies: great-grandfather was a field hand and his wife was a house servant; they lived in Louisiana near Shreveport; he ran away once, was found the next day, and was whipped. On occasion, public records, such as newspapers, the census, and deeds, bear out the details of such traditions. This kind of story, though a sensitive issue in a number of families, can prove very important in establishing the family's ancestry another generation or two back in time. One would hope that the older generation, who may prefer to forget such stories, would nevertheless pass them down to younger family members.

In almost every family, somebody claims close kinship with somebody famous: "Great-Grandmother was a first cousin of Robert E. Lee." "We are descendants of the Presidents Harrison." "Great-Grandmother was a close relative of Sam Houston." In truth, Great-grandmother was born a North Carolina *Lea*, in no way related to the Virginia *Lees*. The fact that Great-grandpa's name was Harrison, and he had relatives who lived near Washington, D.C., when one of the Harrisons was President, certainly does not even suggest any kinship. Very often these tales are simply wishful thinking; very seldom are they even useful.

As in the case of the "close relative of Sam Houston," the tradition has come down through several branches of the family and persists in spite of attempts by that family's genealogist to disprove it. After hearing Aunt Sally's claim of kinship with Sam Houston, Charlotte intensified her search in that particular part of her family. She discovered that Grandma Cummings' maiden name was Huston, sometimes spelled Houston, but her father was Almanzon, not Sam. As she presented this at the next family reunion, she was joined by Aunt Sally, who did not contradict her findings, but added, as if to be helpful, that they were descendants of one of Sam Houston's *sisters*. However absurd that sounded to Charlotte, Aunt Sally was confident of its accuracy.

Doing what genealogists are usually cautioned not to do, because it is usually a waste of time, Charlotte found a biography and a genealogy of Sam Houston's family. In this case, she was not trying to work forward from his family to hers; she was simply comparing two families of the same generation. She found that Sam Houston had three sisters, all born between 1797 and 1800 in Tennessee, the last one named Eliza Ann who married a Moore. Her own Elizabeth, born in 1805 in Pennsylvania, married a Huston but was born a Newton. Aunt Sally's story was simply not true.

At the next family reunion, Charlotte was armed with her facts in case the subject arose. However, this time Aunt Sally "remembered" that their Almanzon Huston was one of Sam Houston's brothers or father's brothers, and that was the gospel truth. Charlotte was ready: Sam Houston had no brother named Almanzon. Although the two men were born only six years apart, Sam was born in Tennessee and Almanzon in New York. Sam's father had only one brother, whose name was John, not Almanzon. Even Sam's grandfather's four brothers are not possible links.

Aunt Sally remains undaunted in her belief of close kinship with the state's popular hero, and she is not alone. Other relatives of her generation agree with her, whatever her story is at the moment, and several old newspaper clippings carry the tradition that Sam and Almanzon were "cousins." In her search, Charlotte found that the two men did know each other, Almanzon having been Sam's Quartermaster General in the Texas War for Independence. Perhaps they called each other "cousin" because of having the same last name. Gradually the younger generation is ignoring Aunt Sally's repetition of her tradition each summer at the reunion and concentrates on learning more about their own Huston ancestor.

Another interpretation of the word *tradition* is a set of customs which are repeated year after year, sometimes into second and third generations. These traditions, too, are part of the family history and are fun to collect. In one family, each child receives a small gift when one has a birthday. In some families the birthday-person has the honor of choosing the menu for the evening meal, or where the family will go to dine out. One family hands down an antique quilt to the Sarah in the next generation; it has the embroidered signatures of related Sarahs dating back some 200 years.

Holidays, especially, are full of traditions. One of my grandfathers had what his family considered a very peculiar custom of having salt mackerel each year for Christmas breakfast. One of my grandmothers always served boiled custard as a holiday treat; and the other grandmother always wanted charlotte russe for Christmas dessert.

Holidays, of course, are often a time for family reunions and gatherings where these traditions are shared and continued. For the genealogist, the occasions are golden opportunities for asking questions, sharing and gathering information, writing down or taping stories, taking photographs, getting autographs, and showing what progress has been made on the family history.

7
Life History:
Beginning to End

As you gather and put in place the middle of your puzzle, what information do you want? Vital statistics, yes, but there is much more to family history than lists of names and dates. For example, if you have a pet, it surely has a name. What did Dad call his dog when he was a boy? What did Great-grandma call her cow? What did Great-grandad call his mule?

Each answer may suggest new questions. If you are really listening, you begin to wonder, "Well, why did he do that?" or "How did they do that?" or "What did it look like?" Ask.

There are hundreds of questions you can ask about each generation. The farther back you go, the fewer answers you receive. But a few answers will give you some picture. The questions suggested here will stretch over many visits and letters. Each person may answer several, but no one could be expected to answer them all. Some of the questions will produce unexpected responses: "Heavens, child! How old do you think I am!" or "Good grief, yes!" or "For crying out loud! Do you think we lived like the Queen of England?" Okay, we live and learn. That is why we ask questions.

You can start with yourself and make notes on your own history. Ask your parents about their childhoods, schooling, teen years, and early married life. Ask grandparents and anyone else who can contribute to the middle of the puzzle. Notes on these questions will be easier to keep in their proper time periods if you indicate at the top the time period you are dealing with: Notes from Grandma Metcalf about her childhood; notes from Grandma Metcalf about her mother's childhood; notes from Great-aunt Wilmer about Grandaddy's early life, 1895–1915; notes from Mahala Yancy on the 1930s.

It is helpful to keep in mind that these questions serve basically two purposes: to extend the information on your charts and to gather life history. Information which contributes to these goals is desirable. Some pieces of information are more important than others. Some are more interesting. Historians seek any pertinent information, but the family historian will want to be careful not to intrude into someone's private territory and not to pull out of the closet skeletons which might cause harm or embarrassment. Family histories must be truthful, but families may prefer to leave some chapters closed where it is unnecessary to mention the information at all. We must honor their wishes.

There are incidents which may have caused embarrassment at one time but which we can laugh about now; these stories add spice to the history. One example is the story of a little girl's mischief. Maggie was five at a time when it was strictly improper for a lady, whether five or fifty, to speak of the body and its parts. Maggie learned a limerick from her older brother and made the mistake of sharing it with her mother. Mama, being concerned with propriety and horrified at Maggie's indecency, washed the little girl's mouth out with soap. The limerick was

> There was a young lady named Mable,
> Who loved to dance on the table,
> But she blushed very red
> When the gentleman said,
> "Oh, look at the legs on the table."

Another little girl in the same family was about seven when the bishop ate Sunday dinner with them. Imagine the disgrace she suffered when, at a lull in the conversation, she addressed the guest, "You wanta hear me drink like a horse?"

The following questions are suggestions for researching a person's life history.

Childhood

1. Gather letters or stories about yourself when you were an infant and a child: firsts, growth, funny incidents, curiosity, likes and dislikes, vocabulary, habits, diseases, accidents.
2. Brothers and sisters: names, your relationship with

them. What stands out about them in your memory of childhood?

3. What is your earliest memory of your house, your family, your town, world affairs?

4. Who were your playmates, pets? What games, toys, celebrations, and playmates were your favorites? How important were television, movies, radio, bicycles in your childhood?

5. Where was your house? If in a city, what address? What county? State? Is the house still standing? What did it look like? How many rooms? Which ones? Describe the house and furnishings: one- or two-story? frame? brick? painted? porch? garage? yard? outbuildings? fireplaces? kind of floor, wall coverings?

6. How easily or often did you get into mischief? Why? What punishments did you incur? Were your parents strict? What rules did you have to follow?

7. What are your most vivid memories of childhood?

8. What relatives do you remember and what stands out in your mind about them? What trips did you take to visit relatives?

9. What chores were yours to do? Did you get an allowance? How did you get your spending money? What did you do with it? What was the financial condition of the family?

10. How did you celebrate birthdays, Christmas, Thanksgiving, July 4, or other holidays?

11. What were family customs for weekends? Sundays? summer days?

12. What unusual events do you recall (fires, storms, moving, etc.)?

13. How far was school from your house? How did you get to school? During what hours were you in school? When did school start in the fall and let out in the summer? What subjects did you like best? least? Were you able to attend school regularly? What do you remember about your teachers? Does any one stand out in your mind as having a large influence on you? How good were your grades? Did you feel pressure to make good grades? How did you spend recess? What memories stand out in your mind about elementary school? junior high school?

14. What did you do in the summer or when you were not in school? trips? sports? scouting? camping?

15. Did you study music, art, dancing? What hobbies did you pursue?

16. What were your childhood favorites: foods, clothes, sport, story, movie, hero, people?

17. What part did church and religious activities play in your childhood, both at home and away from home?

18. What were your dreams or plans for the future? Which have become reality?

19. What experience did you have with death as a child? What funeral or burial customs were followed by the family or area?

20. What neighborhood gatherings, social or working, do you recall?

Teen Years

1. What high school did you attend? Where? How long? Did you graduate? Did you go to college? Where? How did you choose your college? How did you finance your education? In high school (or college), what were your favorite or least favorite subjects? Is there someone from these years who had great influence on you? How large was the school? What clubs or sports did you participate in? Did you enter contests? (Explain.) What do you recall about teachers? classmates? What were some of the school rules? dress code? How did you get to school? How far was it from home? What did you do for lunch? What courses helped you the most?

2. What kinds of parties did you attend? Where did you go on dates? When did you start dating? What rules governed dating at your house? What did you enjoy most for recreation?

3. What clothes were in style when you were in high school?

4. What were your plans or desires at that time of your life? Have you done those things?

5. What chores were your responsibility at home? (Describe.)

6. Did you have pets? What kind? names?

7. What did you read?

8. What unusual or special events do you recall?

9. Where did you live? Was it the same house you lived in as a child? If not, please describe it.

10. Did you enjoy music? dancing? art? other hobbies? Did any of the family sing or play musical instruments? Did you make any of your own clothes? Were you in the school band?

11. Did you have a job? Doing what? How much money did you earn? How did you use your

earnings?

12. What did you do in the summer?
13. What rules governed your household? Were you allowed to play cards? date without a chaperone? stay out past dark? go to movies? dance? eat with the adults? wear slacks to school? Were you required to go to church on Wednesday nights as well as Sunday? stand when adults entered the room? What was considered ''proper'' Sunday or Sabbath conduct? What were considered ''proper'' manners? ''proper'' dress?
14. Did you attend religious services? Where? What other religious activities did you participate in?
15. Did you participate in any service projects? (Explain.)
16. What neighborhood gatherings do you recall?
17. What experience did you have with death as a teenager? What funeral or burial customs do you recall?

Adulthood

1. When did you get married? Describe the wedding, clothes, attendants, parties, gifts, etc.
2. What can you tell me about your courtship and dating? How did you meet your husband (or wife)?
3. What jobs have you held? What jobs has your husband (wife) held? Have wages changed much since you first worked?
4. What trips have you taken? Which have you

enjoyed most?
5. What church, civic, club, political, or service activities have you participated in?
6. What is your political affiliation?
7. What is your church affiliation?
8. Do you enjoy participating in music, art, gardening, handicrafts, needlework (knitting, crochet, tatting, etc.), sewing, carpentry, etc? Which members of the family do (did) which of these activities?
9. How does the family celebrate holidays such as Thanksgiving, Christmas, July 4? What other traditions have you established in your family? What other holidays do you celebrate? How?
10. What kinds of cars have you had? When did you get your first car? How much have the cars cost?
11. What are your favorite recipes?
12. What do you consider your special talents or abilities? What do you do best?
13. What gives you the most pleasure?
14. What are the favorite family stories?
15. When and where were your children born? What stands out in your mind about each one as a small child? as a teenager?
16. Where have you lived? Tell me about each house.
17. Do you have grandchildren? Who?
18. What rules did you set for your children?
19. Do you enjoy entertaining? friends? relatives? business associates? What kind of entertaining do you do?

History as the Family Lived It

In filling in the middle of a family puzzle, the family historian seeks to fit the family into the history of the city, county, state, and nation. The general political, economic, and social history of these areas can be found in published books and newspapers; but only the family can share their own reactions to the public events. For whom did *they* vote? What prices did *they* pay? What jobs did *they* hold? When did *they* get electricity? a telephone? a car? a radio? a television? air-conditioning?

Many of the questions in this section deal with events discussed in history textbooks. Yet many people living during the period were unaware of these events, or were unaffected by them, or did not consider them important. To keep history in perspective, we must balance textbook history with what ordinary people thought and experienced.

The following questions are divided roughly into decades. Some of the public events, well-known people, and customs are included in the appropriate time periods. The questions are aimed at finding out about the family in each period. Use your imagination and add other questions as you think of them. A sample interview sheet is shown in Figure 6.

1940s

1. Did you or members of the family participate in World War II? If so, who? In what capacity? Where? What rank(s) did you hold? In which branch of service? Did you fight? In more than one place? List. What stories can you share about these experiences? Did the family lose members in the war?
2. What did you think of President Franklin Roosevelt at the time? Did you support him at election time, especially the third and fourth times? How did you feel about his third and fourth elections? Have you changed your opinion since then? How effective was he as President in the 1940s?
3. What did you think of President Truman?
4. What did you think of Churchill, Stalin, Hitler,

Eisenhower, Patton, MacArthur, or other political or military leaders?
5. How did the war affect your own plans or life? Did you have to leave school or change your way of life very much?
6. Who in your family had jobs in war industry? In what job did you (they) work? Where? How many hours a day or days a week did you (they) work? How did you get to work? Was it easy to find a job or change jobs?
7. How did you feel about rationing? Did you know people who cheated or otherwise did not co-operate? What items were the hardest to get? What items were not so scarce? Did you raise, can, or preserve any of your own food? What sacrifices did you make? What items did you miss the most?
8. How much was rent? How much was gasoline? How much were food prices? wages? How difficult was it to find housing?
9. Did you travel? for business or pleasure? How did you travel? Was it difficult to get tickets or space on public transportation? Did you have a car? Did you have difficulty getting gasoline, tires, or parts?
10. What part did radio, movies, or sports play in your life during the 1940s? Who were your favorite personalities and programs?
11. What pleasant or funny family stories can you share from the 1940s?
12. What did you think at the time when you heard about the dropping of the atomic bomb? How necessary was it? How necessary was the second bomb? Have you changed your opinion since then?
13. Do you have and can you share any letters or diaries from the period?
14. How did you stay cool in summer without air-conditioning? Do you have air-conditioning now? When did you get it?
15. What were you doing when you heard about the

Pearl Harbor attack? What was your reaction? Do you think we would have entered the war without the Pearl Harbor attack? What was the effect of the news on your area?

16. What were you doing when you heard about Roosevelt's death? What was your reaction?

1930s

1. To what extent did the Depression change your habits, way of life, schooling, plans? Did you "feel" the Depression? Was there a difference in the way the Depression affected people living in cities and people living in the country or small towns?

2. Which family members had jobs? Doing what? What was your pay? Were you paid in cash, goods, or scrip? How much was rent? Was it difficult to find housing? to find jobs?

3. At the time, what did you think of presidents Hoover and Roosevelt? Have you changed your opinions since then? For whom did you vote in 1928 (Hoover or Smith), 1932 (Hoover or Roosevelt), 1936 (Roosevelt or Landon)? Why?

4. Did any family member work for one of the New Deal agencies, such as the CCC, the WPA, or the PWA? If so, who? which agency? Doing what? How long? Where?

5. Did the family raise or hunt, can, or preserve any of its own food? If so, what? What food items did you find scarce or plentiful? Did you live on a farm, in a small town, or in a city? Did you notice any difference in the availablility of food in rural and urban areas?

6. What part did radio, movies, or sports play in your life? Who were your favorite stars? When did you see your first movie in color? When did you see your first sound film? What was your reaction to these new developments? How much were movie tickets?

7. What sacrifices did you make? Why?

8. Did you have a car? If so, what make or model? How much did it cost? How much did gasoline cost? Did you limit your driving? Did you have to give up your car during the Depression? If you did not have a car, what kind of transportation did you rely on?

9. Did you have any money in a bank before or during the Depression? If so, did you lose any of it? If not, why not and where did you keep any

cash you had? Did you lose any stock in the stock market crash?

10. Did the family sew, or do its own carpentry, building, etc?

11. How have your experiences during the Depression affected your attitudes of the present?

12. What games, toys, pets, playmates, etc., did the children have?

13. To what extent were church, school, and family gatherings part of your life? What church and school activities were you involved in?

14. Do you have and can you share any letters or diaries from the period?

15. What recollections and stories can you share about your experiences?

16. Did you hear Orson Welles' *War of the Worlds* on radio on 30 October 1938? What did you think of it at the time? Did you fall for it? Why or why not?

17. Did the family move during this decade? Why? How frequently? Where? What conveniences did you have or lack?

1920s

1. To what extent were you aware of the "Roaring" Twenties at the time? How aware were you of Al Capone and gangster activities? How aware were you of Prohibition? Did it change your own habits? Did you favor it at the time? To what extent do you feel it worked or did not work? Did you obey it? Why or why not?

2. What electrical appliances or conveniences did you acquire for the first time during the decade? What was the first electrical appliance you bought? Did you have a washing machine? indoor plumbing? hot and cold water? What kind of cook stove did you have? What kind of heating? Did you have a car? If so, what make and model? What color? Do you remember its price or the cost of gasoline? How did you buy groceries? Were groceries delivered to the house? Did you shop at different shops for different food items? To what extent did you feel yourself part of the general "prosperity" of the decade?

3. What games, toys, pets, and playmates did the children of the family have?

4. Where did the family live? City or farm? What city, county, state? Did you move during the decade? How frequently? Why?

5. What part did radio, movies, or sports play in the life of the family? Who were your favorite stars? When did you get your first radio? What was your reaction the first time you heard a radio? Was there ever any family restriction on movie-going? Where were movies shown? How much was admission?

6. What did the older family members feel about the fashions and youth of the "new age"? Were they alarmed or did they adjust to the changes pretty well? What do you feel were the greatest changes of the decade? What invention or development do you feel caused the greatest change?

7. What kind of house(s) did the family have? Describe it (them). How much was rent? Out-buildings? electricity? furniture?

8. What part did church, school, and family gatherings play in your life? What church and school activities were you involved in?

9. To what extent were you aware of political scandals of the decade? Whom did you support for President in 1920 (Harding or Cox), 1924 (Coolidge or Davis), and 1928 (Smith or Hoover)?

10. How did the family celebrate holidays, weddings, birthdays?

11. What did the family do for recreation?

12. Do you have and can you share any letters or diaries from the period?

13. What provisions were made for the older family members?

14. Did you find it difficult to acquire new cars? Was it easier to get used cars? How available were they?

World War I

1. Did any family member fight in the war? If so, who, where, what rank(s), how long?

2. To what extent were you aware of Wilson's efforts to get the United States into the League of Nations? What was your personal opinion of these efforts? Did you favor League membership?

3. To what extent were you aware of anti-German feelings and activities in the United States during the War? Did any take place where you lived? Were you affected by any of these?

4. How did the family participate in celebration at the close of the war?

5. Did the family grow a "Liberty garden"? Did you observe "wheatless" and "meatless" days? What did you substitute for meat, wheat, and sugar? Did you have trouble getting these foods? Were any other foods scarce? Did you buy "Liberty bonds"?

6. To what extent did church or school activities influence your attitudes toward the war or your participation?

7. Did your family or any friends receive any special government allowances which some state governments awarded to families of servicemen overseas?

8. Were you aware of any exemptions to the draft policies? Were you aware of any physically handicapped men being drafted?

9. The Spanish flu epidemic of 1918 hit most of the United States and Europe. Estimates have said that it took twice as many lives as the war did. Was your family affected by this flu epidemic? Were there family deaths from it? (Explain.)

1900–1920

1. Where did the family live? How did they earn a living? Did any women of the family work outside the home? In what job? Did the family move during the period? How frequently? Where?

2. If you lived on a farm, what crops and animals did you raise? Which ones were raised for sale? Garden? Orchard?

3. Can you describe your house? When did the family get indoor plumbing for the first time? running water? electricity? Did each house have these conveniences? What kind of stove, heating, and lighting did you have? Outbuildings?

4. When did you get your first car? What kind? New or used?

5. Were the children in school? What do you remember of school subjects, rules, activities, hours, sports, clothes, holidays, homework, pep squads, etc?

6. What games, toys, pets, and playmates did the children have?

7. What part did church, school, or family gatherings play in your life? What church and school activities did you participate in?

8. If you lived in a town or city, did you have such improvements as paved streets, street lights, sidewalks, parks? Describe. When did your town add each one? What was it like without them?

9. How would you classify your economic status at the time? On what do you base this decision?

10. To what extent were you aware of or sympathetic

DEPRESSION 1930's   Interviewer _Emily Croom_   Date _May 1970_

Name _Mrs. H. O. Metcalfe_

Age group during most of the 1930's (circle one)   Child (Adult) Teenager

Family Size (family with which you were living in the 30's) _4_

Residence in the 1930's _Marfa, Texas_   urban rural (small town)

Educational level in the 30's (circle the appropriate) high school student/(graduate)
  other _husband – college graduate_   college student/graduate

If you were a student during the 30's, how did the depression affect your education?
  Were you able to continue?* ___ How did you finance your education (scholarships,
  jobs, parents, etc.)? Did you or your friends drop out temporarily?*no permanently?
  *daughter in college did continue – financed her education with
  scholarships, summer + school-year jobs, + help from parents.

For each job you held, what were the wages and hours? Please list chronologically.

Job	Location	Days/week	Hours/day	Wages or Salary
1. housewife	Marfa			
2. husband lawyer	"	as necessary –		varied
3.		(self-employed)		
4.	He always said people fight more + get into disputes more			
5.	in bad times than in good so lawyers did okay – were kept			
	busy.			

What jobs did other members of your family hold?
husband – lawyer + U.S. Commissioner   *note: Many hobos came by + we fed them too. Everybody in town did.*

                    the family
Were you self-supporting? was Did you help support your family? _____
  Did you have trouble finding a job when it was necessary to change? _____
  How were you able to find another?
→also attended reviews, polo games, etc at the   *Mr. Raetzsch owned Palace movie
army post, frequently went down to "meet   theater + we went to movies some-
the train," followed the fire truck.   about 10-15¢ admission. Didn't
What did you do for recreation or entertainment? get good radio reception except out on
  little dinner parties, bridge parties, young people had   road to stock yard – so up went there.
ice cream parties + tennis + baseball + basketball.

Did your family raise, (make), can, preserve any of its own food? _yes_ If so, what?
  bread, desserts   Canned peaches + other fruit. Made preserves.
Which food items were most difficult to obtain? easiest to obtain?
  Could get what we were accustomed to having before.
Which commodities (clothes, appliances, tools, toys, etc.) were most difficult to
obtain? easiest to obtain? What luxury items did you have to sacrifice?
  appliances – scarce   did without luxuries anyway
  money – scarce [note: daughter says she was excellent manager]
Was your family a "do-it-yourself" group to save money? _Yes_ What did you make?
  Sewing most of the clothes for the 2 girls + myself.
Did you or your family own a car? _yes_ More than one? _no_ What make? c 1925 Chevy
  Do you remember the price of gasoline, or of the car? No but 5¢/gallon on the
              (about 15¢-20¢/gallon) army post in town
Were you able to buy on credit? _yes – nearly everything_ – groceries,
  cleaning, gasoline, drug store. Paid on first of each month.
Did you travel? yes – summer By what means? _car mostly_
  Were the trips mostly for business or pleasure? (Comments are welcome.)
  to visit relatives in San Antonio.

How have your experiences during the depression influenced your attitudes of the
  present? Made us appreciate the value of money more.

toward minority groups during this period? Did the town or area practice segregation? How did you feel about immigrants? about restricting immigration?

11. To what extent were you aware of urban and industrial problems of this period? To what extent were you aware of reformers, muckrakers, progressives, and their efforts? Did you hear of *The Jungle* or read it? To what extent did you support or know about these reform efforts? To what extent were you affected by them?

12. What were the rules, restrictions, and etiquette governing your household?

13. What did people wear? Did the family make any of its own clothes? Did the ladies wear their hair long? use cosmetics? wear jewelry? Explain.

14. What relatives did you visit? What stands out in your mind about these relatives, especially older ones? How did you travel?

15. What part did mail-order catalogs play in your life? Which catalogs did you use?

16. What recollections stand out vividly in your mind from this period?

17. How did the family celebrate holidays, weddings, birthdays?

18. What household chores were assigned to various members of the family?

19. Do you have letters or diaries or stories to share about events during the period, such as fires, storms, disease, or special achievements?

20. When did the family get its first telephone? What was your reaction upon hearing a telephone for the first time?

21. How did you wash clothes before you had a washing machine? How did you stay cool in the summer? How did you get groceries?

22. Describe fashions of the period. What were the hair styles? Did the men wear beards and moustaches?

23. Were the children of the family or young people allowed to play cards? date without a chaperone? stay out past dark? go to movies? dance? eat with the adults? wear slacks to school? Whose job was it to iron? wash clothes? wash dishes? chop wood? Were you required to go to church on Wednesday nights as well as Sundays? stand when adults entered the room? Was it customary to bathe on Saturday night? in the kitchen or in a bathroom? What were the special rules or

customs for Sundays and / or holidays?

24. What did you think when you saw your first car? What funny or interesting experiences did you have with cars and roads during this period?

Before 1900

1. Where did the family live? How did they earn a living? Did they move? How frequently? Where? Why? Did any women of the family work outside the home? Doing what? What was the family attitude toward women working? toward single women in the family?

2. What provisions were made for older family members?

3. What kind of house did you live in? Describe it.

4. Were you or other family members in school? If not, why not? If so, what do you remember of school subjects, rules, activities, hours, sports, clothes, holidays, homework?

5. What games, toys, pets, playmates did the children have?

6. What kind of clothes did the children wear? the adults?

7. What part did church, school, and family gatherings play in your life? Describe these.

8. Did any member of the family fight in the Spanish–American War (1898)? What was the family's attitude toward this war?

9. Do you remember any special celebrations at New Year's when 1899 gave way to 1900 and a new century?

10. What were the hair styles? Did the ladies wear jewelry or cosmetics? What kind? Did the men have beards and moustaches?

11. Were the children or young people allowed to play cards? date without a chaperone? stay out past dark? go to movies? dance? eat with the adults? wear slacks to school? Whose job was it to iron? wash clothes? wash dishes? chop wood? Were you required to go to church on Wednesday nights as well as Sunday? Were you supposed to stand when adults entered the room? Was it customary to bathe on Saturday night? in the kitchen or in a bathroom? Describe.

12. Did the family have electricity, running water, indoor plumbing, telephone, or gas lights before 1900? If not, what did you use? What kind of transportation did you rely on?

13. What Civil War stories have been handed down

in the family? Did any family member fight in the war? If so, who? Where? How did the war affect the family? Which side did the family support? Where did the family live during the war? Did they move soon after the war? Why? When? To where? Did any family members die in the war or because of the war?

14. What family traditions still exist from the period before the Civil War? How did the family earn a living? Did the family own slaves? Was the family caught up in the "westward movement"? Can you identify the various places they lived at various times?

Immigration

1. Who was the immigrant ancestor, couple, or family of this particular branch of the family? Where did this person, couple, or family originate? When and why did they come to this country? Are there family stories or records about where they sailed from, what ship they came on? Are there family stories about their coming and their early experiences here?

2. Does anyone know the names or locations of relatives still in the old country? Are there family Bibles, letters, or other records which give genealogical or geographical information about the family left behind in the old country, or ancestral information from the old country?

3. What traditions does the family preserve from the old country? Names? Recipes? Customs? Costume? What vestiges of the former language still exist in the family? What language did the family speak before coming to this country? Are there pictures or personal belongings still in the family from the immigrant generation, or things they brought with them to this country?

See Bibliography, Appendix B, for resources to help you in searching for your immigrant ancestor.

Black Families

1. According to tradition, which family members were slaves? Where did they live as slaves? Who were the slave-owners? Do you know the name of the plantation or farm or town where they lived, the county, or any landmarks near the residence? How did each one choose his or her last name? If you cannot recall the slave-owner's name, would anyone recognize it if he or she heard it? Were family members at the same plantation or farm for more than one or two generations?

2. Did family members leave the slave-owner's farm after the Civil War? (or perhaps during the Civil War?) Where did they go? Did they go very far away? How did they choose where to go? Was there a particular skill represented in the family which would help one or more find jobs? (For example, blacksmiths, coopers, seamstresses, tailors, carpenters, etc.)

3. After the Civil War, or emancipation, did family members keep the given names they had as slaves, or did they change their names? If they changed their names, do you know what the earlier names were? Do you know the names of slave mothers in the family? Is there any family tradition or record of emancipation prior to the Civil War? Are there family traditions or stories about various places where family members have lived at various times in the past? Can you name any of those places or the approximate time period when family members were in that location?

4. After the Civil War, or emancipation, where did family members live? Work? Were any self-employed? Who were brothers and sisters of the former slaves? Did a group of relatives live together as an extended family after emancipation? Do you know where the family or individual family members were living in 1870, 1880, 1900? What family traditions or records are there about education, religious participation or membership, and professional or social organizations to which family members belonged between 1865 and 1920?

5. Is there family tradition of where any family members came from to the United States? Or when? Did any immigrate as free men and women? Did any immigrate to this country after 1865? From where? When? Are there family names which are traditional in several generations which might give clues to places of origin, either in this country or elsewhere?

6. Are there family traditions or records of intermarriage with white, Indian, or other racial or ethnic groups? Do you have names of any of these ancestors who were non-Black? Do you know anything about any of them?

7. Who is the oldest living member of this side of the family? Interview him or her if at all possible.

Any information you can gather from these and similar questions can help you, even if the information is limited. See Appendix B, Bibliography, for additional books which can help you with your search.

As black men and women became free, they chose their own family names. Some wanted to be known as Freeman or Freedman. Others named themselves in honor of great Americans such as Washington, Jefferson, or Jackson. Some used the name of their former master or of someone who helped them after emancipation.

Slaveowners often mentioned their slaves in their deeds and wills. Slave mothers were often listed with their children in these records. Slaves were listed, though not always by name, in the 1850 and 1860 census records in separate slave schedules which are available on microfilm at the National Archives and many genealogical libraries. Of course, after the Civil War, former slaves and their children are enumerated in the regular "Population Schedules" of the 1870, 1880, 1900, and 1910 censuses, all of which are available to the public.

Before the segregation of churches and before the Civil War, church registers sometimes included servants and slaves in birth, death, and baptism records. Newspapers carried notices of runaway slaves and apprentices, usually including a physical description and sometimes giving their names. Such documents may be very useful for the black genealogist, especially if he can determine the name of a former slaveowner or plantation, or the approximate location of the place where his slave ancestors lived.

9
What Were They Like?

One of the most interesting aspects of the family history puzzle is discovering some of the personality traits and physical features which made up the family. You can probably answer these questions yourself for the relatives you know. In an effort to know something about those who are no longer living, you can try some of these questions on the people who did know them.

Personal Appearance

1. Do you have a photograph of him (her)?
2. Was he (she) tall, average height, or short?
3. Was he (she) thin, average size, stocky, heavy, fat?
4. Was his (her) face stern, pleasant, wrinkled, sad, etc?
5. Was he bald? Did he have a beard or moustache? How did she wear her hair?
6. Was he (she) healthy? sickly? In what way?
7. Was he handsome? Was she pretty? What color skin, hair, and eyes did he (she) have?
8. What feature of his (hers) stands out in your mind?
9. Were there physical features that showed up in more than one member of the family, such as a "drooping left eyelid" or flat feet or blindness?
10. Is there a history of certain diseases in the family?

Habits and Personality

You may find it convenient to use a number scale in answering these questions. To what extent was he or she _____? You could use **0** for *never,* **1** for *rarely,* **2** for *sometimes,* **3** for *frequently.*

1. How often did he / she / you . . .
smoke, chew tobacco, drink, curse; travel, read; enjoy housekeeping, enjoy cooking; play tennis, golf, or other sports; ride a bicycle; skate, ski, etc.; raise animals or pets; like or raise cats; like or raise dogs; sleep late, rise early, stay up late, or go to bed early?
2. How often did he / she / you . . .
play cards (what games?), tell jokes, tease others, play practical jokes, create nice surprises for others, entertain, correspond, visit friends, manipulate people?
3. To what extent or how often did he / she / you . . .
smile, frown, laugh, get mad, cry, complain, gossip, see the bright side, dwell on the past, experience failure or success, look to the future for happiness, enjoy today, have a one-track mind, start projects and not finish them, get things accomplished, work long hours, stay busy, work hard, make mountains out of mole hills, imagine crises which were not really crises, organize well, worry, have common sense?
4. Did he / she / you have a nickname? What?
5. If he / she / you had a few hours to pursue an activity for pleasure, what would the activity be?
6. What were his / her / your special talents? abilities?
7. To what extent was he / was she / were you . . .
a worrier, a loner, a hypochondriac, the life of the party, a good conversationalist, a willing worker, a perfectionist, a spendthrift, a stern disciplinarian, a good story-teller, a leader, a follower, a manager?
8. To what extent was he / was she / were you . . .
demanding of self, demanding of others, hard (easy) to please, hard (easy) to work with, neat (sloppy) in habit and dress, absent-minded, scatterbrained, literal-minded, argumentative, clever, ingenious, logical, shallow-thinking, lazy, ambitious, industrious, energetic, diligent, consistent, flexible, responsible, efficient, artistic, musical, creative, dramatic?
9. To what extent was he / was she / were you . . .
possessive, sharing, affectionate, generous, warm-hearted, kind, stingy, miserly, critical, jealous, blunt, outspoken, softspoken, clever with words, silly, open-minded, narrow-minded, forthright, angered easily, talkative, out-going, understanding, empathic, sympathetic, henpecked, bossy, hard (easy) to get along with, hard

(easy) to talk to, quiet, considerate, courteous, radiant, concerned about others, concerned about what others thought, aloof, confident, intuitive?

10. To what extent was he / was she / were you...
moody, even-tempered, grumpy, gruff, self-centered, eccentric (explain), lonely, finicky (explain), stubborn, suspicious, philosophical, religious, strong in faith, jolly, serious, light-hearted, cruel, nervous, relaxed, carefree, thrifty, hurried, stern, angry, happy, courageous, cheerful, egotistical, humble, honest, sensitive, temperate, temperamental, modest?

11. How did he / she / you feel about...
pregnancy, working women, housekeeping, hobbies, yard work, gardening, travel, death, sewing, spending money, daughters going to college, daughters getting married, single women living alone, women staying single, provisions for older members of the family?

10
Checklist of Family Sources

Family sources vary a great deal from family to family, and your search for information may turn up new sources long hidden in an attic, trunk, or closet. Use this chapter as a checklist of these family sources.

Relatives you already know are the first most obvious source of family history information: parents, grandparents, great-grandparents, cousins, aunts and uncles, great-aunts and great-uncles, brothers and sisters, nieces and nephews. Make an effort to contact these people to tell them of your project, to ask their help, and to share what you are learning. Often they can contribute valuable information, and sometimes they will want to participate in the search with you.

Long-time family friends can occasionally add as much information as relatives can.

Family Bibles and prayer books containing a register of births, deaths, and marriages may be available in several parts of the family so check around for more than one. The most reliable of these sources is the record made at the time of the event. Look at the publication date of the Bible to determine whether the family entries pre-date or post-date the publication date. If the family dates pre-date the Bible itself, it is clear that the family entries were made some time, perhaps years, after the events themselves. In the course of time, dates may be remembered incorrectly.

Family letters, diaries, memoirs, and autobiographical sketches are often excellent sources of births, marriages, deaths, migrations, illnesses, education, daily life, church membership, and observations on contemporary events. My Elliott Coleman even wrote in a letter to his sister the weight of all his children! After all, sister Lucy had never seen his family, and he was describing everyone to her, and to us! He also expressed his opinion that "the plow should never have been brought west of the Brazos River." Written in one of the drier years of the 1880s, the letter is evidence of the problems that farmers had in adjusting to the West Texas and Great Plains environment.

Such letters also furnish us with signatures and handwriting samples that may tell us more about the writers themselves.

Scrapbooks often contain newspaper clippings, funeral cards, party or wedding invitations, letters and postcards, speeches and essays, birth announcements, certificates and awards, photographs, graduation announcements and programs, diplomas, recital programs, and other mementos of important events in the person's life and family. They may yield vital statistics, family relationships, and "spice" for your family history.

School and college yearbooks and other school publications usually contain photographs of students and faculty and give a good picture of school life, both academic and extra-curricular. From these you may learn what Granddad's senior debate topic was, or that Grandmother was elected Most Beautiful Freshman. These books can often be found at the library of the institution itself if the family does not have copies.

Photographs often have identifying labels and clues. They may be labeled with names you have not heard of before, which may be those of relatives after all. Pictures may also show the photographer's address, which could be a clue to the residence of the family in the pictures. People who moved away from home and family, whether across country or across the ocean, sometimes exchanged photos with family members who remained at home. These pictures could help you identify the place from which an immigrant came or the place to which part of the family immigrated. Clothing styles, automobiles, buildings, or signs in the photos could help date them.

Family papers can be a wide variety of items, including deeds, land grants, copies of wills, birth certificates, marriage licenses, oil and mineral leases, voter registration cards, records of naturalization, records from a family business, household accounts and budgets, school report cards, school transcripts, old driver's licenses, membership cards from social and professional organizations, inventories made for insurance purposes, insurance papers, and other documents. These papers probably will give you some vital statistics, signatures of various ancestors, and interesting socio-economic data on the family.

Living relatives that you may not know when you begin your family history puzzle can be very valuable sources. With the help of parents, grandparents, and cousins, you can usually find second and third and even more distant cousins who want to share in the family history project. Second cousins share a common great-grandparent; third cousins have a common great-great-grandparent.

My dad's first cousin in Tennessee still lives in the same town where the family moved in 1845. She herself was not particularly interested in tracing family history, but she helped me in many ways: providing me a place to stay when I went searching, sharing her own memories with me, introducing me to other cousins in her area, and passing along a letter from a distant cousin we had never heard of before. A Mississippi lady had traced some of her great-grandmother's Coleman brothers to Katherine's town, using family letters and the photographer's address on old pictures in her great-grandmother's album. She wrote to the local historian trying to find someone who might know about these Colemans. He gave her letter to cousin Katherine to send to me, and we were "reunited" with our very own distant Coleman cousins. We were able to identify the children in the photos as some of our Elliott's children and were allowed to copy them. The trunk of century-old family letters in Mississippi proved invaluable in piecing together our common history. Likewise, my search had found some information that was new and helpful to her.

Our task now is to interest the younger generation in maintaining the ties which we have re-established. One way families can do this is through **round-robin letters.** The first family sends a letter to another family of relatives; they add their letter and send both to a third family. The third family adds theirs and sends all three letters to a fourth, and so on, until all who have agreed to participate have received the packet. The last family returns the packet to the original family, who replaces their original letter with a new one and sends the packet around again. Each family in turn replaces their previous letter with a new one.

Another method of exchanging information and keeping up with each other is through a **family association.** Some family associations are highly organized, with officers who have specific duties. Others are less structured, with one or two people taking the lead. Some families have a **periodic reunion** or publish a **periodical newsletter**—bimonthly, quarterly, semi-annually, or yearly—as a means of sharing information among their own group and any others searching the same surname.

A Texas genealogist has compiled a list of some 600 family newsletters and periodicals published throughout the country. Her list also includes a number of newspaper genealogy columns that appear in papers in Alabama, Arkansas, California, Florida, Georgia, Indiana, Kansas, Louisiana, Maine, Maryland, Missouri, Michigan, Nebraska, Ohio, Oklahoma, Pennsylvania, Texas, Virginia, Washington, and West Virginia. The 1988 edition of *Family Periodicals* costs $5.00 and is available from Mrs. Merle Ganier, 2108 Grace Street, Ft. Worth, Texas 76111. Subsequent editions are planned.

Family periodicals sometimes have a rather short life-span, and they vary considerably in quality. However, if your surname has a periodical available, a subscription could put you in contact with people who can help you in your search. Many of the family newsletters do deal with the various spellings of their name. Figure 7 lists some of the family newsletters available.

Checklist for finding distant relatives with whom to exchange information:

1. Relatives you already know and family friends can often help you find second, third, or more distant cousins.
2. Family papers and letters may contain addresses, at least town names, which may help you locate any of the family still in that area.
3. Family association newsletters.
4. Queries in newspaper genealogy columns in your research locale.
5. Ads in newspapers of your research locale.
6. Queries in genealogical periodicals. *The Genealogical Helper* (The Everton Publishers, Inc., Logan, Utah 84321) is one periodical which devotes considerable space of each issue to genealogists all over the country wanting to exchange information on particular families. Regional genealogical society periodicals contain queries about families from that county, district, or region. Membership in a society in your research area is often money well spent.
7. Surname lists of genealogical societies. Genealogical

societies often publish with their membership rosters the surnames that each member is searching. These lists are sometimes for sale from the society office. A useful book for locating a genealogical society in your research area is *A Directory of His-*

torical Societies and Agencies in the United States and Canada (Nashville: American Association for State and Local History, latest edition). Sometimes a letter to the public library or other agency in a town inquiring about a genealogical society in the area may help you find one.

8. Hereditary society membership rosters. If you have an ancestor who could qualify you for membership in an organization such as the Daughters of the American Revolution or the Daughters of 1812, you may be able to obtain membership records of other relatives who have also qualified by being descendants of that same patriot. With current membership rosters or the help of the chapter from which the relative joined the society, you may be able to get in touch with these distant cousins. To know whether anyone has joined from your particular ancestor's family, check the ancestor or patriot index for the society.

DAR Patriot Index. Washington: National Society of Daughters of the American Revolution, 1966.

DAR Patriot Index. Vol. II. Washington: National Society of Daughters of the American Revolution, 1980. (Supercedes Supplements 1, 2, and 3.)

1812 Ancestor Index (Eleanor Stevens Galvin, Compiler). Washington: National Society of United States Daughters of 1812, 1970.

The Hereditary Register of the United States (The Hereditary Register Publications, Inc., Jerome Francis Beattie, ed., latest edition) gives addresses for the many hereditary societies, a list of family associations and their publications, genealogical societies, and certified genealogists.

9. Published or privately printed family histories which pertain to your families may contain the address of the author or the publisher, from whom you can sometimes get a current address for the author.

10. Telephone directories, whether in your own area or that of your ancestors, can sometimes give you the names of people who have the same surname as the one you are researching. Contacting these people may or may not lead you to a relative; but I have met some very helpful people by using this technique.

11. Photographs labeled with the photographer's address or containing some other clue to the place where the photo was taken may in turn give a clue

---

Some Surnames in *FAMILY PERIODICALS*

Alford	Graves	Odom
Alexander	Green	Overholser
Arnold	Gregg	Parke
Ashby	Hardy	Pate
Ball	Harrington	Penney
Barron	Harris	Perkins
Bean	Haskell	Phillips
Bell	Hawkins	Potter
Bennett	Haynes	Powell
Berry	Heller	Price
Blalock	Holmes	Purcell
Bland	Houser	Rice
Bunker	Jolly	Riley
Campbell	Joseph	Robertson
Carmack	Kelso	Robinson
Carpenter	Kershner	Rowe
Carroll	Knight	Sample
Clark	Knowles	Self
Coffey	Lamb	Shirley
Collier	Lawson	Simpson
Cook	Light	Sparks
Crane	Lipscomb	Stephen(son)
Cullum	Little	Strong
Daniel	Locke	Taft
Davis	Love	Terrell
Dawes	Madden	Thompson
Dodd	Martin	Thornton
Droddy	Mattocks	Townsend
Eagle	McCrary	Turner
East	McCutcheon	Underwood
Edwards	McKinney	Upchurch
Elkins	McKnight	Valentine
Elliott	Mercer	Van Aken
Ellis	Miller	Wade
Estes	Moore	Walker
Evans	Morrell	Weatherly
Fields	Newton	Williams
Flynt	Nelson	Wolf
Garner	Nichols	Womack
Gebhart	Nye	Wright

to the residence of the family, which can in turn give you a locale in which to search, using some of the techniques already listed.

Spice from Family Sources

Your family history puzzle takes on depth and character in proportion to the amount of ''spice'' you add to it as you search. There are many extras you can add to the information you collect.

Some families are fortunate enough to inherit antique furniture as part of their heritage; others receive smaller personal belongings, such as books, crocheted work, teaspoons, and jewelry. Each of these items takes on new meaning as you learn of its past and its former owners. If these items belong to other family members, you can photograph those you wish to include in your history.

Photography offers a wide range of extras for you, from furniture to houses, from tombstones to people still living. Some photographs are already taken and waiting to be claimed. These are often unidentified faces in albums, tintypes in an old trunk, or water-stained sketches hidden behind later pictures in a frame. With the help and permission of older family members or those who own the pictures, you can label the photographs and have copies made. They make nice surprise gifts and preserve an important side of family history.

When photographs are not preserved, you can create your own pictures by sketching such things as houses or household items. Descriptions of houses, inside or outside, can come from those who lived in them. With their careful observations and your careful notations, together you can provide sketches or floor plans for future generations. An example is the floor plan of the Blalock house of Whiteville, Tennessee, which housed four generations of that family. The house is no longer standing, and there are few photographs of it. The sketch provides the descendants one view of their ''ancestral home.'' (See Figure 8.)

More difficult to find but equally entertaining are handwriting samples from your ancestors. I enjoy collecting their signatures. These are most readily found in old letters, as were the two illustrations shown in Figure 9, written in 1855 and 1854, respectively. Handwriting may also be identified in a family Bible, on original copies of deeds, wills, or other documents, on birth certificates, or on old report cards from school.

Reverend Henry Metcalf made it easier for his descendants to find his signature by signing and returning to the county courthouse the marriage license for each couple whose wedding ceremony he performed.

Studying the old letters can tell you something about the people who wrote them. Did he (she) consistently misspell the same words? Was he (she) consistent in the way he formed his letters? Is he academic or free from rules in matters of punctuation, grammar, spelling, and choice of words? Are the lines of writing straight or slanted? Did he think faster than he wrote, as shown by words which he added when he proofread the letter? Is the letter neatly executed? Is the writer sentimental? Does he express his affections? Does he express his hopes and dreams? Does he reveal his faith or religious beliefs? Does he gossip? Does he give advice? Does he feel a duty rather than a desire to write? Does he mention any enjoyment or pleasure? Does he concentrate on health and greetings, or on business? Nineteenth century letters can say less in more words than we can imagine; they mention receipt of letters, apologies for delays in answering, wishes for good health, inquiries into the health of each member of the family, and greetings to everyone in the family. If they have not run out of space by the end of the page, they may share a little of the ''nuse'' of the neighborhood: weddings, births, parties, and always illnesses and deaths.

Here is a letter written from Sommerville, Tennessee, 2 February 1848, to a brother in Buckingham County, Virginia.

> Dear Brother,
> Yours of date 15 of Jan reached us on the 31rst, you seem to be repenting that you had not writen to me before asking me to forgive you I will if you will not do so again I havent much nuse to communicate, but will answer you and make it an invariable rule to answer all the letters I get as soon as I possibly can and ask the same of all my correspondents You stated in your letter you were at Fathers a few days before you wrote and they were all well, except Sister Lucy I am sorry to hear her health is bad. I am afraid she grieves too much after our dear and affectionate mother. I hope she is better off. so it is useless to grieve after her but endeavour to follow her—You wrote Aunt Susan was to be married to Wm Miller sometime during this month. If she has her choice I haven't a word to say but wish her all the happiness this world can afford You spoke of coming to this country [sic] I came in the summer I don't think

BLALOCK HOME

WHITEVILLE, TENNESSEE
1830's - 1946
HOME OF
JESSE BLALOCK, I,
PITSER M. BLALOCK,
JESSE BLALOCK

HEN HOUSE

WELL

N

LOG
SMOKE
HOUSE

FENCE

ADDED WING

NEW KITCHEN

PANTRY

NEW DINING

BOYS BEDROOM

OLD KITCHEN
(GIRLS BEDROOM)

ORIGINAL BEDROOM

ORIGINAL FRONT ROOM

BRICK FIREPLACE

ORCHARD

PLUM TREE

GARDEN

ORCHARD

BRICK WALK

ROSES

SHUTTER WINDOWS

ORIGINAL BEDROOM

ORIGINAL BEDROOM

NO WINDOWS

SECOND FLOOR

EAC.
AS DESCRIBED BY
KATHERINE BROOKS

it prudent for a person to leave their friends unless they can better themselves. If you will let me know what you are doing or in other words what wages you are getting and I can tell whether you can do better here than you can in Va Cotton is selling for a very low price from 5½ to 6 very little selling at present All that can are holding on until spring thinking it will be higher negroes are selling very low compared with the sales twelve months ago there is a trader in this place by the name of Brooks with a drove of negroes he cant get first cost for his negroes corn is selling from 1.75 to 2.00 dollars cash, pork from 4 to 4¼ dull at that I delivered your message to Catherine she requested me to send her love to you in return for yours says you must write to her and she will answer. This leaves us well present my best love to all enquiring friends and relations and accept the same yourself. I must conclude as I havent anything more to write adiue [sic] dear brother I remain your devoted brother

E G Coleman

What can we learn from this letter?
1. It took 16 days in January for Archer's letter to reach Tennessee.
2. Elliott disciplined himself to answer correspondence. He wanted to hear from family.
3. Their mother had recently died. (Bible record shows that she died on 24 December 1847, about five weeks before this letter was written.)
4. Elliott loved his mother and his family.
5. Elliott could face death around him without over-grieving.
6. He apparently thought Aunt Susan was making a mistake in her choice of a husband. Other records show that this aunt was his father's sister.
7. Aunt Susan planned to marry in February, 1848.
8. Elliott left home and moved to Tennessee in the summer (several years before the letter was written).
9. Elliott realizes and advises that moving away from home is a pretty permanent break and such a move should be well considered and investigated.
10. His wife Catherine was making an effort to know her in-laws, whom she had never met.
11. Elliott followed the standard patterns of expressing his love and concern for his family and their health.
12. Punctuation did not concern him.

Another interesting addition to your puzzle is a map showing the movement of your family within the United States. A dot can be used to locate each place the family lived. Highway maps or atlases can help you locate the cities or counties within each state. If you know when the family arrived at each location, you can write the year of arrival beside the dot.

After placing the dots on the map, connect them with a line. Begin with your own residence and work backward, in order, to the earliest known location. If you trace more than one family per map, use dotted or dashed lines to distinguish them clearly. You may wish to use a different color for each family. In a legend or key, explain your marks and identify each date with the name of the city or county.

The example shown in Figure 10 is of the Croom and Coleman families, which were united in 1900. As was the case with numerous families, whose descendants later married each other, these two families had lived in the same county in the eighteenth century, had gone separate ways, and had ended up in the same county again a century later.

The extras which can add spice to your history are numerous and depend on how much depth you want your history to show and how much effort and time you want to give to it. The results are always enlightening. These efforts, when shared within the family, help strengthen family ties, broaden understanding, and increase appreciation for each other and for your common heritage. Even my uncle who wants no part of the search or the results does his part by providing me a place to stay when I travel his direction to do research.

Margaret Catherine Patton
m.
Elliott G. Coleman
parents of Mary Catherine Coleman Blalock

This leaves all well – hopeing
this may find and all the
family in the enjoyment of
the same blessing. I must close
write soon —

Your Affectionate
Son —
E. G. Coleman

Sister write soon we feel so lonely and distresed tell
Sister Mary that I just received a letter from her and
will answer it soon give my love to all of the family
and except a portion your self   no more.
    but remains ever the same
            your affectionate Sister untill death
            Catharin M. Coleman
                Adieu Sister Adieu

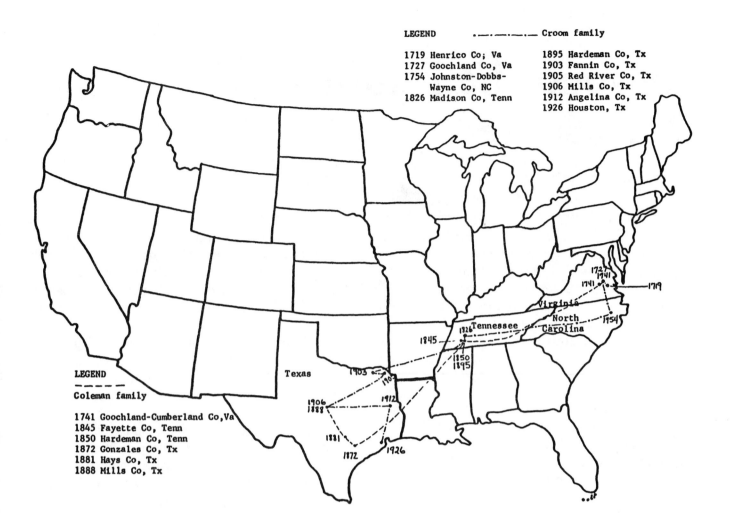

LEGEND .—.——.—.— Croom family

1719 Henrico Co; Va   1895 Hardeman Co, Tx
1727 Goochland Co, Va   1903 Fannin Co, Tx
1754 Johnston-Dobbs-   1905 Red River Co, Tx
     Wayne Co, NC   1906 Mills Co, Tx
1826 Madison Co, Tenn   1912 Angelina Co, Tx
                             1926 Houston, Tx

LEGEND

— — — — —
Coleman family

1741 Goochland-Cumberland Co,Va
1845 Fayette Co, Tenn
1850 Hardeman Co, Tenn
1872 Gonzales Co, Tx
1881 Hays Co, Tx
1888 Mills Co, Tx

11
Beyond the Family:
Local Sources

After you have filled in the middle of your family puzzle, especially the five-generation chart, at least back to 1900, with information from relatives and family papers, you are in a good position to begin consulting the many public sources available to genealogists. By this time, you will know what data you lack and what information you want to look for; and you will have some facts to use in finding the answers. From this point on, you can use family sources and public sources together; genealogists never really finish with either kind.

You may decide to pursue the "line" of your favorite grandparent or the only great-grandmother you ever knew or the grandparent you know the least about. Or you may want to try to fill in one complete chart before extending any one line back beyond your great-great-grandparents. However you decide to proceed, you have a good chance of meeting and working with distant cousins you have not met before. They may have family papers which can help you, and you may know pieces of information that they have been seeking. You never really run out of family sources if you continue looking for them. At the same time, the public sources are invaluable; and you certainly never run out of them.

Among the public sources are city, county, and state records, which include such things as deeds, tax lists, birth and death certificates, wills and probate records. Federal records include especially military records, some land and pension records, passports, immigration and naturalization papers, and the federal census. Fraternal and labor organizations and institutions, such as churches and synagogues, schools and colleges, prisons, businesses and newspapers, have valuable data for you. Cemeteries are excellent sources that are usually accessible to the public. Libraries and archives contain a great variety of special sources; but these should not necessarily be the first sources you try.

Let's say you have filled in the first three columns

on your five-generation chart rather completely, through your grandparents. From relatives and family papers close at hand, you may have the names and vital statistics of most of your eight great-grandparents and perhaps a few of your great-great-grandparents. Where do you turn now?

You have a number of choices. Much depends on how much time you can devote to the search and on what sources are most available to you. If you live in the same general area where some of your ancestors lived, you can begin by visiting the cemeteries, local historians, newspaper offices, and courthouses to gather whatever you can on those particular forebears. If you live farther away from their hometowns, you may wish to plan a visit of at least several days to consult these sources. A library close to you may have copies of information from these same sources on hand. If you can use the original records, you have a much better chance for accuracy and a more complete search than if you have only the copies, which do contain mistakes and which are seldom complete. Let's consider first the primary sources available at the local level.

Cemeteries

Tombstones are excellent sources of dates, birth places, husbands' and wives' names, maiden names, parents' names, evidence of children who died young, and even military service. I try to locate and photograph the tombstones for as many ancestors as I can. Family members were often buried in a family plot; so, locating one ancestor's tombstone may give you access to many more with good information. Of course, not all family members were buried in the same plot or the same cemetery; the search may lead you over a wide area.

Larger cemeteries often have files or maps to help you find a particular stone. Without such aid, your alternative is to walk up and down the rows reading each stone, checking for the person's name. You may have to check both sides of the stones, for in older cemeteries, tombstones in the same row may face different directions.

When you are lucky enough to find the stone you are seeking, copy the information carefully. A photograph of it offers additional proof. If you are not sure of a letter or number, you may need to make a rubbing of it. (See Figure 11.) To do this, put a piece of paper over the stone and rub the paper with a crayon or pencil. Then study the rubbing. Be sure to title your page of notes with the name and location of the cemetery and the date you were there. If the cemetery is large or the stone is difficult to locate, you may need to sketch a map to show its location for future reference. When visiting cemeteries, follow the courtesies of not removing or damaging any stones.

If you know which cemetery to go to, take along an older relative who can take you directly to the family graves. If you do not know which cemetery to look in, consult older residents of the area, local funeral directors, published histories of the area which

may contain cemetery listings, obituaries, and death certificates of the ancestors whose graves you are seeking. If none of these narrows the search, you may have to visit a number of cemeteries. Detailed county maps, such as those printed by the state highway departments, show most of the cemeteries. Ask local residents about any cemeteries not listed on these maps.

Our search for our great-great-grandfather Harrison's tombstone took us to many cemeteries and eventually gave us the dates of his life; but the search had two other very valuable and unexpected "payoffs." Our Orgain ancestors, whom I had found unexpectedly in a Tennessee county where we had relatives from the other side of the family, had moved to Texas; but we did not know where. We had temporarily laid aside that search to concentrate on the Harrison line. In the county where the Harrisons had lived, we had searched all the cemeteries that we could find, without any luck, and had just completed a second search of the Hutto City Cemetery. As we stood debating what to do next, my brother-in-law,

Fred, squinted ahead and said he thought he saw tombstones on a little rise in the distance. I was sure he was seeing a mirage, the kind you see when you close your eyes and see nothing but weeds after you have been weeding the garden all day. But we decided to follow his hunch. A dirt road led us somehow right to the gate of a tiny, very old and overgrown cemetery. We split up to speed the search. I did not recognize any name I saw and found no Harrison; but soon my sister, Judy, called out, "Hey, have you ever heard of a Reverend Sterling Orgain?" Shrieking with delight, I plunged through the tall weeds toward her voice and her treasure; and there it was: a double stone for Reverend Sterling Orgain and Mary E. Orgain, his wife, complete with dates! We had caught up with him again, at last. When I calmed down, I had presence of mind enough to copy and photograph the stone, to copy other stones around it (which did turn out to be of relatives too), and to map the little place so that I could take my 80-year-old great-uncle to see what no one else in the family had known existed, and in a place where we would never have thought to look.

We were still searching for the Harrison tombstone but felt better about visiting so many cemeteries. We returned to search a second time near the tiny town where the Harrisons had lived. The feed store was about the only business open that Saturday; so we stopped there and asked where we might find a local historian who could give us some information about other cemeteries in the area. The man pointed to a house within view and said that the couple who lived there had been in town forever. So we knocked on their door and explained our mission. Mrs. Richardson invited us in, and we visited: Where are you from? Do you have relatives near here? Oh, one of you now lives in the county? Has your family ever lived here? Oh, your grandparents once lived in Georgetown? We used to live there too. Who are your grandparents? Then there were looks of great astonishment on their faces. Mr. Richardson grinned: "I used to date your grandmother when your grandaddy was courting her sister." And Mrs. Richardson added, "And I was your grandmother's maid of honor in their wedding!" What a visit we had!

Before we could get back to the community to search again for the Harrison tombstone, that dear couple went to the city cemetery, found our stone, which we had overlooked because it was facing the opposite direction from all the others around it, copied it, and drew us a sketch of where to find it. From all this effort, we did learn the birth and death dates and burial place of that Harrison ancestor; but we also found birth and death dates for the two Orgain ancestors and met the lovely couple who shared with us so much about our grandparents.

Then I started looking for the parents of this Harrison ancestor. From the 1850 census, I learned their names and the fact that they were living in Victoria. I could hardly wait to go to Victoria. At the cemetery, on her tombstone there, I learned the mother's birthplace: Nottoway County, Virginia. That one piece of information led me to her marriage record, her maiden name, and to nearly two centuries of Bland ancestors in Virginia.

These two early experiences made me a firm believer in the value of cemetery research and introduced me to the value of local historians and the elders of any community. In a small Tennessee town where I have many relatives, whom I met through genealogy, and where I have spent several very special vacations, I used to spend hours in the private library of the "resident historian." He had a sizeable collection of letters, diaries, and other papers from local residents. He let me read and make notes from these, as they pertained to my family. I hope that since his death, his family has given these to the local library or historical society. He himself was able to show me one house that had been in the family during the Civil War.

One day, in the same town, I was walking around to find various old buildings I had been reading about. I had just learned that my great-grandmother had been christened in the little Presbyterian church in town where her mother had been a charter member. I was anxious to see and photograph the church. As I stood in front, the door opened and a very elderly lady emerged from the sanctuary where she had been "straightening up." I introduced myself and told her why I was interested in the church, and she invited me in. The most exciting part of the visit was her letting me play the little pipe organ which was 100 years old. She sat down at the piano, which was more or less in tune with the organ, and by ear and from memory played with me any hymn that I started. Not only was it enjoyable to play this antique instrument, but this was the same organ that my great-grandmother, whom I never met, had heard each

Sunday. And this was the same sanctuary where she and her parents had worshipped together. This was a whole new experience for me, as it would be for many people from the "newer" cities where not much still exists that stood 100 years ago, and for those of us who grew up knowing very few relatives, in an area where no relatives had lived before, and never seeing a family artifact more than 50 years old.

Experiences like these are not rare; there are "old-timers" everywhere who are happy to share their communities with those of us who are sincere in wanting to know about them. All it takes is asking and listening.

Newspapers

Some of the most entertaining historical and genealogical information comes from the gossip columns and social news of small town newspapers. That's where I learned that Elliott Coleman had brought to the editor two of the "largest cucumbers ever," and that "The Presbyterian ladies' ice cream and raspberry festival will be tonight at Mrs. Metcalf's home." If your ancestors were Presbyterians in that town, or if you are a descendant of Mr. Coleman or Mrs. Metcalf, you have found some "spice" for your family history.

Advertisements in the papers give us such items as banking hours, the circus schedule, the drug store's new stock, and the piano teacher's new address. One issue announced that five months' tuition for primary school was $17; in another, Mrs. M. E. Hodge offered room and board for $20 a month.[1] Times have really changed!

The papers give birth, marriage, and death information. They announce school functions, church services and socials, lodge and club meetings, civic meetings, and special town projects. The editorial remarks sometimes commend individual efforts: "We notice that A. S. Coleman with a good force has been planting young shade trees in and around the public square this week... We hope Alf will live long to enjoy the fruits of his labor and the thanks of fellow citizens... He will spare no pains to make his work a full and complete success."[2]

From similar editorial comments we learn that this young bachelor was a busy carpenter, a volunteer fire-fighter, a cook at all the barbecues, a volunteer on civic committees, an officer in the Odd Fellows Lodge, a member of the Presbyterian church and the Sons of Temperance, and a "sterling" Democrat. Then the editor announced in February, 1882, that "Alf Coleman has started for Texas with his celebrated Gate Hinge. Success and safety to him."

The editors made announcements of public interest which help us understand life in the town. The Gonzales, Texas, *Inquirer* of 29 May 1880 mentioned that the census takers would begin their work that week. These men were paid $6 per day and were required to visit each house personally. The editor urged citizens to give complete and accurate information. Refusal to answer questions could carry a fine of up to $100.

Seldom do we hear about taxes going down! The Bolivar *Bulletin* of 19 January 1872 informed its readers that the poll tax had gone down from $1.00 to $.50. The tax for having more than one dog per family was $2.00.

The local columns presented amusing and not necessarily scientific observations: *Fewer men in Texas chew tobacco than in other Southern states.*[3]

The editors frequently passed along "sound" advice to their readers: *Farmers should spread wood ashes on their fields. It makes good fertilizer.*[4]

They shared jokes. *"Blessed is he who does not make a cent, for he will have no income tax to pay."*[5] *"The Illinois girl who lately lost her speech...has had 40 offers of marriage."*[6]

One favorite habit of the editors gives us insight into urban problems and city needs. They loved to give their opinions. The Gonzales *Inquirer* of 1 May 1880 reported that on Sunday 200 to 300 horses had stampeded through town. *"It is a shame that such things are tolerated."*

The Bolivar *Bulletin* of 9 May 1873 announced that eight street lights had arrived and would soon be up. *"We want them no less than eight feet above the ground."*

The same editor on 13 June 1873 warned boys of Bolivar not to stand and smoke in front of the churches, either day or night. If this practice did not

---

[1] Bolivar, Tennessee, *Bulletin*, 27 January 1866; 5 January 1867.
[2] *Ibid.*, 13 March 1874.

[3] Gonzales, Texas. *Inquirer*, 4 May 1878.
[4] *Ibid.*, 27 November 1880.
[5] Bolivar *Bulletin*, 2 February 1867.
[6] *Ibid.*, 27 October 1866.

stop, he would print names!

The small town weekly papers usually contained about four pages. Of course, at least one was advertisements; two were national and state news; and one, local news. By examining a few issues, you can tell where the local items are found. You can save time by turning directly to that section. The newspapers are usually not indexed; so you must read each issue.

When taking notes from these papers, record the name of the paper and the date of each issue as you take notes from it. These papers become very brittle with age; so handle with care.

Ask first in the newspaper office to use their files for research if they include the dates you want. In some cases, the files are in the public library or the county courthouse. Some have been given to university libraries. Some, of course, have not been kept at all. University, public, and historical society libraries and state archives often have microfilmed newspapers from a number of towns in the area.

County Courthouse

Different counties organize their materials differently, but you can generally start at the office of the county clerk or registrar. Explain that you are working on family history and ask permission to look up some marriage records or wills or deeds. The clerks are usually glad to show you around, but they cannot search for you.

Marriages

Consult your list of what you are looking for. For example, you want marriages of all Campbells in that county up until 1900. The marriage books are usually indexed at the front of each volume. Begin with the earliest volume and record all Campbell entries. Record bride, groom, date of marriage, and the name of the minister or person who performed the ceremony. If witnesses are listed, copy those.

Caution! In many marriage books, three different dates may be given: the date the couple obtained the license or bond, the date they married, and the date the marriage was filed at the clerk's office. If you want only the marriage date, be careful that you copy the date they were ''united in holy matrimony.'' In some older books, only the date of the bond or license is given. Copy this. Usually the wedding took place within a few days after that.

Wills and Probate Records

Usually in the same office, you can look through will books and probate records. They are usually indexed at the front of each volume. However, there may be one general index for a number of volumes. If you find a will or probate record from an ancestor, it will probably save time for you to have a photocopy made of the entire document. The cost is usually nominal.

A will usually names the person's children and/or grandchildren. It is therefore proof of kinship. In the will, the testator distributes his property among his heirs and friends. You can learn such things as what property he owned, his religious beliefs, his wishes for burial, and his instructions on the division of his estate.

In characteristic style of the period, Isaac McFadden of South Carolina began his will in 1818:

> I, Isaac McFadden,...feeling the firmities of old age and the wastes of disease making progressive advances upon my bodily frame, yet possessing a competent soundness of mind, do conceive it to be dutiful to make the annexed arrangement of my worldly concernments.[7]

In traditional order, Isaac continued in a style which shows his practicality as well as his faith. He commended his ''soul to God (from whom it was received) resting on the efficacious mediation and merits of our glorious redeemer.'' He wished his ''body to be committed to the dust in a decent and Christian manner, without parade or unnecessary expense in the hope of the resurrection from the dead, the reunion of Soul and body and the final admission of both into the abodes of bliss in the immediate presence and enjoyment of God.''[8] After requesting the payment of debts, he divided his property among wife and fourteen living children.

After one's death in the nineteenth and earlier centuries, and occasionally in the early twentieth century, the estate was often inventoried. Each knife and fork, each head of livestock, each piece of furniture, and each tool was counted and recorded. From these inventories in the probate records, you can learn something of the lifestyle or the financial status of the family. Sometimes the estate was sold. In the reports

---

[7] Chester County, South Carolina, Wills, Book 2-G, 50.
[8] *Ibid.*

of the sale, you can learn who bought each item and how much they paid for it. There are also estate settlement records concerning the division of money, land, and personal property among the heirs. There are records dealing with the guardianship of minor children. These records give a picture of family relationships, activities, and even quarrels. They are valuable sources of information.

Deeds

There are several types of deeds, but two are common. One is the transfer of ownership of land, buildings, or, before 1865, slaves. It may record a sale or a gift of this property. The other is a deed of trust, which can be written for various sets of circumstances. A common nineteenth century deed of trust was made by a man in debt who was trying to pay his creditors or was paying off a mortgage. In effect, he put up certain property as security to insure the payment of the debt or mortgage. In the language of the deed, he sold this property to a friend or relative for a dollar or two. If he could not pay his debts or the mortgage by a given date, then the friend or trustee was authorized to sell the property and use the money to pay the debt.

Deed books are often indexed in separate volumes. There are two kinds of indexes. The grantee index alphabetizes the buyers; the grantor index lists the sellers. You should look in both lists and write down the volume and page number for each one you want to read. As you read each one, check it off your master list.

The language used in deed records looks frightful but is usually understandable when you get used to the form. Here is a fictitious example in the standard form and language:

Made this 20th day of August in the year eighteen hundred and eighty	date
four between Paul Parker of the county of Coleman in the state of	seller where
Texas of the first part and G A Keahey of the county of Coleman in the	buyer where
state of Texas of the second part, witnesseth that I, Paul Parker for and in	
consideration of two hundred dollars	price
lawful money of the United States to me in hand paid by said G A Keahey, do hereby sell, grant, and	

release unto the said G A Keahey and his heirs and assigns forever all my interest in land in this county, district 6, containing one hundred acres, known as the Patton place (description follows)...together with	# acres & where
the appurtenances and all the estate and rights of said Paul Parker in and to said premises, to have and to hold the premises herein granted unto said G A Keahey and his heirs and assigns forever. In witness hereof, I have hereunto set my hand and seal this 20th day of August eighteen hundred and eighty four.	

In the presence of		witnesses
Thomas B. King	*Paul Parker*	&
Charles W. Metcalf	(signature)	signature

The notes you take when reading the deed should contain all the important facts about the transaction: who, what, when, where, how. What to write down is suggested by the column of words to the right of the deed. Here are sample notes:

Volume B, 217–218.   Coleman Co, Tx Deeds

dated 20 Aug 1884

Paul Parker of Coleman Co,
for $200   to G A Keahey of Coleman Co,
sells 100 A in Coleman Co, district 6, called Patton place (description of land here, if desired)

Wit: Thomas B. King, Charles W. Metcalf

Signed by Paul Parker

If Paul Parker could not write his name, his signature would have appeard thus:

his
Paul **X** *Parker.*
mark

Your notes would mention that he signed with his mark.

If you want the detailed description of the property, copy or photocopy it. It may help you locate the property on a visit, or it may help you identify family relationships if other people and property are given in the descriptions.

Other Courthouse Records

In the county clerk's office you may also find birth and death records. These records usually begin after 1900 although scattered records before 1900 do exist. They may furnish such information as parents' names, cause of death, birth date and place, death date and place, occupations, place of burial, place of birth of one's parents.

In large cities, these records are often kept by the city health or vital statistics office instead of by the county. Birth and death certificates and sometimes marriage records may also be obtained from the state vital statistics office in the capital city. Two very helpful source books for this kind of information are: *Where To Write For Vital Records: Births, Deaths, Marriages, and Divorces,* a United States government publication, and *The Vital Record Compendium.* (See Appendix B.)

In the courthouse, you may want to use the tax records. They can help you determine what part of the county the family lived in, what taxable property they owned, such as land, horses, cattle, or carriages, or when they moved into or out of the county. Say they moved away between 1870 and 1880, as you know from census records. If 1875 is the last time you find them in the tax records, you can suggest that they moved away in 1875 or 1876. Tax records are not usually indexed but can often be worth the time it takes to go through them.

Also in the courthouse, you may want to look at the various court records in the minute books. These contain not only civil and criminal justice cases but estate divisions, juror records, evidence of local residents hired to do work for the county, applications or papers for naturalization of new citizens, and records of fees paid or charged by various businesses such as taverns and ferries. The court records are often not indexed and may be difficult to find. One such set I wanted to see was stored in the old county jail. The only man who had a key was in the hospital for two weeks. Another set was stacked in a dark storeroom in a state of absolute chaos with no labels on the front of any volume to help locate the desired material.

Occasionally, you can find family information in mortgage records, registers of license and professional fees, books of livestock brands, and other records which vary from county to county and state to state. Sometimes you can find the actual voting records which show who voted for whom. I have seen these polling lists recorded in deed and will books, in unlabeled books, and in bundles of loose papers tied with string.

Sometimes it is necessary to write a letter asking for information from a courthouse office, newspaper office, local historian, or other source. The letter should be typed, double-spaced, in good form, using correct grammar, and it should be short. Enclose a self-addressed, stamped envelope for a reply. Give as much information as is necessary to help the person answer your question. It is best to ask only one or two questions, for the staff cannot do research for you. There may be a charge for what you want, especially if you request a copy. If you need numerous pieces of information, it is advisable to visit the office yourself or hire a recommended researcher to search for you.

Dear Sir,
In searching for family history, I am looking for a marriage record for Samuel Black and Keturah Shaw, probably between 1797 and 1803. Do your records give a date for this marriage? If so, what is the cost of obtaining a copy?
Thank you very much.
                                Sincerely,
                                Susan Metcalf

Local Public Libraries

Public libraries are generally centers for more secondary research sources than primary sources. That is, they do not contain many original records, but copies or abstracts of them. It is best to use the primary sources whenever possible, but they are not always accessible. So, most genealogists use a combination of the primary and secondary sources.

Some public libraries have set aside an entire wing or room for their genealogy collection. Smaller libraries may have one section of shelves for these materials. Some maintain a file in which local families or their descendants can place their Bible records, family papers, and family history charts for other searchers to use. Occasionally the public library is the depository for back issues of the local newspapers and local archives. Of course, there are public libraries with large and extensive genealogy collections. Some of these are included in the appendix for your convenience.

Most public libraries cannot handle genealogical research by correspondence. In many libraries, the staff is not trained to do genealogical searching; and in most libraries, the staff simply cannot take the time to answer all the requests they would receive if they offered such a service. However, you may want to inquire whether they have genealogical records and periodicals, family papers, back issues of local newspapers, and local or county history, including cemetery inscriptions, census transcriptions, or church records. This information can help you plan a visit to the area.

Another way to find out about libraries in your research area is to consult the *American Library Directory* in your own public library. It is a fascinating volume which describes each library, state by state. It will tell you if your chosen public or college library has a special genealogy or local history section or collects church archives or local newspapers. The directory could also inform you of a genealogical or historical society library which could be helpful in your search.

When you visit your ancestral-home towns, include a stop at the local public library. You may be pleasantly surprised at what you can accomplish there, and you may be able to contribute to their holdings. To make the most efficient use of your research time in the library or county courthouse, make a list of the sources you want to use and the information you hope to find.

If the historical and genealogical material in the library is extensive, the card catalog can tell you what sources they have on your research area. The genealogical materials are often cross-referenced: (1) under the *subject*, i.e., cemeteries, census, deeds, genealogy, history, indexes, inventory of church archives, inventory of county records, archives, manuscripts, immigration, microfilm holdings, militia, tax lists, naturalization, passenger lists, wills, newspapers, etc; and (2) under the *name* of the city, county, state, family, or country to which they pertain.

Local Schools and Colleges

If you know or can learn which school or college a particular ancestor attended, you have a variety of additional sources, often in the institution's library or archives, from which to learn about his or her life: the school yearbook, newspaper, or literary magazine;

school catalogs and information bulletins; a school history or scrapbook of clippings; graduation programs; departmental records; faculty and/or student lists; and transcripts.

The federal privacy law of 1974 has restricted our access to transcripts. For the most part, only the student himself can now request copies of his transcript. If your older relatives are agreeable and if you are interested in transcripts as a part of the family history, it might be wise to request them while these former students are living. The handling of records of deceased students, especially one's ancestors, is not clear in the law. Some schools will not release records of deceased students without a court order, which is expensive. One college sent me my great-grandmother's transcript without delay. Another university refused to send my deceased grandfather's record without his signature! They finally released the transcript when my grandmother, as executor of his estate, although no longer able to sign her own name, made her very feeble mark on a request as witnessed by a third

Sources of "Education" Information about an Ancestor:
— local newspaper stories about schools, teachers, sports, graduation, contests, school-sponsored programs and activities
— history of city, county, school or college; student or alumni lists
— family letters, diaries, scrapbooks
— interviews with older relatives and family friends
— 1850 and later census asked which children attended school during the year and whether each adult could read and write
— 1890 and 1900 censuses recorded whether each individual could speak English
— wills or estate settlements or guardian accounts, which sometimes mention tuition and schooling for the children
— wills, deeds, other documents, which show whether each party could sign his own name or had to sign with his "mark." (Of course, if a person signed his name to some documents and signed his will or later deeds with his mark, the change would suggest blindness or other infirmity rather than a lack of schooling.)

relative who had power of attorney over her affairs. You should contact the school in which you are interested to learn what its policy is.

Local Churches

Occasionally local institutions maintain records old enough to be of use to genealogists. When you find records from an ancestor's church, you may find dates for baptisms, confirmations, marriages, deaths, removals, transfers in or out; names of parents or children; and perhaps minutes of the governing body.

Local church records are not always easy to find. If you know which church your ancestral family attended, then ask the pastor, secretary, a lay leader, or officer in the church whether there are records from the period you are interested in and where you might find them. A few state-level or regional church offices maintain archives. A diocese office sometimes stores older Catholic or Episcopalian records; a conference office may have Methodist archives. In some cases, the individual church simply stores or discards their records as they choose, or as the pastor chooses. In one Texas Methodist church, the preacher's wife got tired of storing "that old junk" at the parsonage and burned it all, including my mother's baptism record which she had hoped to use in proving her existence in order to get a delayed birth certificate.

Other congregations have their own ex-officio historian who keeps the old record books; some store their files in the church office or in a bank vault. A number of libraries, especially at church-affiliated colleges and universities, have church history or archives collections, which may contain records from individual congregations. If you find no church records in the town where your ancestors lived, you might try the closest denominational college or office.

Small rural Methodist, Baptist, and Presbyterian congregations who had circuit rider preachers may have had no records in the first place beyond the preacher's own register, which his family or descendants may or may not have saved.

A number of church records have been published, including many Episcopalian, or Anglican, church vestry books and parish registers from the colonial and early national periods, and many Quaker records. Gravestone inscriptions from individual churchyards and records of early congregations appear occasionally in genealogical periodicals. Check the index or contents of such periodicals from your research locale.

The Religious Society of Friends began about 1644, and hundreds of its members, called Quakers, came to the British colonies during the seventeenth and eighteenth centuries. The majority arrived at Philadelphia and spread southward through the Shenandoah Valley and eventually into the Northwest Territories. Thanks to the founder, George Fox, who required each local "meeting" to keep detailed records, genealogists today have a wealth of records to search for vital statistics and migrations of Quaker ancestors. The best source of such information is the records of the Monthly Meetings, which list births, marriages, deaths, transfers, committee reports, infractions of the rules, and members "disowned" for marrying a non-Quaker (marrying "out of unity") or being married "contrary to discipline" (being married by a civil servant or minister of another denomination).

Because the Quakers did not believe in rituals, their "weddings" were not ceremonies; nor did they have baptisms or funerals or tombstones. They did not enter military service or leave personal and financial records. Yet, it is possible to find them in census records and sometimes in tax, land, probate, and court records in county courthouses.

In order to use the Quaker records, you must know where your Quaker ancestors lived and to which monthly meeting they belonged. These civil records will help you locate your ancestors in a county and town so that you can identify their monthly meetings.

Some records of monthly meetings in North Carolina, Pennsylvania, Virginia, and Ohio have been published: William Wade Hinshaw, *Encyclopedia of American Quaker Genealogy,* 6 volumes, 1950, originally distributed by Friends Book and Supply House, Richmond, Indiana. These volumes are available at many genealogical libraries. The Friends Historical Library at Swarthmore College, Swarthmore, Pennsylvania, has the largest collection of Quaker records. See Appendix C for other Quaker collections. For a thorough discussion of searching for Quaker ancestors, see *Our Quaker Ancestors: Finding Them in Quaker Records,* by Ellen T. and David A. Berry (Baltimore: Genealogical Publishing Company, 1987).

The most unusual aspect of Quaker meeting records is their notation of dates. Until 1752, Britain and the American colonies, and therefore the Quakers, officially used the old Julian calendar, under which each new year began on March 25. (See pp. 85–86 for a more complete discussion of the calendars.) Under the "old style" calendar, March was the first month; April, the second; and so forth. The Latin names of the months called September, October, November, and December correspond to their places in the year as the seventh, eighth, ninth, and tenth months. Because the names of the other months were derived from pagan origins, the Quakers chose to substitute the numbers for the names of the months in their records. They usually listed the day, then the month, then the year, as much of the world still does, but in their own style: *12da 5mo,* or 12th day of the 5th month, which was July under the Julian calendar but May under the "new style" Gregorian calendar. The chart below compares the Julian and Gregorian dates, using the Quaker style of writing them.

Here are several other sources for church records:

1. Indexes or inventories of genealogical or historical collections such as *Handy Index to the Holdings of the Genealogical Society of Utah,* which has church records from all over the country.

2. Guides to research in a particular state, such as *Research Material in South Carolina: A Guide.*

3. *The Vital Record Compendium,* which shows the location of hundreds of church records and Bible records throughout the United States.

4. In the card catalog, especially of large collections, look under "Inventory of church archives of _____ (state)" or "_____ (state)—church records."

To find out which church or denomination...

—interview older relatives, family friends.

—read family letters, diaries, scrapbooks, funeral cards, wedding announcements or invitations. Funerals and weddings often, but not always, took place at the family's church, as did special anniversary celebrations.

—check the family Bibles, especially the register page, a gift inscription, bookplate, or identification information.

—read the local columns of contemporary newspapers, where you may learn who attended the Presbyterian ice cream social or who organized the Catholic bazaar, or where you may find a family wedding or anniversary story or obituary which identifies their church.

—read marriage records, estate settlements, deeds. These can mention where events took place, which ministers performed their ceremonies and services, gifts they made to churches, church officers conducting church business.

—check county and church histories for lists of members, officers, families.

—search church records of your research area whenever you find them.

Date as written in a record book	Date under "old style" Julian calendar	Date under "new style" Gregorian calendar
12da 5mo*	12 July	12 May
1da 10mo	1 December	1 October
24da 1mo 1702/03 †	24 March 1702	24 Jan 1703
(5 days later)	(5 days later)	(5 days later)
29da 1mo 1703 †	29 March 1703	29 Jan 1703
7da Feby 1728/29	7 February 1728	7 February 1729
1da 11mo 1750 OS	1 January 1750	(OS applies only to the Julian calendar.)

*When only the number of the month is given, you cannot know which name it stands for until you know which calendar was in use.

†The dual dating of the year applies only to January, February, and March. After March 25, the year was the same under both calendars.

Checklist of Local Sources

In searching for your family history, you are the judge of what you want to accomplish and how extensive your search will be. You may decide simply to fill in your charts with basic vital statistics on most lines while you study only one at a time in depth.

Of the many local sources available to genealogists as a group, perhaps only a few will give you information on a particular ancestor. You may find newspapers which enlighten you on two ancestral families, church records for three others, and school records for only one. It would be unrealistic to expect to find information in all these sources for all your ancestors. Of course, some searchers gather only vital statistics for each ancestor (birth, marriage, death dates, and spouse's name); they don't really collect family history. Consequently, they may never try many of the available sources, and they miss out on a lot of fun. Likewise, some searchers, by preference or necessity, do not visit the local hometowns where so much information is often found. They too miss a lot of fun and satisfaction, as well as information; for much of the local data is not available elsewhere.

The checklist presented here does not cover all possible sources but is intended as a guide to the most commonly available ones.

Checklist of local sources in the community or county where the ancestor lived:

1. Cemeteries (tombstones)
2. Funeral home files
3. Elders in the community: for their stories; memories; directions to and descriptions of houses, buildings, and cemeteries.
4. Newspaper files or microfilm copies in local, state, historical society, or university library.
5. County Courthouse, especially county court clerk, circuit court clerk, or registrar's office:
    a. Marriage records
    b. Birth records
    c. Death records
    d. Wills, inventories, estate settlements, estate sales records, guardianship records, orphans' court and other probate court records
    e. Deeds, mortgages
    f. Tax lists
    g. Various court minute books
    h. Polling lists, license and professional fee books, registration of livestock brands, etc.

6. City vital statistics registry at health department or registrar's office; duplicates at the state level
7. Church parish registers, vestry books, and other religious archives
8. Papers of families or businesses of ancestor's community on deposit in local, state, historical society, or university libraries
9. Local school records, college records and publications
10. Local historians or local historical society
11. Local genealogical library or public library with genealogy and/or local history collection
12. Local genealogists or genealogical society
13. Published county or city history, especially one with biographical sketches. Goodspeed Bros. of Chicago and Nashville published a number of these as state histories with county by county biographies, mostly in the 1880s. Many of the county history and biography sections have been reprinted in recent years, or microfilmed.
14. City archives: tax rolls, law enforcement records, city censuses, etc.

As you prepare to visit libraries or archives or courthouses, you may find it helpful to use a Quick Reference Chart, as shown in Figure 12. Not only can this chart serve as an index to your five-generation and family group charts, but it can also be a guide to each state, county, or region in which you are searching. As shown in Figure 12, a search in South Carolina records can be more efficient and more thorough with a Quick Reference Chart of your various South Carolina families. The example also lists ancestors from North Carolina counties who had South Carolina spouses or who have shown up in South Carolina records because they lived close to the border.

As you search for the ancestors of your primary interest, you may find other names which "ring a bell." Rather than copy a lot of information simply because it pertains to someone of the same surname as one of yours, refer to your chart. If your William Richardson lived in South Carolina in the mid-1700s, there's little reason to copy information about a William Richardson born in South Carolina in 1873. Especially for those families, such as Richardsons, Pattons, McFaddens, Bufords, Culps, and Gastons, who are numerous in South Carolina records, it is valuable to have at your fingertips the information on your specific ancestor so that you don't spend time unnecessarily "barking up the wrong tree."

Of course, it may prove advantageous to write down all the information you find about contemporaries of your ancestor who had the same surname if it is rather unusual. They may or may not be related to you in the long run; but it's generally easier to get the information the first time than to keep re-reading your sources.

It is probably wise to write down all information you find about people of the same name and time period and place as one of your ancestors. Certainly, not all the early eighteenth-century eastern Virginia deeds bearing the name Daniel Coleman belonged to the same man; but studying all available information may help the family historian sort them out. In the late eighteenth century, numerous men were named Samuel Black and William Shaw. In looking for your Blacks or Shaws, somewhere in North Carolina, you may run across many Black or Shaw families scattered over many counties. You may need to gather information about several of the families who lived at the same time in an effort to narrow down the search for your particular Samuel or William.

Interlibrary Loan

You may be able to obtain considerable information from the counties in your research area by renting books or rolls of microfilm on interlibrary loan. A number of public libraries offer this service to their local patrons at a nominal fee. This process allows you to read microfilmed local records, census reports, family papers, and newspapers, made available by city, county, state, or university libraries.

An excellent source of such microfilm is the Mormon Church's vast collection in Salt Lake City. Through one of their own branch libraries, located throughout the country, you can rent county, census, family, and other records from all over the United States and some foreign countries. Consult a telephone directory under "Church of Jesus Christ of Latter-day Saints" or write to the main library in Salt Lake City for the branch library nearest you. (See Appendix C: Utah.)

When You Travel

When you travel to ancestors' counties for research, you might want to contact a Texas-based guestroom exchange network called Visiting Friends, Inc., P.O. Box 231, Lake Jackson, TX 77566. Begun by genealogists, the network has members, most of whom are genealogists themselves, in more than 100 locations in the United States and several in Canada and England. For a small lifetime membership fee and a nominal fee for each guest-visit, members have the privilege of staying in private homes when they travel and of being hosts to other genealogists or sightseers in return.

The purpose of the organization is "to introduce people of similar interests, to enable them to meet new friends in other places who will offer a safe private home for them to visit while they research or sightsee." To protect the privacy of members, no directory of names and addresses is published. Visits and exchanges are arranged through the office, considering the preferences and needs of both guests and hosts.

QUICK REFERENCE — ALPHABETICAL ANCESTORS

Surname or Maiden Name	Given Name	Birth Year	Death Year	Primary Residence	Location on 5-Gen. Chart	Family Group
North & South Carolina						
Blalock	Millington	1741	1827	Granville Co NC	5	
"	William	1764/69		m 1795 NC ? Granville Co	5	
Buford	William	1747	1810-11	c 1765 Williamsburg Dist	3	Richardson
Garner						McKennon
Hitchcock	Hester			b SC m Daniel Jaggers	4	"
Jaggers	Daniel		1808	b SC d Hardin Co KY	4	"
"	Mary (Polly)			m John McBride	4	"
Judah	Daniel ?	1790-1800		b SC Dale Co Ala	Metcalf	
"	Henry/John			b SC Dale Co Ala		"
Lea	Rosanna's father			1812- Johnston Co NC	5	Blalock
Lee	John			Jones Co NC	28	
"	Fanny			m James Steele	28	McFadden
Metcalf				Rutherford Co NC		C.W.M
McBride	John	1791	1857	NC ? Maury Co Tenn	4	
McFadden	Isaac	1753/4	1820	Chester Co SC	28	
"	Candor ?	c 1727			28	
MacFarlane	Alexander	Manchester Eng		Via Nova Scotia Charleston 1798	2	
McKennon	William	17__	17__	SC	4	
"	John	1745	1801	1801 Chester Co SC	4	
"	Elizabeth	1750	1845	1801 Chester Co SC	4	
Patton	Thomas	1794	1852	Chester/York SC Fayette Co Tenn	28	
Richardson	William	1743 Va	1786	m 1768 Charleston d Clarendon Co SC	2	Mood
Steele	Alexander		1752	wife-Mary Onslow Co NC	28	
"	Peter		1792	wife-Martha Jones Co NC	28	

12

Beyond the Family:
State and Federal Sources

In chapters 10 and 11, we examined family and local primary sources for searching family history. There are also state and federal primary sources.

Checklist of State Sources

Just as local sources will not always be available or practical to search, so state sources may be limited. You will not be able to use all these sources for all your ancestors, but they could help you determine a period or place of residence, a place or date of birth, or other significant information.

Some of these sources may be available at county courthouses, or within the appropriate state agency, but older records will probably be in a state library, state archives collection, university library, or state historical society library. If the records have been microfilmed or published, you may find them at university, public, or genealogy libraries. (See Appendix C for a listing of libraries and archives.)

A number of state and university archives depositories have published guides to their holdings and update them periodically. The guide can be an extremely useful tool to own if your research is concentrated in a particular state.

1. Colonial, territorial, or state census records. Many of the states have had one or more state-prescribed census. Many of these name only heads of households and group family members by ages or sex; others give everyone's name, age, occupation, birthplace, etc. (See Appendix D for the location of these records.)

2. State land records, primarily in the state-land or non-public land states: the Original Thirteen states, Kentucky, Tennessee, West Virginia, Hawaii, Maine, Vermont, and Texas. In these states, land was originally held by the colonial or parent state government, or in Texas, by its national government. Land records of the public-land states are in the National Archives. Revolutionary War

bounty land warrants issued by the states.

3. Correspondence of colonial, territorial, or state officials which sometimes deals with individuals, such as your ancestors, and their problems or achievements.

4. Indian records, especially in Oklahoma pertaining to the Five Civilized Tribes. Contact the Oklahoma Historical Society or the Oklahoma Genealogical Society for their specific holdings, many of which are copies of records from the National Archives. Another source may prove helpful: Spindel, Donna, *Introductory Guide to Indian-Related Records (to 1876) in the North Carolina State Archives.* (Raleigh, NC: Division of Archives and History, Department of Cultural Resources, 1979).

5. Tax rolls, from counties or from state assessments.

6. State pension records: (Revolutionary War pension applications which were denied may be in the county court minutes.) State pensions granted to Revolutionary War veterans and widows as well as claims against the state for losses incurred during the Revolutionary War. Confederate veteran and widow pensions from the Civil War (former Confederate states only). Of course, not all who were qualified for pensions applied for them.

7. State militia rolls and records.

8. Pay warrants issued by the state.

9. Vehicle registrations.

10. Voter registrations, poll tax records.

11. Cattle brand registers (sometimes in county courthouses).

12. State law enforcement, department of public safety, or correctional institution records.

13. In the South, Confederate records, both civil and military. Many of these records were copied by the federal government in their attempt to identify all those who were guilty of treason against the U.S. by their participation in and support of the Confederate cause, 1861–65. The National

Archives has on microfilm the *Unfiled Papers of Civil War Soldiers* and a master index, *Consolidated Index to Compiled Service Records of Confederate Soldiers.* It was possible for a Confederate veteran to apply for a pension from the southern state in which he lived after the war; if he moved to another southern state, he could apply again in his new residence.

14. Vital statistics registry, primarily birth and death records at the state level. (Marriage, birth, and death records are often available in the counties.) Birth and death certificates are usually available at the Department of Public Health or Bureau of Vital Statistics. A useful resource for locating these records is published by the U.S. Department of Health and Human Services: *Where to Write for Vital Records: Births, Deaths, Marriages, and Divorces* (Hyattsville, MD, 1982), available from Superintendent of Documents, U.S. Government Printing Office, Washington, DC 20402, or from a U.S. Government Bookstore in large cities.

15. Other state agencies, such as state hospitals, departments of education, state courts.

16. County records which may have been transferred to or copied by the state archives.

17. Family and business papers which may be housed at state or university archives. Ask about an index or guide to the manuscript holdings. An index might show your ancestor's name. A guide might show papers or records from his hometown, his school, his church, his employer, or an organization to which he belonged.

18. Colonial government and Revolutionary War records, many of which were copied by the federal government to replace and reconstruct records destroyed in an 1805 fire in the War Department and in the 1814 burning of the capitol and looting of War and Treasury Departments, which held the Revolutionary War records, by the British.

19. Miscellaneous records: memorials and petitions to the state legislature, election records, charters granted by the state, interments in the state cemetery, notary public files, bonds and oaths of office. Bryan, Mary, and William Dumont, *Passports Issued by the Governors of Georgia, 1785-1820,* Vol. 1: 1785-1809, Vol. 2: 1810-1820 with Index...1785-1820 (Washington: National Genealogical Society, 1959, 1964). Potter, Dorothy Williams, *Passports of Southeastern Pioneers, 1770-1823: Indian, Spanish and Other Land Passports for Tennessee, Kentucky, Georgia, Mississippi, Virginia, North and South Carolina* (Baltimore: Gateway Press, 1982).

Federal Sources

The National Archives and Records Service is the home of millions of records of individuals and their dealings with the United States government. These include military service and pension records, immigration and naturalization papers, ships' passenger lists and passports, civil service employee records, homestead and bounty land warrant records, Indian annual census rolls and "removal" lists, some tax files, and census schedules.

Two pamphlets which are helpful in learning about the archives holdings and services are free upon request:
1. *Genealogical Records in the National Archives,* General Services Administration, General Information Leaflet #5.
2. *Military Service Records in the National Archives,* General Services Administration, General Information Leaflet #7.

Both are available from the National Archives and Records Service, General Services Administration, Washington, DC 20408.

A much more comprehensive survey of the records in the National Archives is the book *Guide to Genealogical Research in the National Archives.* (Washington, DC: National Archives and Records Service, 1983). Another useful resource is *Microfilm Resources for Research: A Comprehensive Catalog.* (Washington, National Archives Trust Fund Board, 1986).

Scattered throughout the country are branches of the National Archives which hold regional records and microfilm copies of some records stored in Washington. Write to the one in your research locale to learn what they have that may help you in your search. (See Appendix E for their addresses.)

Federal Census Records

Perhaps the most valuable of the federal records for the greatest number of genealogists is the federal census. Whenever I learn the names of "new" ancestors, I like to find them in a census record as soon as possible, as if this record makes them real people. The census is a good place to begin your use of public records.

The United States Census is a list of families and individuals living in each county and each state; the list has been compiled every ten years since 1790. Congress has designated one day in each census year as census day. The enumeration has begun that day and has included all persons living in each household on that one day, regardless of when the censustaker actually visited the dwelling. Persons who died after census day but before the census taker came were to be listed as if they were still alive. Babies born after census day were to be omitted!

Census Day 1790–1940	
1790, 1800, 1810	Apparently the first Monday in August
1820	First Monday in August (August 7)
1830, 1840, 1850, 1860, 1870, 1880, 1890, 1900	June 1
1880 — Indian Schedule	October 1
1910	April 15
1920	January 1
1930, 1940	April 1

Through 1840, only the head of each household was named, and the other members, both slave and free, were grouped by age, sex, and race. Beginning in 1850, each individual was named or listed by initials with his age, sex, race, occupation, birthplace, ability to read or write, schooling during the year, and infirmities, such as blindness or deafness.

The slave census schedules for 1850 and 1860 are separate from the general population schedules. Many libraries have microfilm copies of these schedules, and they can be purchased from the National Archives. (See Appendix D.) The records contain the slaveowner's name and the age and sex of each slave. The slaves were listed by number rather than by name in almost all cases; however, a few census takers did record slaves by name or initials.

The 1890 census was almost completely destroyed by fire. Some areas have a census-type record compiled from other existing records, such as tax lists. Some states took their own censuses between 1880 and 1900, and these form a useful substitute for the missing federal census. Still in existence is an 1890 Special Census of Union Army veterans and widows that was made in each state.

The 1900 census contains very helpful informa-

tion: each person's month and year of birth, the number of children born to the mother, the number of her children still living, and how long a couple has been married.

See Chapter 13 for more specific information on census records.

Soundex

The 1880, 1900, and much of the 1910 census records are indexed by state using a code that is based on the sounds in the last name; this indexing system is called Soundex. It is most often available as a microfilm of the cards on which the information is written. Soundex is especially useful when you do not know where the family was living in 1880, or 1900, or 1910. It will show you what county and what community they lived in and where you can find them on the census. When you find the family in the Soundex, write down *all* the information given, especially the enumeration district number, the supervisor's district number, the precinct, page, and line numbers, as you will need these references when looking for the family in the census itself. One drawback of the 1880 Soundex is that it includes only families with children under 10 years of age. If Grandpa's children were already over 10 or were grown by 1880, you will not find Grandpa in the Soundex, unless he lived with a family which had small children.

The Soundex coding system groups letters by the way they sound. Similar letters are given the same code to account for spelling variations. In this way, Medcalf, Midcalf, Metcalf, Metcalfe, and even Mitchell all have the same code number and are grouped together in the Soundex. The code begins with the first letter of the surname; that letter is not coded with a number. Only the consonants are used as key letters to make the code; you may cross out all vowels (*a, e, i, o, u*) and *y, w,* and *h*. Double letters that come together are coded as only one digit. If you run out of key letters before you have a three-digit code, you simply add zeros. Practice coding your own family names.

Code Number	Key Letters
1	b, p, f, v
2	c, s, k, g, j, q, x, z
3	d, t
4	l
5	m, n
6	r

Examples of Soundex Coding

C A M PB E LL
C   5   1   4

C 514. Double L and PB are coded as one digit. Other names with same code: Cambell, Camblin, Champlin, Campellona, Canfield, Camfield, Chamblee, Chambless (–iss), Chamblin.

C A R P E N T E R
C   6   1   5 –   –

C 615. Disregard the last three letters since you already have a three-digit code. Other names with same code: Corbin, Craven(s), Crippen, Carbone, Cherrybone, Carabine, Cherubini, Charbonneau.

L Ø D E N
L   3   5   0

L 350. Add zero to complete three-digit code. Other names with same code: Layton, Lawton, Litton, Latham, Letton, Ludden, Ladin, Ledden, Lauten, Leyden.

M A TT H E W S
M   3   2   0

M 320. Add zero to complete code. Double *T* counts as one letter. Other names with the same code: Mathis, Mathews, Mattes, Mutz, Muths, Metts, Metz.

R A Y
R   0   0   0

R 000. Add three zeros since there are no key letters. Other names with same code: Rhea, Rea, Roe, Roehe, Rowe, Roy, Rue, Rye, Rey, Riewe.

S H Ø E M A K E R
S   5   2   6

S 526. Names beginning with *Sc,* such as Schumacher—S 526, are treated the same way they would be if the double letter appeared in the middle of the name. Other names with same code: Shomaker and other variant spellings, Smucker, Smyser, Singer, Shinker, Shanker, Sanker, Schanzer, Schen(c)ker, Schwinger, Schwenneker, Sangree, Sanacora, Songer, Schmucker.

T A Y L Ø R
T   4   6   0

T 460. Add zero to complete the code. Other names with same code: Tolar, Toler, Tyler, Tiller, Tillery, Theiler, Teller, Tealer.

W H I T E
W   3   0   0

W 300. Add two zeros to complete the code. Other names with same code: Whitt, Wyatt, Wythe, Watt, Wheat, Witt, Witte.

There are entries in the census and other records in which the surname was written incorrectly, spelled with a *C* instead of *K*, or minus a final syllable, or spelled phonetically instead of correctly, or misunderstood for another name. My great-grandmother's marriage license gives her name as Ann Maria *Robertson*. Her mother's second marriage record gave her name as Mrs. Elizabeth *Robinson*. Ann's brother was listed in the 1860 census as T. J. *Robberson*. To this day, we do not know which name is correct. That dilemma is, of course, part of the challenge of genealogy.

If your name can have several spellings, especially with a different initial letter, or could be spelled phonetically in several ways, or could be mistaken for another name, it would be wise to look under all the variations when reading the Soundex or any index. Soundex codes which are almost the same, such as 450 and 452, are often grouped together. Sometimes prefixes such as *von, van, de, de la,* and *le* are omitted in coding.

Names that are similar, with different initial letters:					
Ostien	O 235	Garner	G 656	Croom	C 650
Austin	A 235	Carner	C 656	Krume	K 650
Otwell	O 340	Riggins	R 250	Ebert	E 163
Atwell	A 340	Wiggins	W 250	Hebert	H 163

Names which may be confused with each other:					
Garner	G 656	Larson	L 625	Saddler	S 346
Gardner	G 635	Lawson	L 250	Sandler	S 534
Rich/Richey	R 200	Robinson	R 152	Carson	C 625
Ridge/Ritchie	R 320	Robison	R 125	Carlson	C 642
Ridgeley	R 324	Robertson	R 163	Kallsen	K 425
Wooley	W 400	Oren	O 650	Finch	F 520
Woodley	W 340	Owen	O 500	French	F 652

In the library, when you want to read a particular roll of Soundex microfilm, you can ask the librarian for it in this way: "I'd like to read the 1900 Soundex for Texas for the code H 452." "I'd like to see the 1880 Kansas Soundex for K 620."

Census records such as the 1790 and much of the 1850 have been published and indexed and are available at various libraries. The rest are available on microfilm at many libraries. Use the indexes whenever possible to save time, especially when reading the 1880 or later censuses; but do not stop with the index. Read the real document.

In order to look for your particular family, you must know which census year you want to read and which state and county the family lived in. You would tell the librarian you want to read, for example, the 1850 census for Williamson County, Texas, or the 1870 census for Montgomery County, Ohio. She will give you a roll of microfilm that probably has several counties on it. You must scan until you find the beginning of your county, usually marked with a divider card and the name of the county.

If you do not have access to an index, your alternative is to read the entire county, family by family. The process is long but sometimes very rewarding. That's how I found my Sterling Orgain in Madison County, in western Tennessee, although everyone had thought he lived in central Tennessee. I usually prefer to read the whole county for censuses of 1860 and earlier, or for counties where I know there were many related families of different surnames. Besides, the census can be as entertaining as an encyclopedia or dictionary. You will find people with very interesting names, such as two of my favorites, the two men in Dale County, Alabama, named Green Bird and Bright Bird. You will probably find people with the same names as people you know today. You will learn who was in jail, who the doctors and teachers were, and will get a "feel" for the county: where most of the residents were born, or where they came from most recently, or which foreign countries were represented, which given names were most popular, which occupations were prevalent or represented by only one or two individuals.

Census reading poses its own special challenges. One that you meet quickly is handwriting. Some people write English as if it were Arabic. Nineteenth-century writers adhered to a standard style more often than contemporary writers do, but they had a few quirks that trip us up if we are not careful. For example, the old style double *s* looked like an *fs*. Capital *J*'s and *I*'s are sometimes indistinguishable. Names such as Lemuel and Samuel may be difficult to differentiate, or Daniel and David, if the script is angular and disjointed. However, with caution and common sense, you can generally decide the writer's intentions.

Form 4, a Census Check, is useful in capsuling the information gained from each census record for each family. The ancestor shown in Figure 13 has not been located in the 1830, 1840, or 1850 censuses. An extensive search of the 1850 census may locate him yet and lead his descendants to his father's name and to the appropriate 1840 and 1830 rolls. Meanwhile, in one place, you have the information which can save you time and effort in the search. Perhaps it will even save you from that most irritating of mistakes—spending several hours reading a lengthy census record only to discover (afterwards) that you had already read it!

Military Records

Military records in the Archives fall into a wide variety of categories. They cover regular Army, Navy, and Marine Corps personnel service records, service records of volunteers, pension applications and records, bounty land records from lands offered to Revolutionary War veterans, and the special 1890 census of Union Army veterans and widows, available for the states falling alphabetically between Kentucky and Wyoming and the District of Columbia. The service records pertain to the Revolutionary War, soldiers under the United States Command from 1783–1811, the War of 1812–15, the Mexican War (1846–48), the Indian wars, the Civil War (1861–65), and the Spanish–American War (1898). Coast Guard records date from 1791–1919. Civil War files include many service records and pardon petitions of Confederate soldiers. Useful published sources to aid in the search for military records include:

1. National Genealogical Society, *Index to Revolutionary War Pension Applications in the National Archives.* Washington, 1976.

2. United States Senate Document 514, 23rd Congress, 1st Session, *Report from the Secretary of War in Relation to the Pension Establishment of the United States.* (Washington, 1835. Baltimore: Genealogical Publishing Co., reprint, 1968). Short Title: *Pension Roll of 1835,* 3 vol.

3. United States Senate Executive Document 84, 47th Congress, 2nd Session, *List of Pensioners on the Roll January 1, 1883.* (Washington).

CENSUS CHECK ON WILLIAM FRANCIS MARION HOLMES FAMILY

Born 3/4 FEB 1829   Where Bible record says Jackson Co Miss   First Census 1830

Father's Name _____ HOLMES   Age in First Census 1 year

Married 2nd - 1861   Spouse MATILDA Y. BROWNE   Died 7 MAY 1903

CENSUS YEAR	COUNTIES SEARCHED/ NOTES	COUNTY WHERE FOUND/ NOTES	PAGE
1830		age under 5	
1840		age 10-15	
1850	Mississippi index & all Holmes shown in index. All Texas Holmes shown in index. Try Tenn or Ark. (A Thomas Holmes b Va & wife Millie b Ga, Winston Co Miss, p 367 R.)	age 21	
1860	Gonzales Co Tx	Gonzales Co Tx in household of A.S. Miller, employed as overseer, single, age 31, says he was born in Miss.	Pr. Pg 117 written Pg 95
1870	Gonzales Co Tx	Gonzales Co Tx with Matilda 30, William 7, Sam H 5, Mary E. 3, alvie 9 months. WFM age 42, says he was born in Tenn.	Pr. Pg 478 written Pg 6
1880	Gonzales Co Tx	Gonzales Co Tx with children. Says he was born in Tenn, father in Va, mother in Ga. WFM—age 51	Pr. Pg 476
1900	need to read Gonzales Co Tx		

The military service records may contain valuable vital statistics, family relationships, children's names, and other information. Copies of the records that relate to service that ended at least 75 years ago can be requested by submitting Form 6751, Order for Copies—Veterans Records. The forms are free on request from the National Archives, General Services Administration, Washington, DC 20408. In order to have a search made for these military records, you must supply certain identifying information, such as the serviceman's name, the war in which he served, the state from which he entered military service, and if possible, file numbers or pension application numbers. Some of the information you need can be found in these books, which can be found at most libraries with genealogical and research sources:

1. *Index to Revolutionary War Pension Applications in the National Archives*

2. *Report From the Secretary of War in Relation to the Pension Establishment of the United States,* or *Pension Roll of 1835,* 3 volumes

3. *List of Pensioners on the Roll January 1, 1883,* 5 volumes

Records relating to more recent service, generally for those personnel who were discharged (''separated'') after 1917 (Army officers), 1912 (Army enlisted personnel), 1947 (Air Force personnel) 1902 (Navy officers), 1885 (Navy enlisted personnel), 1895 (Marine Corps), 1928 (Coast Guard officers), 1914 (Coast Guard enlisted personnel), and for civilian employees of the Coast Guard's predecessor services (1864–1919), are housed in the National Personnel Records Center (NPRC), General Services Administration, 9700 Page Boulevard, St. Louis, Missouri 63132. Inquiries for information from these records may be submitted on Standard Form 180, Request Pertaining to Military Personnel Records. The files are not available for public use and are restricted to members of the veteran's immediate family or the veteran himself/herself. If the veteran is still living, his/her written consent is necessary.

The Atlanta, Georgia branch of the National Archives houses the file of World War I draft cards. A search for an individual name can be made for a $5.00 mailing fee, if you can supply the person's full name, town and county of residence at that time, and date of birth.

Federal Land Records

Land records in the National Archives pertain mostly to the thirty states created from the ''public domain,'' land acquired through purchase or in treaties following wars: all states west of the Mississippi River except Texas and Hawaii, states created from the old Northwest Territory, and the old Spanish and Indian lands which became Florida, Alabama, and Mississippi. The land records, mostly 1800–1974, include entries from several types of grants; the ones containing the most genealogical information are usually bounty land warrant applications and homestead applications.

Bounty land warrant applications in the National Archives are based on a man's wartime military service between 1775 and 1855. As an inducement to enlistment, first in the Revolutionary War, some of the Thirteen Colonies and the Continental Congress promised free land to those who served until the end of the war or to the widows and heirs of soldiers killed. Bounty land grants were also authorized after the Revolutionary War, War of 1812, the Indian Wars, and the Mexican War (1845–48). Warrants for such land grants were issued under laws passed between 1796 and 1855; qualifications varied from time to time, and some people made more than one application. In order to apply for the warrant, the veteran or his heirs had to document his service. This documentation process is the source of most of the genealogical information in these files.

Some of the Thirteen Colonies issued warrants for grants on their own unsettled lands and western lands which they claimed. In this way, North Carolina granted land in Tennessee, and Virginia made land grants in Kentucky. Virginia also issued warrants for grants in south central Ohio, in an area known as the Virginia Military District. Central Ohio became the location of bounty lands for soldiers who had served in the Continental Army, under the authority of Congress rather than individual states.

Applications for Virginia warrants for land in the Virginia Military District of Ohio and the Register of Military Certificates located in Ohio and Kentucky are in the Virginia State Library. The federal Bureau of Land Management, Eastern States Office, has record copies of the Virginia Military District patents. See Willard Rouse Jillson, *Old Kentucky Entries and Deeds,* ''Virginia Warrants used to patent Kentucky land, 1782–1793.'' (Baltimore: Genealogical Publishing Co., 1969, reprint of 1926 edition, pp. 313–392).

The American Library Association has published indexes to many of these early land records: Clifford Neil Smith, *Federal Land Series: A Calendar of Archival Materials on Land Patents* (Chicago: ALA, 1972–73, 1980, 1986). Volume 3 is an index to Revolutionary War Bounty Land Warrants, 1799–1835, and Volume 4, part 2, indexes Grants in the Virginia Military District of Ohio.

Among the early land records are also those dealing with **individual claims.** Many of the people making these claims had land grants or purchases from foreign sovereigns (French, Spanish, Mexican, British mostly) and settled the land before the United States acquired it. The United States had to decide who owned each tract and had clear title to it. The records of these claims are published and indexed: Walter Lowrie and Matthew St. Claire Clarke (eds.), *American State Papers: Public Land Series: Records relating to individual claims presented to federal authorities, 1790–1837. . .* (Washington: Gales and Seaton, 1832-61). Federal authorities who handled these claims included district land offices, district courts, U.S. Court of Claims, the General Land Office, the Supreme Court, and the Court of Private Claims (for Mexican lands).

In Florida, Oregon, and Washington before the Civil War, the government began giving land to people who would settle in order to strengthen the United States claim to the area when ownership was disputed with another country. Because this land was given or donated to the settlers, the records of the grants are called **donation land entries.** The files in the Archives contain records for Florida, 1842–1850, and for Oregon and Washington, 1851–1903.

A fourth kind of land record in the Archives is **homestead entry papers.** The Homestead Act of 1862 allowed settlers on public domain lands to obtain a free homestead farm of 160 acres for a small fee. In order to obtain title to the land, the homesteader had to live on the property for five years. In applying for this grant, a man gave certain information which the genealogist may find useful: name of the applicant and his wife, size of the family, residence, age or date of birth, the location of the land, and the date acquired. If he was of foreign birth, he gave evidence of his naturalization or his intention to become a citizen. His entry papers would include this application, his certificate of intent to make a claim, the testimony of two witnesses, the claimant's own testimony, the final certificate authorizing him to obtain a patent, and his naturalization papers or a Union Army discharge certificate.

The handling of land grants and the sale of former Indian lands was done at land offices. These offices in the early years were sometimes quite distant from the lands they sold. The index to the Public Land Series identifies these land offices: Philip McMullin, *Grassroots of America.* (Salt Lake City: Gendex Corporation, 1972). The National Archives has a 4-volume index which lists the land offices responsible for a given region at a given time.

Titles to public domain land was transferred from the government to its new owners through deeds or patents, which were recorded in **tract books** in the land offices. The land offices east of the Mississippi River eventually transferred their tract books to the General Land Office, now the Bureau of Land Management in the U.S. Department of the Interior. The tract books for the thirteen public land states east of the Mississippi River and the first tier of states west of the river are kept at the Bureau's Eastern States Office, 350 South Pickett Street, Alexandria, Virginia 22304. The Bureau also has a 5-volume index to Ohio tract books, 1800–1820, and microfilm of all the tract books, eastern and western, for use at their office and for sale. The National Archives does not have this particular microfilm set. Searching and copying from the Bureau's files can be done for you by mail for small fees.

Some of the western tract books are kept in the Bureau of Land Management regional offices in Phoenix, Anchorage, Sacramento, Denver (Lakewood), Boise, Billings, Reno, Santa Fe, Portland, Salt Lake City, and Cheyenne; other western tract books are in the National Archives, state and local historical societies, or state archives.

The National Archives and the Bureau of Land Management both have records of land patents from about 1800–1908, although not identical files. Entries after 1800 are indexed by names for Alabama, Alaska, Arizona, Florida, Louisiana, Nevada, and Utah. Entries for other public-land states are indexed for years after 1908. The post-1908 entries are in the National Archives. The first two volumes of Clifford Neil Smith's *Federal Land Series* (A.L.A., 1972–73) deal with land patents between 1788 and 1814 and contain subject, tract, and name indexes.

From 1800–1820, public lands were sold on credit; the National Archives contains the Credit Entry files from 1800–1820 and the Credit Entry Final Certificates, 1800–1835. The Archives also has the Cash Entry files for 1820–1908 with a master card index for Alabama, Alaska, Arizona, Florida, Louisiana, Nevada, and Utah.

Archives Materials for Black Genealogists

Records in the National Archives pertaining to Black genealogy are extensive. Of course, military records form an important source. Military records include such files as compiled service records and indexes, disallowed military claims of Colored Troops, 1864–1893 (in Record Group 217), records of Colored Troops in the Adjutant General's Office (Record Group 94), and compiled service records of volunteer Union soldiers who served with U.S. Colored Troops (Record Group 94). Two references which have been developed from these files are:

1. Debra L. Newman (comp.), *List of Black Service Men Compiled from the War Department Records,* Special List 36 (Washington: National Archives and Records Service, 1974).

2. Aloha South, *Data Relating to Negro Military Personnel in the Nineteenth Century,* Reference Information Paper 63 (Washington: National Archives and Records Service, 1973).

Among the records of district courts held in the Archives are files of the U.S. District Court for the District of Columbia relating to Slaves, 1851–1863. For residents of the District of Columbia in the Civil War era, the Archives has manumission papers (by which a slaveowner freed his slaves himself), 1857–1863, and emancipation papers (by which slaves were freed by law, 1862–63. Records from South Carolina during the Civil War include lists and register of slaves who worked on fortifications in the Charleston and Georgetown harbors from August, 1862–September, 1863, and for the first half of 1864. The register contains names of the slaves and slaveowners. Among papers taken from the Confederate government by the War Department are records of Black civilian laborers, 1861–65 (Record Group 109).

The district and field offices of the Freedmen's Bureau after the Civil War maintained all kinds of records, including some marriage records mostly for Arkansas, Kentucky, Louisiana, and Mississippi. The Archives now has these files and such others as the registers of depositors in the Freedmen's Savings and Trust Company, 1865–1874.

Additional resources for Black genealogy, in and out of the National Archives, include these books:

1. Blockson, Charles L., with Ron Fry, *Black Genealogy* (Englewood Cliffs, NJ: Prentice–Hall, 1977). Sources in the National Archives, Library of Congress. Bibliography of black newspapers, black history, sources by state and country. Excellent guide for an extensive search.

2. Rose, James and Alice Eichholz, *Black Genesis* (Detroit: Gale Research Co., 1978). Gale Genealogy and Local History Series. State by state sources, including books, articles, newspapers, family papers, archives. Chapters on oral history, slave records, National Archives and federal records. Interesting and very useful.

3. Streets, David H., *Slave Genealogy: A Research Guide with Case Studies* (Bowie, MD: Heritage Books, 1986).

Indian Records

Indian records in the National Archives include annual census rolls from 1885–1940, lists of members of the Five Civilized Tribes (Cherokee, Choctaw, Creek, Seminole, and Chickasaw) who moved west between 1830 and 1846, enrollment cards for the Five Civilized Tribes, 1898–1914 (Record Group 75), and the census roll of the Cherokee Indians east of the Mississippi (with index) for 1835 (Record Group 75). Record Group 75 contains the files of the Bureau of Indian Affairs. Among the publications of the National Archives is a 1973 pamphlet describing data available on microfilm of the *Indian Census Rolls 1885–1940* (M595 of Record Group 75).

Other records pertaining to Indians include some marriage cards and registers, heirship records, land allotment files, Indian school records, annuity payrolls, and Eastern Cherokee claim files, 1902–1910.

Some Indians served with the regular army during the Revolutionary War. Their service records and resulting bounty land warrant applications are also on file, as is a special 1880 census of Indians in Washington, California, and Dakota Territory. The Regional Archives branches in the western states have the field office reports from the Bureau of Indian Affairs. For more detailed information on Indian records in the

National Archives, consult such sources as these:

1. Hill, Edward E., "American Indian Records in the National Archives," *World Conference on Records and Genealogical Seminar.* (Salt Lake City: The Genealogical Society of the Church of Jesus Christ of Latter-day Saints, Inc., 1969).

2. Hill, Edward E. (comp.), *Guide to Records in the National Archives of the United States Relating to American Indians.* (Washington: 1981).

3. Hill, Edward E., *Preliminary Inventory of the Records of the Bureau of Indian Affairs, No. 163.* Record Group 75. 2 Vol. (Washington: 1965, reprint 1982).

Immigration and Naturalization

Records of immigrant arrivals are often found in ships' passenger lists. Ship captains had to file a report of their passengers who had embarked in a foreign port and were disembarking at a United States port. Before 1820, captains reported this information to the customs office in the port of entry. Few of these records still exist; those which have been found are published in a number of different books and periodicals. Lists of passengers arriving after 1820 were filed with the Bureau of Immigration. Those which still exist can usually be found in the National Archives and Regional Archives, as well as in published sources.

In Record Group 36, the U.S. Customs Service, Department of the Treasury, are passenger lists and indexes from vessels arriving at Baltimore (1820–1897), Boston (1848–1891), New Orleans (1853–1899), New York (1820–1846), Philadelphia (1800–1906), and a supplemental list of arrivals at Gulf and Atlantic ports between 1820 and 1874. Record Group 85, Immigration and Naturalization Service in the Department of Justice, contains passenger and crew lists, and indexes by ports, for the late nineteenth century and this century up to about 1945.

In order to find **naturalization papers** for your ancestors, you need to know when they arrived in this country. Passenger lists, census records, land records, family papers, and county tax lists are some of the sources that can help you establish the arrival date. Ancestors arriving in this country before the American Revolution generally did not go through a naturalization process; in fact, many were already British citizens who were simply changing their residence within the British empire. Before the first naturalization law in 1790, the states handled the process on their own.

The first step toward becoming a naturalized citizen was to file a Declaration of Intention. Before 1906, an immigrant could file his "first papers" at any federal, state, or local court. Many did this in their port of entry soon after their arrival in this country. After 1906, the Declaration had to be filed in a federal court.

The second step was to file "final papers," which included a Petition for Citizenship, an Oath of Allegiance, and papers proving residency for the required number of years. The residency requirement varied from time to time but generally was five years. The final papers did not have to be filed in the same court as the Declaration of Intention. The process was complete when the court issued the Certificate of Naturalization.

Records of naturalization before 1906 are scattered among state and federal archives, historical societies, libraries, and courthouses. Indexes and guides to each collection may help you locate the records you need. Papers filed after 1906 are usually kept with the records of the court which handled them. If you do not know which court your ancestor went to, inquire at an office of the Immigration and Naturalization Service for the proper form and procedure for having a search made.

Among the Records of the District Courts, filed in the National Archives, are Naturalization Petitions to U.S. Circuit and District Courts for Maryland, 1797–1951. Indexes to these records are available on microfilm, as are petitions presented to courts in Alaska, Colorado, Oregon, Pennsylvania, Washington, and South Carolina. Record Group 21 contains Records of Admission to Citizenship in the District of South Carolina, 1790–1906, and the Naturalization Records of the Territorial and Federal Courts of Montana, 1868–1929.

An excellent source to consult on immigration and naturalization is James and Lila Lee Neagles' *Locating Your Immigrant Ancestor.* (Logan, Utah: The Everton Publishers, Inc., 1975), which suggests sources in the United States and in the country of origin for your search.

Other Archives Sources

The Archives maintains records of the Continental Congress and Confederation Congress from the years prior to the writing of the present Constitution, as well as the papers from the Constitutional Convention.

Territorial Papers of the U.S. Senate, 1789–1873, are available on microfilm as are some of the Territorial Papers of the United States, for Iowa, Minnesota, and Oregon. This collection is documents and records pertaining to the areas which were at one time official territories of the federal government, as most of the public land states were. These papers have been published with indexes, under the name of each territory: Clarence E. Carter (ed.), *The Territorial Papers of the United States,* 27 vol. (New York: AMS Press, reprints of 1962 edition).

In the Internal Revenue Service, Record Group 58, you can read on microfilm the assessment lists for 1862–66, by state; within the records of the U.S. General Accounting Office are the Civil War Direct Tax Assessment rolls for Tennessee. The non-population census schedules for Tennessee, 1850–1880, and the federal mortality census schedules, 1850–1880, are available in Record Group 29, Records of the Bureau of the Census under the Department of Commerce.

The holdings of the National Archives are enormous, and many of those records are available on microfilm. The Archives publishes catalogs of these microfilm records for users and purchasers. One roll of interest to genealogists is #T325 (no record group number), *Examples of Records in the National Archives Frequently Used in Genealogical Research.*

Other Federal Sources

Records of civil service employees are somewhat restricted, but inquiries about service which ended after 1909 may be made to Civilian Personnel Records (NCPC), General Services Administration, 111 Winnebago Street, St. Louis, Missouri 63118. The few existing records pertaining to employees before 1909 can be found in the National Archives. Inquiries should contain the employee's full name, the name and address of the agency where he or she worked, and the approximate dates of that employment.

Passport applications filed between 1791 and 1926 may be found in the National Archives. Limited searches can be made for age and citizenship information in the records which are at least 75 years old. Such searches require the applicant's name and the place and approximate dare if his application. Inquiries for information from passport applications less than 75 years old should be made to the Passport Office, Department of State, Washington, DC 20520.

Microfilm from the National Archives and Branches

The Southwest Regional Archives in Fort Worth, Texas used to handle inter-library loan of microfilm from the National Archives and the other branches. This practice was discontinued at the end of 1981. Microfilm is no longer available on loan from the National Archives, but can be purchased. Currently, the price is $20 per roll, payable in advance. Submit orders on Form 36–Microfilm Orders or institutional purchase orders. Orders must include the microfilm publication number, roll number, and price. Send check or money order payable to Cashier, National Archives Trust Fund Board, Washington, DC 20408. Orders may be charged to Visa or MasterCard.

Through a privately-owned company called National Archives Microfilm Rental Program (P.O. Box 30, Annapolis Junction, MD 20701-0030) and for nominal fees, you can rent census (1790–1910) including slave schedules, Soundex (1880, 1900, 1910), the American Revolutionary War service records and index, pension applications, and bounty land warrant applications. Your local library's inter-library loan department can tell you which library nearest you participates in this program; or you can contact the company at the above address or at 301-604-3305 for the library nearest you which participates.

13
Where Do I Look for That?

As you fill in the middle of your puzzle for each generation and each ancestor, you will obviously find some pieces much quicker than others. You may know quite a lot about your grandfather from 1900 forward but absolutely nothing about his life before then. You may have found the vital statistics for your great-grandmother after she married, but still be "in the dark" on her maiden name, place and date of birth. This chapter suggests where to look for the most commonly sought information, using both public and family sources.

Birth Date and/or Birthplace

Family sources for birth date and place include Bible records, interviews with older relatives and family friends, family letters, diaries, scrapbooks, birth announcements, driver's license, voter registration, contemporary newspaper accounts of the event which have been clipped and saved, tombstone, or auto-biographical sketch or memoirs. Sometimes another family member has written biographical sketches of brothers and sisters or parents; ask distant cousins about sources in their part of the family.

Public sources which may give you birth date and place include published Bible records in books or periodicals, church registers (manuscript or published), tombstone, birth certificate, driver's license, hospital birth record, voter registration, school or college records, newspaper files which might have a birth announcement or obituary, military record, Social Security record, club or organization membership application or membership record, death certificate, passport or passport application, pension application, homestead application, ships' passenger lists which sometimes show the age of each person, state censuses, or the federal census. Of course, some of these sources give a person's age on a given date: his age when he died, or his age when a particular census was taken. The searcher must be alert to this possibility and simply calculate the approximate birth date from what is given.

Two booklets which are helpful in searching for birth dates and places are available from the Superintendent of Documents, U.S. Government Printing Office, Washington, DC 20402, or at a Government Printing Office Bookstore, in many cities. One is *Age Search Information,* which gives addresses for where to write for birth and death records in the U.S. and outlying areas and suggests many sources of birth or age information and where to find them. The second booklet is a combination of several former pamphlets: *Where to Write for Vital Records: Births, Deaths, Marriages, and Divorces.* It includes addresses, cost of copies, and the years covered by the particular records. It contains some suggestions for obtaining birth, death, and adoption records overseas.

The United States census records are very valuable sources for genealogists. For age information, the census can be very helpful but is not always accurate, as you will see later in this chapter. The 1790 census is of only general help in determining age; it shows that the head of household was alive and over age 16 (usually) as of the first Monday in August, 1790. It gives the number of males (not specified as sons, or even as relatives) in the household over 16 or under 16; females were not grouped by age at all.

The 1800, 1810, and 1820 censuses divided everyone into age groups: up to 10, 10–16, 16–26, 26–45, and over 45. Only the head of household was named, but he or she was not always the oldest person in the family. The 1820 census had a column for males between 16 and 18. The next column was for males between 16 and 26. The males in the 16–18 age groups are listed under *both* columns and are not to be counted twice. Census records for 1830 and 1840 again name only the heads of household and group everyone in these age brackets: under 5, 5–10, 10–15, 15–20, 20–30, 30–40, 40–50, 50–60, 60–70, 70–80, 80–90, 90–100, and over 100. If your Jeremiah Johnson had only three sons and his 1830 census return shows 3 males aged 10–15 and none in the other columns, you can be relatively sure (not positively certain) that those three males are his sons. You would know then that they were all born between 1815 and 1820, if their ages were accurately reported and recorded. At least you have something to work with as you look for proof of their birth dates.

Beginning in 1850, each free person was named, and the age reported on the census was supposed to be his age as of June 1 of that year. This census is your earliest opportunity to find specific individuals with age information in the federal census. Of course, ages were not always reported accurately; and sometimes a child got left off the list altogether. Furthermore, the law said to omit any child born after June 1, 1850, and to include anyone who had died after June 1. Any baby less than one year old as of June 1 was to be reported by age in months, or a fraction of a year: $^2/_{12}$ for two months old, $^7/_{12}$ for seven months old, or $^0/_{12}$ for less than one month old. When these ages are accurate, they can help you estimate the birth date more closely.

These same procedures were followed for the censuses of 1860 through 1900, and through at least 1940 except that the cut-off date changed from June 1 to a variety of others after 1900. (See Chapter 12.) The 1870 and 1880 censuses did ask for the month of birth to be specified for babies born within the census year, that is between 1 June 1869 and 1 June 1870 or between 1 June 1879 and 1 June 1880. The 1900 census is the most helpful, specifying month and year of birth for all persons. The 1910 census reverts to almost the same process used in 1850, asking only for age, but this time giving the fraction of a year for babies under two.

The 1880, 1900, 1910, and 1920 censuses also asked for the birthplace of each person's parents. This information helps you narrow the search for the preceeding generation.

Here is one way you can use the census records in finding someone's birth year. You will notice that there are obvious discrepancies in the ages of this man from one census to the next. In 1850, Johnson Godwin reported that he was 50 years old; ten years later he was only eight years older. Why? Different people could have given the information to the two census takers; the census taker could have written the age incorrectly; many people rounded off their ages to the nearest 5 or 0. From census figures, therefore, we can determine only approximate birthdates. The chart illustrates the case of Johnson Godwin. Subtracting

the age from the census year in each illustration gives you a possible birthdate.

Using the Census to Find an Approximate Birth Year		
Census Year	Age Given	You figure the suggested birth year
1830	30–40	1790–1800
1840	30–40	1800–1810
1850	50	1800
1860	58	1802
1870	67	1803
1880	74	1806

According to the figures, his birth occurred between 1790 and 1806. Since 1800 appears three times in the chart and 1802 and 1803 are also suggested, it is likely that he was born between 1800 and 1803. Unless we find more information to go on, we have to give his birthdate as "about 1800–1803."

When actual birth records and census data are not available, you can sometimes gather birth information from deeds, wills, tax rolls, marriage records, and other public documents. When Colonel Thomas Ballard of York County, Virginia wrote his will on 26 September 1706, he gave us some useful information on his children. He left a plantation on the York River to his son Matthew. The other four sons, he said, were all under age, that is, under 16. This statement would probably indicate that Matthew was indeed over 16. We would be able to figure, then, that Matthew was born by 1690, and his brothers Thomas, Robert, John, and William were born between 1690 and 1706. Then the colonel named daughters Katherine and Mary, both under age, and two married daughters, Elizabeth, wife of William Smith, and Anna, wife of John Majors. Although it is possible that Elizabeth and Anna were, one or both, under age and married with father's consent, it is more likely that they were already at least 16, with birth dates before 1690. This will does not give precise birth information, but it does steer us toward an educated guess.

When Elliott G. Coleman gave his consent on 14 January 1817, in Cumberland County, Virginia, for his daughter Mary D. Coleman to marry John A. Allen, he left us at least the indication that the bride was not yet 16.

When William Harrison and Nancy Vaughan promised to marry each other and signed a marriage agreement which went into the Petersburg, Virginia, deed book, Nancy's father David Vaughan witnessed the proceeding, but made no consent statement because the bride was probably already of age. The youngest daughter of William and Nancy was Virginia Harrison, "an infant of tender years" in February, 1819, according to another record in the deed book. We know that she was born before her father wrote his will in May, 1812. The 1810 census indicates that she was born between 1800 and 1810. Other census records suggest that her brother George was born about 1800-1801. If she were born in 1802, she would already have been 16 in February of 1819. With only these documents available, we can place her birth between 1803 and 1810. Other census records may help narrow the gap if no tombstone or Bible record is found.

A person's age may also be suggested in the county tax rolls. Depending on legal taxable age at that time and in that place, his presence on the roll as a "poll" would indicate that he was "of age," whether 16, 18, or 21.

Christening or Baptism

Bible record, church register, certificate issued by the church at the time of the event, old letters and diaries, scrapbook, clippings from church or local newspapers announcing the event.

Marriage Date and/or Place

Marriage records of the county where the marriage took place, Bible record, church register, contemporary newspaper announcements of the event, original marriage license in possession of family or county, interviews with older relatives and friends, old letters and diaries. Occasionally a tombstone shows a marriage date, but this is not common. The couple may have married in a different county from the one where they made their home; check surrounding counties.

If no other records give a wedding date, you can sometimes suggest a marriage year by using the census records; but these records are not proof of the date. The 1850 and 1860 censuses have a blank to check if the couple married within that year. The 1870 and 1880 censuses asked for the month of marriage if the couple married within the census year. The 1900 census asked for the number of years married; and the 1910 census asked for number of years of the present marriage.

Say your great-grandparents are listed in the 1880 census, ages 32 and 30, with children ages 8, 6, 5, 3, and $2/12$ (2 months). Their eight-year-old was born about 1872. Great-grandmother would have been born about 1850 and could have married as early as age 16 or about 1866. If no miscarriage occurred before the birth of the eight-year-old, and no older child had died, the marriage could have taken place in 1870 or 1871. An easy way to narrow the possibilities is to find them in the 1870 and 1900 censuses.

If they are listed as a couple in the 1870 census with no children, it is possible that they had been married less than two years. Of course, look for a mark in the column headed "Married within year," which would indicate a wedding between June 1, 1869, and June 1, 1870. If you find these two ancestors living in the households of their individual parents, of course, they had not yet married by June 1, 1870. If they lived until census time in 1900, you may find another piece of helpful information, in the column headed "number of years married." Pooling these puzzle pieces, you can determine fairly closely the year of their marriage.

Example:

1880 — great-grandmother age 30, born about 1850, could have married as early as 1866 (age 16), oldest child age 8 — born about 1872. Marriage between 1866 and 1871.

1870 — great-grandparents shown as a couple, with a baby born in April of that year, no other children. The child must have died before 1880, but its presence in 1870 suggests the couple married in 1869 or before. Narrows down the possibilites to 1866-69.

1900 — both still living, married for 32 years. Subtract 32 from 1900; marriage year of about 1868, which could mean the latter half of 1867.

Other records such as deeds, wills, and estate settlements may help you narrow down a marriage date. William Harrison sold a lot in Petersburg, Virginia, in November, 1784, and his wife Lucy was "privately examined as the law directs" and freely acknowledged the sale; we know, then, that William and Lucy were married before this date. Several documents may be necessary to approximate the marriage date itself, but each additional record will help you make a more educated guess.

Occasionally, the county records give us a marriage agreement, such as the one signed by both William Harrison and Nancy Vaughan on March 26, 1789, acknowledging their "promise to marry each other," and giving Nancy his "mansion house" and other property. We know by this document that the couple married probably in 1789. Because William was giving his new wife the house called Porter Hill "where Harrison now resides," and the couple continued to make their home there, we may guess that they probably married in Petersburg where Nancy's family and Harrison both lived.

In Amelia County, Virginia, Richard Phillips wrote his will on March 14, 1793, naming among his family and heirs his daughters Elizabeth Tolbert Allen and Tabitha Phillips. This document tells us that Tabitha was not married at the time the will was written but that her sister Elizabeth Tolbert Phillips had married a man named Allen before this date.

Death Date and/or Place

Newspaper obituaries, tombstone, death certificate, interviews with older relatives or friends, funeral home files, funeral program or notice, Bible records, church register, old letters and diaries, federal mortality schedules if the person died in a census year. Death date can be suggested by the probate files (wills, estate settlement, guardianship records) of the county where death occurred. In the case of Elliott Coleman, the county probate file contained a number of items which helped to establish his death date, particularly these:

> Accounting of money paid in behalf of Mr. Coleman, deceased, including cost of medical services, coffin, digging the grave, and clothes for burial, dated 17 Feb 1892.

> Bill from the doctor dated 18 Feb 1892 for visits to Mr. Coleman between 16 Dec 1891 and 3 Feb 1892.

These two items alone narrow down his death date to some time between February 3 and 17. If the burial had already taken place by February 17, it is likely that death occurred on the 16th or before.

A more common example is the case of Thomas Ballard Smith of Louisa County, Virginia. He wrote his will on August 13, 1776, and added a codicil (addition) to it on October 6, 1777. The will was probated in court on January 12, 1778. The record indicates that his death occurred between 6 October

1777 and the following January, which was most likely the first time the court had met after his death. You could guess that he died, therefore, in October, November, or December, 1777.

Another use of wills, deeds, and estate settlements is in determining information about other family members. When Richard Phillips wrote his will in March, 1793, he named two grandchildren, John and Lucy Holt, "allowing them to be equal to one of my said children" in the division of his estate, to receive their "deceased mother's" portion. We learn here of a daughter, unfortunately not named, who had married, had two children, and died before March, 1793. This kind of discovery can help in establishing not only the death date of this person who wrote the will, but birth, death, and marriage information for his family members, married names for older daughters, and maiden names, in this case, for John and Lucy Holt's mother.

William Harrison's wife Lucy relinquished her dower right and freely acknowledged her husband's sale of land on 11 February 1786, at her home because she was "about to leave this State and cannot conveniently attend court." Then on 26 March 1789, William signed a marriage agreement and deed of gift to Nancy Vaughan, a young neighbor girl. We cannot tell what had happened to Lucy, his former wife, in just these two sources, but we can realize that divorce was rare, especially for a clergyman, as William was. Besides William and Nancy named their second daughter Lucy a few years later, and Nancy had no sister named Lucy to honor with such a namesake. It seems more likely that Lucy died during the three years between the documents.

Names of a Person's Children or Parents

Old letters and diaries, wills and other probate records, estate settlement and guardianship records, newspaper obituaries, funeral notices, Bible records, interviews with older relatives and family friends, birth announcements and wedding stories from newspapers, court minutes and other court records. Deeds can be especially helpful: (1) deed for land bought "by my father James Shaw from Isaac Robertson"; (2) deed of gift, "to my beloved son George"; (3) deed of trust, "my share of the estate of my father, the late Ferdinand G. Coleman of Cumberland County, Virginia."

The 1880, 1900, 1910 and later census records

state each person's relationship to the head of the household. The 1900 and 1910 censuses can help you check your list of children for completeness; those two censuses asked how many children the mother had had and how many were still living.

Tombstones in cemeteries near the family residence may identify other children: "infant daughter of M.H. and C.E. Cummings." Remember that family members may be buried in different cemeteries, even within the same community.

Church baptism records often give the parents' names. Some state censuses and federal censuses from 1850 to 1870 can suggest a list of children, who were to be listed in chronological order after the parents and before other relatives by the same last name, children by a previous marriage, in-laws living in the household, servants or employees, etc. Relationship is not specified in those particular censuses. Federal pension applications and bounty land warrant applications sometimes give names of brothers and sisters, or parents, or children. Marriage bonds may show a parent giving permission for marriage for a child who is under age. Birth and death certificates give the parents' names, although many death certificates give incorrect names. Looking up the death certificate for several children of the same family may give a consensus for their parents' names. Sometimes, children's names can suggest the names of grandparents. Isaac McFadden Patton, Thomas Patton Coleman, and Pitser Blalock Croom were all named for their maternal grandfathers: Isaac McFadden, Thomas Patton, and Pitser Blalock. Of course, other records are necessary to prove the relationship.

Mother's Maiden Name

Bible record; marriage record; interviews with older relatives and family friends; birth or death certificates of her children; newspaper articles on birth, marriage, death, or other occasion; will of the parent listing the daughters by their married names; sometimes a deed of gift from a parent to a married daughter. The tombstone which reads "Denisha Jane Turley, wife of Sam Brelsford," indicates Turley as the wife's maiden name.

Sometimes you can get a clue from the names of her children or grandchildren: Peter *Talbot* Phillips, William *Darby* Orgain, Sarah *Warren* Orgain, Catherine *Ewing* McFadden, and William Lucius *Heath* Harrison. One Virginia boy, *Archer Allen* Coleman,

seems to bear the maiden names of both his maternal grandmother and great-grandmother.

A wife's maiden name is sometimes suggested in a census record by the presence of a person with a different surname living next door to or with the family. Johnson Godwin, living with George and Effie Keahey in 1870, turned out to be Effie's father. Elizabeth Brelsford, living with Gracey and Young Colvin in 1860, was Gracey's mother. Young people listed after the immediate family in a census may be younger brothers or sisters, nieces or nephews, or cousins of the husband or wife.

Tombstones in a family group, even with several different surnames, are sometimes members of the same family; one of an earlier generation may be the wife's mother.

Perhaps you are trying to find the maiden name of your great-grandmother Cordelia Cummings, wife of Moses Cummings. You check the county marriage record first and discover Moses Cummings married Mrs. Cordelia Everett. This indicates that Cordelia had been married before; so you look for a Cordelia somebody marrying a somebody Everett. No luck. From the 1880 census you learn that Cordelia was born about 1830; so she could have been married to Mr. Everett by 1850. The index shows a number of Everett families in the 1850 census of Texas, where Cordelia lived at least after 1860. After reading several of these in different counties, you find Cordelia Everett, age 17, born in Pennsylvania, married to William Everett, a carriagemaker! They are living in St. Augustine County, not at all where you expected find them. As you read the other families on the page, you find one other family with some members born in Pennsylvania, namely the mother and a son older than 17. What an interesting coincidence that this family is named Huston, and Aunt Sally keeps saying that you are a close relative of Sam Houston. So you decide to write down that family just in case they might be relatives, somehow. You also notice the mathematical possibility that Cordelia could be a child of this family, fitting in between the children still at home.

This census shows Cordelia in a different county from the one where you have read the marriage records; so you try the marriage records for the new county. There you find Cordelia Huston marrying William Everett in 1847!

The Huston parents you copied from the census

were named Almanzon and Elizabeth. On the chance that other records of St. Augustine County may link Cordelia with this family, you visit the courthouse one day and decide to check the probate index but find nothing. The deed index shows Almanzon Huston in numerous transactions but not with an Everett or Cummings as the other party. Rather than read all those instruments in as many as 20 different volumes at this time, you decide to check other sources. Finally, an 1834 census of The Republic of Texas shows in the town of St. Augustine Almanzon and Elizabeth Huston with six children, including Cordelia, age 3. The 1860 census of the same county lists Almanzon and Elizabeth Huston and Cordelia, age 26, the other Huston children, and Elizabeth Everett, age 7, and Almanzon Everett, age 5. Thus, evidence indicates that Cordelia really was the daughter of Almanzon and Elizabeth Huston.

Since it is closing time for courthouse and library, your visit must end, and you wish you had planned another day or two in this town, where there is bound to be more good information. We genealogists never really finish.

Back in the town where Cordelia lived after 1860, you find the city cemetery which you had not visited before. A little road leads through the middle of this small, well-kept cemetery; so you drive to the highest point and get out of the car. Amazingly, the first tombstone you see is a double grave with two names: Alma, the 8-year-old daughter of Moses and Cordelia Cummings, and Elizabeth Austin, née Huston, age 73, the two having died on the same day. Could this older lady be Cordelia's mother Elizabeth? "Née Huston" ordinarily means "born Huston," but how could that be? The person you think is Cordelia's mother married a Huston; was she born one, too? And Austin? She must have remarried. You copy all the tombstone information that could possibly pertain to the family (as you know it) from other stones in the cemetery before leaving.

Another day, and on home territory, you visit the courthouse and look in the probate index for Elizabeth Austin. The file includes her will and estate settlement, listing her 14 Huston children and heirs, including Cordelia Cummings. The names all match the several census records you have copied. Hooray! Cordelia's parents really were Almanzon and Elizabeth Huston. The tombstone, "Elizabeth Austin, née Huston," remains a mystery, but you know that

Cordelia was "née Huston."

Visiting the one-block "downtown" of Cordelia's little town, you visit the newspaper office (finding nothing) and the library. You ask the librarian if they have any genealogy records from the area. She leads you to a filing cabinet full of local family records. You immediately scan the headings and see Watters–Huston, McShan–Huston, Usher–Huston, and you know you are in the right place. Bible records, clippings, pictures, and notes abound, further solidifying your knowledge of Cordelia's family, and even yielding one more maiden name: Elizabeth *Newton,* wife of Almanzon Huston. So the tombstone "née Huston" simply meant "formerly Huston," and you have found two maiden names in the search for one! Oh happy day!

Ancestors on the Move

If you are looking for a late nineteenth or early twentieth century ancestor or relative who moved from the family to another place, you can try a variety of sources to identify their new location: interviews with other relatives and family friends, old letters and diaries; newspaper files at the new location (ads, local items, letters remaining at the post office, juror lists); index to state-wide death records; state-wide census Soundex for 1880, 1900, 1910; change of address files or rosters of national organizations; church registers, which may show transfers; college alumni records; queries in regional or national genealogical periodicals for someone working on or with information of the family of _____ (name of person who moved away); papers for an hereditary organization, such as DAR or SAR, filed on the "missing" person's line by a descendant seeking entry into the society.

Alf Coleman was a bachelor in 1882 when the Bolivar, Tennessee *Bulletin* bade him farewell and good luck as he left for Texas with his "celebrated Gate Hinge." At the time we found this notice, the 1900 census had not yet been opened to the public. When that record did become public, the Soundex picked up Alf, still single and living in Dallas.

On the other hand, you may be looking for the birthplace or any former residence of an ancestor in an attempt to work back into previous generations. There are many sources in addition to those listed above which can help you in such searches, going forward or back in time.

Census records can be very useful in this kind of

search; and more and more indexes are being published each year for censuses without Soundex (1790–1870). Two particular searches present special, but not unusual, problems.

Case I

Project: Working backward to find a hometown, county, or parent(s) for a blind ancestor, Luther White.

Information at hand: 1870 and 1860 censuses, in Texas, listed his birthplace as Mississippi. The 1860 census indicated, from the ages of the three children, that the family was probably in Illinois or Mississippi in 1850 and came to Texas after 1855.

Problem: Luther not listed as head of household in Illinois or Mississippi 1850 index. (Either living elsewhere or with another head of household).

Plan: Copy all heads of household with White surname, with enough information to read each entry.

Looking for Whites in Mississippi is like the proverbial needle in a haystack. There were Whites in 64 Mississippi counties in 1850! (At times like this, I must remember a favorite quotation from Shakespeare's *Henry V,* Act II, Scene 1: "Though Patience be a tired Mare, yet she will plod on.") With persistence and plodding, I read, entry by entry, all the Mississippi White families, taking the counties in alphabetical order since they are arranged on the microfilm in approximately that way. Almost at the end, in Pontotoc County, I found James White, age 59, and Luther White, age 25 and blind, wife Tennessee (other censuses had listed her as Frances T.), and children Sarah and William. Persistence paid off. Perhaps it will help in taking James and Luther back 10 more years.

Case II

William Francis Marion Holmes was easy to find in the 1860–1900 census records because he remained in one county.

Project: Working backward to 1850 to try to find parent(s) or other relatives, since he was about 21 years old in 1850.

Information at hand: Censuses from 1870–1900 gave birthplace as Tennessee; 1860 census and secondary Bible records said he was born in Mississippi. Had no parents' names to use in searching.

Problem: Indexes in Texas, Arkansas, Tennessee, and Mississippi did not show him; reading all Holmes families listed for Texas and Mississippi turned up

nothing. At last, other sources gave a tentative name for his father: Isham Holmes. I decided to read all families with surnames beginning with *H* and with heads of household named Isham. I found the family listed and indexed as "Haynes" in Tishomingo County, Mississippi. Use of further sources showed that this was indeed the correct *Holmes* family.

Finding parents and families before 1850 is more difficult because the census names only heads of households. If the ancestor you are seeking was a head of household in 1840 and before, you may indeed find him/her in a given location; then you can use other sources to prove it is the same family. If the person you seek was listed in the 1850 or later censuses, you have at least a tentative state of birth in which to start a search.

Specialized sources, such as those described in Chapter 12, can help you locate people in a state or county at a given time. Military and land records which are indexed for multiple states are easiest to check. Newspaper abstracts and state-wide marriage records, deeds, probate records, if indexed, Bible records published as a state-wide project, indexes of state-wide genealogical periodicals, published lists of such groups as landholders, loyalists, taxpayers, veterans of a particular war, "mortalities," pension applicants, or area "pioneers" are other sources to check. If you organize your plan of attack and work on it systematically, your search is much more likely to yield results. These are further sources which may help:

1. *The Consolidated Index of Claims Reported by the Commissioners of Claims to the House of Representatives from 1871–1880.* (Washington: United States House of Representatives, 1892). These records of the Southern Claims Commission, a federal agency, are in the National Archives, Record Group 217; the approved claims, filed by state and county, are petitions, testimony, and supporting testimony and documents submitted as evidence concerning property seized for use by the Union Army from "citizens in the Southern states who remained loyal to the Union." Disallowed claims are found in Record Group 233. Similar claims of "loyal citizens in loyal states" are in Record Group 92, in the Quartermaster General Claims.

2. Revolutionary War claims of civilians against the state for losses incurred during the war or, especially in South Carolina's accounts, soldiers or their

heirs claiming back pay. In Virginia, see Public Service Claims from the Revolutionary War. In North Carolina, consult Revolutionary War Claims. In South Carolina, see Audited Accounts.

3. Loyalists. Murtie J. Clark, *Loyalists in the Southern Campaign of the Revolutionary War: Officer Rolls of Loyalists*...Vol 1: Recruited from North and South Carolina, Georgia, Florida, Mississippi, and Louisiana. Vol 2: Recruited from Maryland, Pennsylvania, Virginia, and Those Recruited from Other Colonies. Vol 3: Recruited from Middle Atlantic Colonies with Lists of Refugees from Other Colonies. (Baltimore: Genealogical Publishing Company, 1981).

Arthur G. Bradley, *United Empire Loyalists.* (New York: AMS Press, reprint of 1932 edition).

Wilbur H. Siebert, *Loyalists in East Florida, 1774-1785.* (New York: Irvington Publishers, reprint of 1929 edition).

Robert O. DeMond, *Loyalists in North Carolina During the Revolution.* (Baltimore: Genealogical Publishing Company, 1979 reprint of 1940 edition).

Robert S. Lambert, *South Carolina Loyalists in the American Revolution.* (Columbia: University of South Carolina Press, 1987).

4. City directories, college alumni lists, county histories, and such collections as state-wide or county-wide cemetery records.

5. Betty Oliveira, *North American Immigration to Brazil: Tombstone Records of the "Campo" Cemetery, Santa Barbara, São Paulo State, Brazil.* (Brasilia: Graf. do Senado Federal, 1978). A number of Southerners moved to this community after the Civil War, including families from Chester County, South Carolina.

Mary Bryan and William Dumont, *Passports Issued by Governors of Georgia, 1785-1809* (Vol 1) and *1810-1820* (Vol 2). (Washington: National Genealogical Society, 1959, 1964).

Dorothy Williams Potter, *Passports of Southeastern Pioneers, 1770-1823: Indian, Spanish and other land passports for Tennessee, Kentucky, Georgia, Mississippi, Virginia, North and South Carolina.* (Baltimore: Gateway Press, 1982).

6. Records of important gateways or "jumping off places" to frontier areas: Hagerstown, MD; Nashville, TN; St. Joseph or Independence, MO; etc.

7. Quaker, Huguenot, Moravian records.

8. Margery Harding (comp.), *George Rogers Clark and His Men: Military Records, 1778-1784.* Frankfort, KY: Kentucky Historical Society, 1981).

Lloyd D. Bockstruck, *Virginia Colonial Soldiers, 1607-1775.* (Baltimore: Genealogical Publishing Co., 1988). Compiled from bounty rolls, enlistment rolls, etc.

Other such compilations of military units, militia records, etc.

9. Books of early land grants, early landholders, early taxpayers, early officials in given areas. One such record for Kentucky is the *Certificate Book of the Virginia Land Commission, 1779-1780.* (Easley, SC: Southern Historical Press, 1981 reprint of 1923, Vol 21, *Register of the Kentucky State Historical Society*). Two such books for Indiana are Margaret Waters' *Indiana Land Entries, 1801-1840* (Vol 1) and *Indiana Land Entries: Vincennes District, Part 1, 1807-1877* (Vol 2). (Knightstown, IN: Bookmark, 1977). For Virginia: W. Stitt Robinson, Jr., *Mother Earth: Land Grants in Virginia, 1607-1699.* (Charlottesville: University Press of Virginia, 1957). For Tennessee: Goldene Burgner, *North Carolina Land Grants in Tennessee, 1778-1791.* (Easley, SC: Southern Historical Press, 1981). For Ohio: Albion M. Dyer, *First Ownership of Ohio Lands.* (Baltimore: Genealogical Publishing Company, 1982 reprint of 1911 edition). For California: Rose H. Avina, *Spanish and Mexican Land Grants in California.* (Salem, NH: Ayer Co. Publishers, 1976). For New Mexico and Colorado: John R. and Christine M. Van Ness (eds.), *Spanish and Mexican Land Grants in New Mexico and Colorado.* (Manhattan, KS: Sunflower University Press, 1980). For Louisiana: Walter Lowrie, *Land Claims in the Eastern District of the Orleans Territory, Communicated to the House of Representatives, January 9, 1812.* (Easley: Southern Historical Press, 1985). For New York: Fred Q. Bowman, *Landholders of Northeastern New York, 1739-1802.* (Baltimore: Genealogical Publishing Co., 1983).

10. Anyone doing research in Virginia must become familiar with Earl Gregg Swem's *Virginia Historical Index*, 2 vol. (Roanoke: The Stone Printing and Manufacturing Co., 1934). This "Swem Index" is a massive project from pre-computer days which indexes the Calendar of Virginia State Papers (1652-1869); Hening's Statutes at Large (1619-1792); Laws of Virginia, Supplement to Hening's, 1700-1750; The William and Mary College Quarterly, Series 1 and 2; The Virginia Historical Register; Tyler's Quarterly;

the Lower Norfolk County, Virginia Antiquary; and The Virginia Magazine of History and Biography.

Occupation

The census records of 1850 and later asked for each person's occupation; and this is probably the best place to begin looking. By 1870, the instructions to the census takers emphasized accurate and precise recording of occupations, including those of children who contributed to the family support with a regular job. By 1900, unemployment during the year could be recorded as well as the person's status as employer, employee, or self-employed.

Other good sources for occupation information include old letters and diaries, interviews with older relatives and family friends, scrapbooks; local newspapers, especially the advertisements; employee records and union membership records; state unemployment records; and published histories of cities, counties, or companies. Occasionally wills or deeds mention a family business or the tools of one's trade. Papers of businessmen, doctors, and families of the area which have been deposited at a library or archives sometimes include accounts with their customers, other businessmen, or employees. In court minutes I learned that my Elliott Coleman had worked for the county repairing the iron bridge and cutting the floor of the courthouse for the cistern. Also in court minutes, we learned that James Shaw owned the ferry across the Cumberland River in early Nashville.

Inventories and estate sales and settlements in the probate records can also be helpful. Many inventories of deceased retailers give detailed lists of their stock and accounts; estate settlements sometimes report the profits of a family business or the receipts for sale of the crops.

Political Affiliation

Local newspaper stories and advertisements, especially during campaigns, give information about volunteer workers, supporters, and candidates. Interviews with older relatives and family friends, old letters, diaries, scrapbooks, photographs of campaign parades, and perhaps local or state party records may give you information. We of the twentieth century, who take the secret ballot for granted, may forget that voting was not always a private matter. Some deed books or other county record books have polling lists which show who voted for whom in various elections.

In one Kentucky county, I stumbled across the election returns (lists of who voted for whom in each precinct) from the Presidential elections as far back as the 1820s. What a gold mine of information that the clerk's office had not even known they had!

Housing or Living Conditions

Photographs in possession of family members or local historical societies, scrapbooks, old letters, diaries, interviews with older relatives and family friends, local archives, published books on houses of the area are basic sources. Sometimes deed records describe or illustrate a house on a particular lot. Church records and parish vestry books sometimes describe the minister's house. If a business has been built on the site of a former family home, that company or the builders of the new building may have photographs of the site before construction. If the home is still standing, the current residents may talk with you, allow picture taking, or even let you visit inside. If the home is still standing, older residents of the community may be able to describe the interior floor plan or tell you what changes have been made over the years.

Inventories and estate settlements in county records often include lists of personal property and furnishings which give an idea of the family's lifestyle: the number of plates and bowls, silver teaspoons, mirrors and candlesticks, sometimes even window curtains, bedspreads, and quilts, or the books that the individual owned. In a will, an ancestor may specify certain pieces of personal property, furniture, or jewelry to be given to particular individuals.

The censuses of 1850, 1860, and 1870 recorded the value of one's real estate. The 1860 and 1870 returns also asked the value of one's personal estate. Beginning in 1890, the census asked whether homes and farms were rented, owned, or owned free of mortgage.

Country of Origin

The more recent the immigration, the easier it will be to find information. Consult census records, naturalization papers, passenger lists, some land records, death certificates, tombstones, obituaries, family Bibles and histories, family tradition, elder family members to learn of immigration since the mid-nineteenth century. (See Chapter 12, Records of immigrant arrivals and Naturalization papers.) Studies of surnames and their origins may suggest translations and alterations of names that have changed after immigration.

Studying the ethnic backgrounds of the area where your earliest ancestor in this country lived may suggest groups to which he might have belonged. Religious groups often traveled in a body, as did members of extended families, or neighbors. People migrated with relatives or friends. Maps in published histories and geographies may show migration patterns of particular ethnic and religious groups, which may give you clues.

Hundreds of books have been published with lists of immigrants from other countries, especially those in Europe. Westland Publications, P.O. Box 117, McNeal, Arizona 85617, has published a number of books and booklets on immigrants from the German provinces and France, including a two-volume set on the *Mercenaries from Hessen-Hanau and Ansbach-Bayreuth Who Remained in Canada and the United States after the American Revolution*, compiled by Clifford Neal Smith, 1976.

A source of current books on immigrants, or any other topic, is the latest *Books in Print* volumes, published by R.R. Bowker Company, 245 West 17th, New York, NY 10011.

Another major source of genealogical books, including many that will help with a search for immigrant ancestors, is Genealogical Publishing Company, 1001 North Calvert Street, Baltimore, MD 21202 (Tel: 301-837-8271). One of their books which is very useful in Irish research is Sir Robert E. Matheson's *Special Report on Surnames in Ireland Together with Varieties and Synonyms of Surnames and Christian Names in Ireland* (1968 reprint of 1901 edition). Listed here is only a sampling of the books from this publisher:

David Dobson, *Directory of Scots Banished to the American Plantations, 1650-1775* (1986).

David Dobson, *Directory of Scots in the Carolinas, 1680-1830* (1986).

David Dobson, *Directory of Scottish Settlers in North America, 1625-1825*, 6 vol (1985).

John Camden Hotten (ed.), *The Original Lists of Persons of Quality...from Great Britain to the American Plantations, 1600-1700* (reprint, 1962).

Ira A. Glazier (ed.), *The Famine Immigrants: Lists of Irish Immigrants Arriving at the Port of New York, 1846-1851*, 3 vol (1983).

John Wareing, *Emigrants to America: Indentured Servants Recruited in London, 1718-1733* (1985).

N. Dermott Harding, archivist, *Bristol and America, 1654-1685* (reprint, 1970).

William Henry Egle, *Names of Foreigners Who Took the Oath of Allegiance to the Province and State of Pennsylvania, 1727-1755, with Foreign Arrivals, 1786-1808.* (Reprinted from Pennsylvania Archives, Second Series, Vol XVII, 1967).

Albert Cook Myers, *Immigration of the Irish Quakers into Pennsylvania, 1682-1750* (Reprint, 1969).

Gary J. Zimmerman and Marion Wolfert, *German Immigrants, 1847-1854* (1985).

Don Yoder (ed.), *Rhineland Emigrants: Lists of German Settlers in Colonial America* (1985).

John Farmer, *A Genealogical Register of the First Settlers of New England*, (Reprint, 1983).

James Savage, *A Genealogical Dictionary of the First Settlers of New England*, 4 vol (Reprint, 1986).

Gary Boyd Roberts, *Genealogies of Mayflower Families*, 3 vol (1985).

Other publishers have added sources for immigration research:

George T. Flom, *A History of Norwegian Immigration to the United States.* (Iowa City, IA, 1909 — publisher not named).

Richard Sallet, *Russian-German Settlements in the United States.* (Fargo, ND: Institute for Regional Studies, 1974).

Bernard H.M. Vlekke and Henry Beets, *Hollanders Who Helped Build America.* (New York: American Biographical Co., 1942).

Marion and Jack Kaminkow, *Original Lists of Emigrants in Bondage from London to the American Colonies, 1719-1744.* (Baltimore: Magna Carta Book Co., 1981).

Albert B. Faust and Gaius Marcus Brumbaugh, *Lists of Swiss Emigrants in the Eighteenth Century to the American Colonies*, 2 vol. (Washington, DC: National Genealogical Society, 1920, 1925).

There are so many books and periodicals dealing with passenger lists and immigrants that whole books have been written just listing them. Write to the publishers who have done some of these; they often have printed catalogs they can send you. Consult the larger genealogical libraries; they sometimes have pamphlets or booklets listing their own sources for this important research topic.

Once you have enough clues to lead to tentative searches into the country of origin, you have many sources to check, but the problems include accessibility, language, difference in types of records, obscure place names, and time or money for travel. The Mormon library in Salt Lake City and a number of public libraries around the country are acquiring more and more foreign records each year, from deeds, wills, and other public records to church and parish registers.

The Everton Publishers, Inc., of Logan, Utah, have published a number of books guiding the genealogist to searches in other countries, such as Austria, Norway, Denmark, Central Europe, Scandinavia, England and Wales, Italy, the German states, and Hungary. You can contact this company at Box 368, Logan, Utah 84321.

The Genealogical Publishing Company in Baltimore also has published a number of these guides to research in other countries. Two of them are by the same author, Angus Baxter: *In Search of Your German Roots* and *In Search of Your European Roots*. This same author wrote *In Search of Your British and Irish Roots* (New York: William Morrow and Co., Inc., 1982).

If your search for immigrant ancestors points to England, you may want to contact a unique company called Family Society Tours, Ltd., 24 Murray Street, Norwalk, Connecticut 06851 (tel: 203-846-8486). The founders are genealogists who know how difficult it can be to search effectively in foreign records and for tiny old ancestral villages unless we have proper guidance. They, therefore, plan family history tours: (1) for family associations to visit ancestral towns and regions, (2) for descendants of English immigrants from a particular area such as East Anglia or Yorkshire, (3) educational tours for Americans to learn about England and English genealogy from English experts. The now-annual "Family History for Americans" course-tours include lectures, small group focus on search problems, excursions to area museums, countryside, and historic sites, visits to area records repositories, free time, and quality accommodations. Lectures have included such stimulating topics as background history for Americans, regional surnames of England and Scotland, religion and "dissenter" groups, the English parochial system, reading old documents, English manorial records, seventeenth and eighteenth century search problems, estate and land records, probate records, census returns and civil registrations, and migration and mobility.

The accepted practice among genealogists when writing letters with genealogy requests is to enclose a self-addressed stamped envelope (SASE) for a reply. When we write to individuals, libraries, or societies in foreign countries, however, we cannot enclose a SASE. The accepted method of providing for their reply is to send *International Reply Coupons*, which can be purchased at the post office, currently for $.95 each. One coupon provides one ounce of surface mail; an air mail reply may require two coupons. Ask your local post office for guidance; different destinations may need different provisions for replies. The post office also sells aerograms, currently for $.39, which are light-weight air-mail paper that you can write a message on, then fold up and address on the outside. They are actually cheaper than sending a letter in an envelope, which costs $.45 for ½ ounce going overseas; however, enclosures are not allowed inside aerograms.

## 14

What's In a Date?

Writing Dates

There are generally two methods of writing dates. The more common one combines month/day/year: 6/6/76 or June 6, 1976. The other system is used in Europe, in military notation, and increasingly by researchers as it eliminates commas and helps prevent confusion in reading. It simply notes day/month/year: 6 June 1976 or 6/VI/76 in which the month is written in Roman numerals. Each writer is usually consistent; so you can tell in a moment which system he uses. If he writes 5/31/15, it is obvious the month is being placed first since there are not 31 months. If you send a questionnaire to someone to fill out, it would be wise to give them blanks to fill out as you want it done:

_____/____/_____ or _____/_____/_____
month day year   day month year

It is wise to write out or abbreviate clearly the month instead of using numbers. This practice prevents confusion.

Reading Dates

In older newspapers or documents, writers sometimes used shortcuts in writing dates. These shortcuts deserve explanation. Say that today is 17 February 1841. An editor writes a memo referring to "your letter of the 8th instant." He means "your letter of 8 February." "Instant" means "this month." If his memo said "your letter of the 28th ultimo," it meant "your letter of January 28." "Ultimo" means "last month."

What if he wrote on 25 January 1841 and referred to "your letter of the 28th ultimo"? He meant 28 December, the previous month. But December was in last year, too—1840.

A writer might describe a wedding which took place on "Tuesday last." He means the most recent Tuesday. He may announce an ice cream social for "Thursday next." He means the nearest Thursday.

What if the editor wrote in April about an event of "February last"? He meant the most recent February, two months ago. "December last" would mean the most recent December, even though it was in the previous calendar year.

Old Style versus New Style Dates

The Julian calendar, the Old Style, was introduced in Rome in the year we would call 46 B.C. and into the Christian world in 325 A.D. It gave the year 12 months and 365 days, with a leap year of 366 days every fourth year, similar to our system today. However, it became obvious to some that the calendar and sun-time were not synchronized as they should be. Man's calendar was gradually getting behind the sun's natural calendar, like a clock losing a little time each day. In other words, each calendar day was a few minutes too long. These few minutes added up to three days over a period of 400 years or ten days by the year 1582. This discrepancy meant that the first day of spring, the vernal equinox, fell on March 11 instead of March 21, and the church's calculations for the date of Easter, which are governed by that equinox, were not right. Therefore, in March, 1582, Pope Gregory XIII revised the calendar to be in accordance with the sun. He "made up for lost time" by moving over those 10 days rather rapidly to catch up with the sun; and the day after March 4, 1582, became March 15 instead of March 5.

To keep the calendar accurate and prevent the loss of three more days in succeeding 400 years, we would omit three leap year days every 400 years. To simplify the process, the Pope chose the double-zero years, the century dividers. The rule is that the double-zero years that can be divided evenly by 400, with no remainder, *will* be leap years: 1600, 2000. The ones in between, which cannot be divided evenly by 400, will *not* be leap years: 1700, 1800, 1900, 2100, etc.

The Pope made one other change, and this is the one which really affects genealogists. New Year's Day had fallen on March 25: March 24, 1532, was followed the next day by March 25, 1533. However, from 1582 on, New Year's Day would be January 1, as it is today.

The changes were confusing to a number of people, and some thought the Pope was trying to shorten their lives by 10 days! Even more confusing, however, was the fact that only Spain, Portugal, and parts of Italy made the change in 1582. When it was April 12 in Rome that year, it was April 2 in London. France followed the Pope's lead later that year; and the Catholic German states in 1583. However, for over 100 years, the countries of Europe, as well as their territories in the New World, operated under two different calendars.

In 1700, the rest of the German states, the Protestant ones, began using the Gregorian calendar, followed shortly by Sweden and Denmark. Stubborn still, perhaps reluctant to follow the lead of a Catholic official, Britain (and thus the American colonies) stuck with the old Julian calendar for another half century. By then, the difference between the two systems was 11 days instead of 10 because the year 1700 had been leap year, with an extra day, in Britain (under the Julian calendar) but not in Rome (under the Gregorian calendar).

Further complicating the situation, some British individuals (and therefore some American colonists) adopted the Gregorian calendar on their own. Thus, you cannot always tell which calendar was used in the particular records you are reading; but it seldom really matters. You can make the distinction in your own notes as necessary or desirable by adding after the date *O.S.* (Old Style or Julian) or *N.S.* (New Style or Gregorian). If you find a date written with a double day, 5/16 April 1704, you know that under the old calendar the date would be April 5; but under the new style, it would be April 16. Likewise, you may find a double year written in an early record, but only for the months of January, February, or March, which could come under either of two years depending on which calendar the recorder used. Thus, 9 January 1688/89 would mean 1688 for a person using the old calendar or 1689 for one using the new or Gregorian system. Technically, George Washington's birthdate could be written 11/22 February 1731/32, which covers both calendars.

When you work with early records, you may find what otherwise may seem to be discrepancies or inaccuracies which can actually be explained by the difference in calendars. If a record is dated "the 5th day of the 5th month of 1729," it could be May 5 under the new calendar but July 5 under the old one, March being counted as the first month in the Julian system.

My own ancestor Patty Field Allen, according to the Bible record, was born on August 25, 1746. Her sister Obedience was born on March 1, 1747. It becomes obvious that the family was not using the Gregorian calendar, for a baby born in August is not followed by another born barely six months later. According to the Julian calendar, still the official calendar of Britain and the colonies, the March following Patty's birth was still 1746. March 25 ushered in 1747; so, March 1, 1747, was another 12 months away, actually 18 months after Patty's birth. Obedience, therefore, could write her birthdate 1 March 1747/48, meaning 1747 under the old system or 1748 under the new one.

Finally, in 1750, Parliament agreed to make the official change to the Gregorian calendar. The day after September 2, 1752, would be September 14, instead of September 3, making up for the 11 days' difference in the two systems. Furthermore, the new year would begin on January 1 instead of March 25.

What Day of the Week?

The five-day work week with a weekend for family and social activities is, of course, a relatively recent phenomenon. Today's predominance of Saturday weddings is surely related to this pattern. On what day of the week did weddings occur in your family's past? Why did Grandma and Grandpa choose Wednesday for their wedding? At least one couple chose that day because the groom, who worked six days a week, found someone who would work for him Wednesday and Thursday. His only free day was Sunday, but no one in that community at that time would have considered having a wedding on Sunday.

Another prospective groom was asked when the wedding would be. The young farmer answered, "Sometime between the peas and the wheat." Apparently any day of the week would do so long as it fell within the slack season.

Some almanacs publish a perpetual calendar by which you can find the day of the week for many dates in the past or future.

However, you can figure it yourself with easy arithmetic. The formula below gives a correct day of the week for any date after 14 September 1752, the day on which Britain and the colonies converted to the Gregorian calendar. Actually, you could use the formula for dates before September 14, 1752, if you then convert them to the old calendar. Here are two examples, using two actual wedding dates:

Formula	Example 1 9 December 1824	Example 2 8 August 1781
Step 1. Begin with the last 2 digits of the year.	24	81
Step 2. Add ¼ of this number, disregarding any remainder.	6	20
Step 3. Add the date in the month.	9	8

Step 4. Add according to the month:

January	1	(for leap year, 0)			
February	4	(for leap year, 3)			
March	4				
April	0				
May	2	September	6		
June	5	October	1		
July	0	November	4		
August	3	December	6	6	3

Step 5.

Add for the	18th century	4		
	19th century	2	2	4
	20th century	0		
	21st century	6		

Step 6. Total the numbers.	47	116

Divide by 7. Check the remainder against this chart to find the day of the week:

	Example 1	Example 2
1 = Sunday	6 with	16 with
2 = Monday	remainder	remainder
3 = Tuesday	of 5. The	of 4. The
4 = Wednesday	wedding	wedding
5 = Thursday	took place	took place
6 = Friday	on	on
0 = Saturday	Thursday.	Wednesday.

Just for the fun of it, practice the formula using September 14, 1752, the day of the great calendar switch-over. Can you imagine the trauma of trying that kind of change in our culture on *that* day of the week? Even daylight-saving time goes into effect in the early hours of Sunday so as to give the least possible confusion. Imagine our making a daylight-saving time change on the same day of the week that the whole calendar changed!

Using Dates

Dates are a useful tool for the genealogist. There are many ways to use them for purposes other than just vital statistics.

Here are some actual cases which illustrate the use and misuse of dates.

Case I

Notes taken from two tombstones in one family read as follows:

Infant daughter
4 September 1891–10 September 1891

Talmadge Ward Campbell
12 January 1892–26 November 1894

Do you see the discrepancy? And this has nothing to do with the old calendar. A daughter born in September and a son born four months later? Hardly. The first note seemed to be correct: the baby girl lived only a few days and was not named. The other was probably copied wrong. It could have been June, 1892, or January of 1890 or 1893. The tombstone was studied again; the stone actually read June instead of January, 1892. The copy contained the error.

Case II

Another tombstone clearly reads:

To the sacred memory of
Rev. William Harrison
who departed this life
20th November 1814...

However, his will, which is dated May, 1812, is recorded in the January, 1814, probate records; and the year 1814 is clearly written three times on the page. So the tombstone must be incorrect and should probably read 1813. His will cannot have been probated before he died. Chances are that he died the November prior to the probate, or November, 1813.

Case III

The original marriage bond in the archives of the Virginia State Library, showing the intent of William Daniel to marry Patty Field Allen, is clearly dated 28 March 1768, as is the attached consent of the bride's father Samuel Allen. Under a Virginia law of October, 1748, if either bride or groom was under 21 and not formerly married, consent of the father or guardian of "every such infant shall be personally given before the said clerk'' of the county, with two witnesses.[1] According to the published Bible record of Patty's brother Archer Allen,[2] Patty's birthdate was 25 August 1746. This date would make Patty 21 years and 7 months old when she married, and not really needing the consent of her father to marry.

At this time in Virginia, it was the law for a wife to be brought to the courthouse when her husband sold land to which she had a claim. The Justice of the Peace or another official took her aside, explained the deed of sale to her, and asked if she willingly signed it. Was the signature hers? Did she wish to retract it? By agreeing to the sale, she relinquished her dower rights to that property.

By law, when a man died, part of his real estate was allotted to the widow for her lifetime, especially if it had been hers before the marriage or if she had inherited it. This property was her dower. By relinquishing her dower right to a particular tract of land, she was acknowledging the fact that the land was no longer theirs or hers and she could not expect to have claim to it if her husband died.

William Daniel sold a tract of land in August, 1761, and no dower rights or wife were mentioned. Probably, William was not married at the time. Then in 1763, at least by September 27 when the deed was recorded, William sold 200 acres also in Cumberland County, to John Daniel. No dower rights or wives were mentioned at that time. However, in the spring of 1765, John Daniel sold this same tract, and William sold 375 acres in another tract. Seven months later, 28 October 1765, John's wife Elizabeth and William's wife Martha appeared in court and relinquished their dower rights to the 200 acres that John was selling, and Martha consented to the sale of William's 375 acres.[3] Why would Martha have any claim to relinquish on John's land unless she was married to William at the time he sold it to John? That sale was in 1763, and suggests that William and Martha were married by that time, certainly by 1765 when the dower rights were relinquished. Yet the marriage record clearly shows their marriage in 1768.

The dates of these documents clearly present a dilemma, and perhaps they cannot be reconciled. A possible answer is that William was married to another Martha before he married Patty, who in later records continued to be called Martha rather than Patty. If this is so, the first Martha would have died in 1766 or 1767, leaving no children. Another possibility, although less likely in light of other county records and family histories, is that another couple named William and Martha were in the county in the 1760s. This is an example of one of the great puzzles of genealogy.

Case IV

After collecting information from many sources, it is helpful to chart what you know and study the possibilities. Form 3, an Outline of the Life of any ancestor, provides convenient space in which to chart the information you have gathered on a particular person. At a glance and in chronological order, you have such information as his birth and baptism, education, marriage, military service, moves from one home to another, the birth of his children, real estate transactions, court appearances, voting record, and other puzzle pieces that you may obtain from public and family records. The outline helps keep these events in perspective, provides a quick review of what you know and what you lack, helps you catch discrepancies, and helps you formulate questions for your next search effort. Your notes, of course, contain the source and documentation for each piece of information transferred to the outline. An example is shown in Figure 14.

Here are some questions which arise from the outline of William Harrison's life:

1. The large gap between his birth and his ordination is an opportunity for study, for search. Where was he educated? Where did he grow up?
2. Did he actually go to North Carolina between 1756 and 1760?
3. Do Surry County records shed any light on his life around 1760–62?
4. Where did he go during his eleven month leave-of-absence in 1772? Perhaps to England? Perhaps to Barbados? For further education?
5. Events between 1774 and 1780, especially in Virginia, must have troubled him greatly, for he resigned his pastorate and switched sides. Are there Cornwallis papers or Governor Nelson papers which might shed light on his change in loyalty from the

---

[1] Hening's *Statutes of Virginia*, Vol 6, p. 82.
[2] Bible record of Archer Allen, in *William and Mary Quarterly*, Series I, Vol 22, p. 95.
[3] Deed Books of Cumberland County, Virginia, Book 3, p. 193, 416; Book 4, p. 60, 67.

American side to the British side?

6. The court records which included Harrison's trial no longer exist. Is there any other source which might tell more about that event?

7. We know he was exiled and that he was later allowed to return to his home. Where did he go during the exile? How long? When did he leave? Immediately or in 1786 when Lucy was "about to leave this state" and could not appear in court?

8. When did Lucy die? What more can we learn about her? These deeds are the only mention of her that has been found so far.

Many more questions can arise as the search continues. They may or may not ever be answered, but looking for an answer is part of the fascination of genealogy.

Each ancestor presents a different set of questions and challenges for you to work on. To correlate the questions and the search for answers, I have found it helpful to use a Problem Search Record, as shown in Figure 15. It provides a central place to keep records of the search for particular information. As shown in the example, three problems presented by William Harrison's outline in Figure 14 are being "attacked."

An effort has been made to discover his birthplace and place of education. The various letters which have been written are listed here along with a summary of the answer from each source. This information is especially useful for those of us who have to put intervals of weeks or months between our opportunities to search. Over a period of time away from your subject, it is easy to forget what you have already accomplished if you do not write it down. Proper use of this chart can help you begin again where you had to stop the time before.

The questions or problems for which the Problem Search Record is most useful are those which require the use of a number of sources or writing a number of letters.

OUTLINE OF THE LIFE OF <u>WILLIAM HARRISON</u>
<u>name of ancestor</u>

Note: Fill in information on marriage(s), children, education, military service,
illnesses, religious milestones, jobs, migrations, family events, deaths, etc.

YEAR	EVENT
c 1730	Born at _Barbados_ (Info from Lambeth Palace Library, London)
19-21 Dec 1756	Ordained deacon + priest by Bishop of London + licensed to officiate in North Carolina, where he proposed to set up a public school.
1760	Minister in Southwark Parish, Surry Co, Va.
22 Nov 1762	Rector of Bristol Parish, Blandford Church, Petersburg, Dinwiddie Co, Va.
Sept 1772	11 months leave of absence — Where did he go?
27 May 1774	Signed the Association protesting closing of the port of Boston
4 Feb 1780	Resigned as rector of Bristol Parish, after 18 years
19 Oct 1781	Captured with Cornwallis, surrender at Yorktown
21 Oct 1781	Gov. Nelson wrote Lord Cornwallis: Harrison has been delivered to civil authorities to stand trial — we can't prevent it.
13 Feb 1782	Gov. Harrison wrote to Attorney for the State in Gloucester Co mentioning an order to prosecute Harrison on charge of high treason.
17 May 1782	Gov. Harrison wrote to Attorney General asking him to be present at trial of Harrison. Harrison found guilty of treason, exiled from Virginia.
Nov 1784 – Jan 1786	Wife Lucy joins him in selling Ravencroft lots in Petersburg.
10 Feb 1786	Lucy "being about to leave the state & cannot conveniently attend court."
26 Mar 1789	Marriage agreement of William with Nancy Ann Vaughan, dau. of David & Winnefred Vaughan.
c. 1792 – 1804 or so	5 children born to William & Nancy Ann — living in Petersburg
1810	Census: William's household in Petersburg, p126 of Dinwiddie Co, including 5 children
29 May 1812	Wrote his will (Later moved to front of his home, Porter Hill. Blandford Church)
20 Nov 1813*	Death. Burial place _____
3 Jan 1814	Will probated. *(Tombstone shows 1814 as death date. Court records indicate he died before 1814 — either 1812 or 1813.)

PROBLEM SEARCH RECORD

THE SEARCH FOR Rev. William Harrison
<u>name of ancestor</u>

PROBLEM	SOURCES TO TRY/ QUESTIONS TO ANSWER
ORIGIN, BIRTHPLACE, + EDUCATION	1. Registrar at Cambridge Univ. - *no record of him* 2. Registrar at Oxford - *no record of him* 29 June 1976 3. Registrar, Barbados- *birth certificate search, April, 1976 - no record of him* 4. Guildhall Library, London - *June 1976 - referred me to Registrar, Barbados.* 5. Bishop of London ★ *Lambeth Palace Library - found ordination papers - 1756 - gave Barbados as birthplace + educated in England.* 6. Church Commissioners London, June 76 - *referred me to Lambeth Palace Library.* 7. Society for the Propagation of the Gospel - ★ *no record of him but helpful suggestions.*
CORNWALLIS PAPERS which might shed light on his appt as chaplain, 1781, especially Orderly Book for August, 1781.	LIBRARY OF CONGRESS, MS DIVISION - *April 1976 referred me to Clements Library, Ann Arbor Michigan.* CLEMENTS LIBRARY - *does not have Orderly Book. Suggested Pub. Rec. Office, London.* GUILDHALL LIBRARY - *June '76 - suggested Pub. Rec. Office, London.* PUBLIC RECORDS OFFICE, LONDON - *does not do any searching - must hire searcher - Alas!*
EDUCATION, BIRTH cont'd.	REGISTRATION OFFICE, Bridgetown, Barbados - *no record of him, suggested their achives. 2 baptism certificates: 1688 too early + 1747 too late.* CODRINGTON COLLEGE, Barbados - *opened 1830, too late. Suggested Central Grammar School + Codrington Grammar School - Sent addresses.* WRITE THEM.
1774 - "Association protesting closing port of Boston"	*Is this the same William Harrison? Were there 2? Was the Rev ever a Burgess?*

## 15

Fitting the Pieces Together

Putting together a family history puzzle involves many strategies, sources, and people. One interview with a major figure will probably not be enough. You may contact the same person time and time again over a period of years. Likewise, use of the public records may call for several visits to the same courthouse as you learn more and ask more questions. It takes repeated use of all these sources to make your puzzle as complete and interesting as possible. Here is an example of an actual search as it began. Notice the combined use of family and public sources.

In a brief visit with Aunt Leona and Mama Edna, we started the family group sheet, with Grandma and Grandpa White as the husband and wife. Their 18 children and step-children were not in chronological order; we listed them as we thought of them and numbered them later. In a few cases, we listed nicknames, leaving space for the full names when we found them. We had time for adding three or four spouses, learning that all the children on the chart were born in the same Texas county, that Grandpa had a brother named Wallace and a sister, and that both grandparents had lost spouses before marrying each other. The visit had to end, but we planned another soon.

Now we had two families to follow, two searches to pursue: Grandpa's family, the Whites; and Grandma's family that we had not yet identified. Between visits, I read the 1880 federal census for their county. I found Grandpa and his first wife with brother Wallace and the sister, who was Olivia. This census gave their ages, birthplaces, and relationship to Grandpa who was head of the household. The census said that Grandpa was born in Illinois! The blank for birthplace of his parents was marked ''unknown.''

Finding that Wallace and Olivia were both born in Texas, I decided to try the 1870 census to see if I could find them with their parents. Since the older brother cared for the younger brother and sister, and no living relative knew of any others, what family were they part of? The 1870 census showed Grandpa,

Wallace, two parents, two more sisters, and another brother! And Great-grandpa Luther was blind! Since Olivia was nine years old in the 1880 census, I did not expect to find her in 1870, and I didn't. She was born after the census was taken, either in late 1870 or 1871.

The immediate question was what happened to the rest of the family between 1870 and 1880? There are probably two alternatives: they moved away or they died. If they moved away, why did they leave the baby of the family with older brother? Since none of the descendants have heard of any other relatives, chances are that the parents of the family died. The sisters could have married and lived in other counties. Was there an epidemic in the county that may have taken several family members in a short time? Some of these questions may never be answered. Meanwhile, we wrote them down, laid them aside, and continued the search for basic information.

Noticing in the 1870 census that one of Grandpa's sisters was born in Mississippi about 1856 and the next one in Texas about 1859, we could calculate the family's migration to Texas between 1856 and 1859. So the next source we checked was the 1860 census of their county; and they were there. To round out the available census information, we read the 1900 census for Grandpa and his brother Wallace and their sister Olivia with their own households.

From the four census records we compiled the information shown at the top of page 93.

In the county records, we discovered marriage records for Grandpa, Wallace, and Olivia, and a second marriage for Great-grandpa Luther in 1873. So we knew that Frances died between December 1870, when Olivia was born, and 1873. We found a deed record, which showed Great-grandpa Luther still living in the county in 1878 but gave no reference to him after that.

As Case I in Chapter 13 illustrates, taking this family back to the 1850 census was a challenge and an exercise in patience. Information from other records suggested that they were probably in Illinois or

Name	1860 Age	Birthplace	1870 Age	Birthplace	1880 Age	Birthplace	1900 Age	Birthplace	Birth Date	Birthplace of parents
Luther White	35	Miss.	45	Miss.					c 1825	
Frances T. "	30	Tenn.	40	Tenn.					c 1830	
William J. " (Grandpa)	12	Ill.	22	Ill.	32	Ill.	51	Ill.	Jan 1849	Ill.
Martha E. "	5	Miss.	14	Miss.					c 1854–55	
Margaret A. "	1	Tx.	11	Tx.					c 1858–59	
Wallace M.T. "			7	Tx.	18	Tx.	38	Tx.	Mar 1862	
James L. "			2	Tx.					c 1867–68	
Olivia Frances "					9	Tx.	30	Tx.	Dec 1870	Ill.

Mississippi in 1850 but did not show Luther as a head of household in the indexes to that census. With absolutely no other clues to go on, there was only one choice: read the several hundred entries for White families in 64 Mississippi counties. In Pontotoc County, there they were: James White (age 59), Luther (age 25 and blind), Felix (age 14), John (age 10), Tennessee (age 26), Sarah (age 5), and William (age 3). This gave us James as a probable father of Luther, Felix, and John, born about 1791 in Tennessee; his younger sons Felix and John, born in Mississippi about 1836 and 1840; Frances Tennessee, Luther's wife; and their children Sarah and William. Sarah, of course, did not appear in the 1860 and later censuses; chances are that she died before 1860.

The surprising information in the 1850 census was that Sarah's and William's birthplaces were both given as Mississippi, although all the other censuses said William was born in Illinois! Even in 1900, William and Olivia both said their parents were born in Illinois. This assumption is probably incorrect, but there may well be a clue in the fact that William's birthplace is given as Illinois during his entire adulthood and even once during his childhood. There are many possibilities: the family lived in Illinois only a short time during which William was born; he and Sarah were both born during a slightly longer stay in Illinois; the parents could have married there regardless of where their children were really born; they may have simply talked about moving to Illinois so much that it became fact in the minds of the children; one or both parents could have lived in Illinois during childhood; etc.

The family sources, for the time being, are exhausted, and the Texas sources are being examined. The Mississippi (and Tennessee and possibly Illinois) sources are, for the most part, untouched but promise a challenging search.

Meanwhile, the other part of the family, Grandma's, was even more intriguing because we knew nothing of it. We knew Grandma's maiden name (Cummings) from her first marriage record; her second marriage record, of course, showed her as Mrs. E. L. Collier (Ella Lee) who married William J. White.

On the way to visit Aunt Leona a second time, we stopped at the county clerk's office in the courthouse and read marriage and deed and probate records for Cummings, our "newest" family name. The only Cummings listed in the deed indexes was Moses Cummings, with his wife Adelia. This was possibly Ella Lee's (Grandma's) father, but we found no proof. The probate records gave us Moses' death date, 1903, at age 77, which suggests a birth year of 1826.

Our second interview with Aunt Leona was rewarding. We copied all information from the family Bible: marriages, births, and deaths, and found that Grandpa William White had died in 1910. No wonder the kids (the ones still living) didn't remember him; they were too small. We finished naming the 18 children of Grandpa and Grandma's combined families, and their spouses, on the family group sheet — as much as we could. We shared with Aunt Leona the surprises found at the library and courthouse.

She guided us through the cemetery where she knew many of the family members were buried. As we copied names and dates, she identified each person: "Ida's husband," or "he was killed in a car wreck," or "an adopted son." She also listed for us the unmarked graves of family members known to be in the cemetery, including Grandpa and his first wife.

All afternoon we recorded stories as fast as she told them, and she was really wound up. Each question brought a 20-minute answer with tales of getting lost in the woods, having 75 to 100 relatives for Christmas, growing up in the tomato patch, a near-shotgun wedding, and the old aunt who griped when the kids fed scraps of biscuit dough to the chickens.

With Aunt Leona navigating, we drove to the old "home-place" where she had grown up, although the house is no longer there; to the school where all the kids got "edgicated"; down the road they used to walk to school on; and by her Grandma Cummings' house! The real house! This opened a whole new area of the puzzle.

Aunt Leona's Grandma Cummings would be our great-grandmother, Ella Lee's mother, but we call her Grandma now, slipping into Aunt Leona's generation. And we fired the questions:

1. What was your Grandma's name? *Grandma.*

2. When did she die? *She lived to be 93; the kids got out of school to go to the funeral.* (**Use this.** Leona was born in 1907 and started to school at six or seven, 1913 or 1914. Her grandma died when she was small but already in school, so after 1913 but probably before 1920, when Leona was 13 and old enough to remember more of landmark events.)

3. Who were Grandma's children? *Mama and a brother Cumby.*

4. What was his real name? *I don't know.*

5. Was Grandma married more than once? *I don't know.*

6. Were there any stepchildren? Did Mama have half-brothers and half-sisters? (Note: from here on, we use Leona's names for these people. "Mama" was our Grandma Ella Lee; "Grandma" was our great-grandmother Cummings. It is easier for people being interviewed to identify relatives by the names they called them.) *Yes, Mama had a half-brother, John Cummings.* (**Use this.** Grandpa Cummings married someone else before Grandma.)

7. We found a John Cummings in the 1880 census with a wife and a baby girl, Elnora. Is that the same John? *Yes, Nora was the only girl. She had 11 brothers, named for Bible characters, including Matthew, Mark, Luke, and John.*

8. Did Mama have other half-brothers or half-sisters? *I don't remember.*

9. What was Grandma Cummings' name? (again) *Grandma.* (again)

10. Did she live on "the place" a long time? *Yes, 40 or 50 years. Grandma needed someone to look after her when she got old, and Mama had too many kids to be Mama and Papa to and run the farm and feed some of her grandkids, too. She simply could not take care of Grandma. So she deeded her half of the place to her brother, Cumby, if he'd look after Grandma.* (**Use this.** Grandma lived there many years, and Mama "deeded" her half. That means they owned the place; they didn't rent. In the deed index, the only Cummings listed was Moses. So Grandma is likely his wife.)

Now we made an effort to sort out what we knew about the Cummings family.

11. What road is the house on? *Old San Antonio Road.* (**Use this.** Moses had at least two pieces of land just outside town on the Old San Antonio Road, shown in deeds we just found at the courthouse.)

12. Did you ever know Grandpa Cummings? *No.* (We had found that Moses died in 1903, before Leona was born.)

13. What was his name? *Never heard anybody say.*

14. Could it have been Moses? *Don't have any idea.*

15. Could Grandma's name have been Adelia? *Hey, yes! But it was Cordelia. Yes, it had to be because sister Delia was named for her.* (Adelia in the deeds makes little difference; recorders can make mistakes.)

16. Moses was Adelia's husband. See these deeds of 1869 and 1870. Let's look at the marriages we copied at the courthouse. Here's M.H. Cummings (could be Moses) marrying Mrs. C.E. Everett (C could be Cordelia) in 1865. Your mama was born in 1867; so these could be her parents.

17. Look at some of the cemetery notes: Nina Cummings, 1872–1945; C.C. Cummings, 1865–1934; Alma Cummings, 1870–1878, daughter of M H and C E Cummings; Christopher Columbus Cummings, died in 1963, age 81. Can you identify these? *Well, Cumby's wife was Nina.* Could Cumby be a nickname for Christopher Columbus? *I don't know; I never heard his real name.*

We decided it could be: M H and C E married in March, 1865. Their son Cumby, if the C C above, could still have been born in late 1865. The child Alma of M H and C E was born exactly three years to the day after Mama was born, but died young. Christopher Columbus Cummings, born in 1882 and living 81 years, could be Cumby's son, a junior; or he could be a son of Cumby's half-brother with 11 sons; but Christopher Columbus is hardly a Biblical name.

18. Do you know any of Cumby's kids or John's kids we could write to for further information? *Yes.*

And she gave us a name and address.

The visit had to end. What next? Study notes taken so far. (I like to underline or star in bright-colored felt-tip pen the parts that pertain to the direct family.) Fill in the new information on the family group sheets. Write down questions that have come up and are still unanswered. Write the man Leona suggested. Re-check the 1880 census for Luther White's second wife Martha or Mattie, as a widow. Re-check the 1880 census for Moses and Cordelia Cummings. Leona's mama, their daughter Ella Lee, was still at home, unmarried, in 1880. Maybe this family was overlooked in first reading. Write Aunt Delia. She's 80 and unable to answer, but maybe her daughter will. Anyway, try. Plan to visit the court-house again for the marriage dates of Ella Lee's eight Collier kids by her first husband and for the marriage of C E _____ (Grandma) to a Mr. Everett, to find her maiden name and marriage.

That part of the search is now complete; Cordelia Huston Everett Cummings was the Grandma Cummings we first heard about from Aunt Leona. Her father Almanzon Huston was a New York-born Catholic innkeeper, stagecoach owner, and mail contractor; her mother was Elizabeth Newton, born in 1805 in northern Pennsylvania. We have most of the vital statistics on this couple and their 14 children and are gathering the "spice," the history, the socio-economic information, checking the tradition that they had lived in Michigan before moving to Texas, and trying to find *their* parents.

## 16

Read It Right

Reading handwriting from the past is a skill all genealogists use. Developing this skill is easier if you are aware of the pitfalls.

In the eighteenth and nineteenth centuries, most lower-case letters were formed about the same way they are today. Individual variations are found, of course, but there was a general pattern for writers to follow.

There were two styles of *r* and *t*, just as there are today:

*Western fork of a branch
running a northernly course*

at my decease

all their future

Sometimes the *u*'s and *n*'s, or *w*'s and *m*'s, looked alike. Like writers today, writers a century ago did not always dot their *i*'s and cross their *t*'s. Because of fading ink, yellowing paper, and the unevenness with which quill pens and pen staffs wrote, these and other strokes in the original are barely distinguishable to us today.

The most unusual characteristic of older handwriting is the double *s*, written as if it were *fs* or a sprawling *ps*. Here are some examples from the nineteenth century.

possessed

division [sic]

blessing

witnesseth

James Harriss, Clerk

Missouri

Missippi [sic]

Agness

Jessee

Miss Polly

Bass

One of these same writers made the *j* of *enjoyment* exactly the same as the first *s* in *blessing*. There is no confusion, however, because it is clear what word he is using.

in the enjoyment of

Another writer in 1903 used the same stroke, but for the letter *g* in *things*:

Some capital letters can confuse the modern reader. The *S* and *L* are very similar and sometimes the *T* is hard to distinguish from them.

Susannah, Sally &

Sister   *Sons*

Subject   *Legacy*

Levi   *Lea*

Lucy   *Thomas*

State of So Carolina

signed Thomas Smith

The *I* and *J* are almost identical. Perhaps this similarity is a carry-over from the Latin and Greek alphabets in which the two letters were interchangeable, or in which there really was no *J*. Words which we spell with *J* often come from Latin or Greek stems beginning with *I*. A prominent example is the pair of Christian symbols *IHS* and *INRI*. The first is the beginning of the Greek spelling of *Jesus*. The second is an acronym from the Latin words for "Jesus of Nazareth, King of the Jews." The three *I*'s here stand for words we begin with *J*.

Another example is the variation of forms of the name John: the German Johannes, the French Jean, the Spanish Juan, the Russian Ivan, the Scandinavian Jan, and the Gaelic Ian. Many of the Biblical names

used in the eighteenth and nineteenth centuries are of Hebrew or Aramaic origin and were originally spelled with an *I*. It was not until the seventeenth century that the *J* was clearly a separate letter in function and form. Is it any wonder then that handwriting reflected this double duty? Here are some examples showing the similarity of *I* and *J*.

January Sessions

I do   *Isham*

Isaac   *Isaac*

Joseph Harrisson

In the first place

J. B. Kirkland

Juliana

John
Isaac Johnston
James
Joshua

Many of the capital letters of the eighteenth and nineteenth centuries are similar to the script type, shown here:

When you find problems in reading the handwriting, let your imagination play with the letters and try different combinations until you decide what the original says. If the letters individually create a problem, look at the word as a whole, or the phrase it is part of. What is the writer talking about? What is the logical word to fit his meaning? Is this the word he is using? Look at other letters of the same handwriting. Try to find the same letter or word written elsewhere by the same person. Can you guess it by comparing its shape with others you already know?

If you cannot decide, try copying the original as closely as possible or put a blank in your copy, indicating an illegible word. If you can narrow the possibilities, put the alternatives in your notes. An example is the two names Lemuel and Samuel, which are sometimes hard to tell apart. In your notes, put ''Lemuel or Samuel'' to indicate the problem and to let you know later that you could not tell which name it was.

Try some sample problems. This word looks frightful by itself. But when you put it with the whole phrase, there is only one possible reading: ''Witness the following signatures and seals.''

This is a signature on a marriage license from 1869:

We know the initial is *P* and the last name is Mullally. The first name looks like it ends in *is*. It cannot be Morris or Travis. The first letter is not shaped like the *M* in his last name, and there are too many humps for *Travis.* If you have access to another source, look to see how someone else wrote his name. His name is Francis.

Another signature to study is the one above Carter H. Trent's name on a contract. The initials are clearly *E. W.* There is a dot for an *i* and the last letter seems to be *s*. The beginning letter, as it turns out, is easily recognized as a large *s* as in the old-style double *s*. But it could give a reader an impression of *J* or maybe a fancy *T.* In this case, it cannot be compared with letters of the same shape on the document because this is a signature added to another man's instrument. But in the rest of the contract, the man's name appears several times, a little different each time:

By comparing three slightly different ways of writing the same name, we must conclude the man was E.W. Sims.

Seventeenth- and early eighteenth-century writing looked very different from the later styles. It was much more square or rounded, not so sleek and flowing. Yet it was elaborate in its own way.

Sten Hughes
Robert Hughes

mercy and merrits [sic] *of my Lord*

Daniel Croom

witnesses hereto

An excellent reference book for the very early American writing is E. Kay Kirkham's book, *How to*

Read the Handwriting and Records of Early America (Salt Lake City: Deseret Book Co., 1961).

Copying older handwriting takes special care so that the message of the original is preserved. An example is found in the marriage record from Madison County, Tennessee. The bride's name is divided and on two lines of the original: Stur-devant. One copier saw only the first syllable and recorded, and published, the name as Steer. The original writing is tiny and the *u* could be read as two *e*'s. But a more careful copier would have seen the rest of the name on the next line. Furthermore, one who had worked with the records of that county would have recognized Sturdevant as the name of several families in the county.

In copying a passage, copy it just as the original reads. If a letter or word has been omitted and you want to put it in, add it in brackets to indicate that you, rather than the original writer, are supplying it. Another method is to write [*sic*] after the word. This is Latin for "thus." It indicates that you know something is wrong, but you've copied it exactly as it was.

"This leaves all well — hopeing this may find [you] and all the family in the enjoyment of the same blessing. I must close write soon — "

"give my love to all of the family and except [sic] a portion your self   no more."

Numbers written in the nineteenth century are very similar to numbers we write now. The major difference is that the older ones sometimes contain a few more flourishes.

Reading old records can be quite enjoyable because clerks often had very polished, clear handwriting. It takes a lot more skill to duplicate their style than to read it. The care with which they wrote may remind us to review the legibility of our own scribbling.

17
What About Computers?

Computer technology entered the world of genealogy in the late 1970s and early 1980s and within a few years offered software programs designed for use on home computers to organize, sort, and store all the names, dates, places, and events that we genealogists collect. The field of computer genealogy has grown rapidly and promises exciting developments in the future. As personal computers become more affordable by more people and software becomes more sophisticated and, at the same time, more "user-friendly," genealogists are becoming more aware of the benefits and the value of computers in our field.

Perhaps the first evidence many of us had that computers were at work in genealogy was the indexes being created by computers for voluminous census records. Gradually, correspondence among us took on the "print-out" appearance with square letters, paper with serrated edges, and the group-letter, less-personal approach of "Dear Friends Searching Jenkins Families." Within a couple of years, such letters began including pedigree and family group charts from the computer.

You do not have to own a personal computer to understand the benefits of having one for use in genealogy. If you have ever spent hours looking up all the family addresses from the last three years' Christmas cards before sending out requests for information for family group sheets, or if you have ever typed, retyped, cut and taped, and retyped a research paper or family history project, or if you have ever indexed anything with little slips of paper in a house with children, pets, or ceiling fans, or if you have ever spent an hour looking up one marriage record in your stack of notebooks in order to answer Cousin Grace's letter and, in the meantime, forgotten three different times just which of Silas Brown's daughters you were looking for, you will be receptive to the idea of computers for genealogy.

With a computer, the appropriate *software* (programs) and accessories, and time spent learning how to use the system, you can store all those family ad-dresses, print them on labels or in lists, and sort them by Zip Code, surnames in alphabetical order, or any number of other ways. With word processing functions, you can rearrange, insert, or delete paragraphs or sentences, change words, correct spelling, update addresses, and improve your letters and papers before you ever print them. You can index your files or books. You can search quickly for specific pieces of information and print it out in many formats. You can easily search through all your data to find the marriage date that Cousin Grace needs and even print everything in the computer's "memory" about Silas Brown.

Of course, the equipment required to do these tasks does not come in one simple package; nor do you need the most sophisticated equipment available. Early 1988 estimates suggested that genealogists buying computer systems were spending about $3500 on hardware,[1] which included much more than the basic computer and printer; but unless you use the system for something other than genealogy, the cost makes genealogy an unnecessarily expensive hobby.

What equipment, then, will do what for you?

The basic computer "hardware" consists primarily of (1) a keyboard with a typewriter layout of letters and numbers and additional keys that perform or allow particular functions, (2) a screen that allows you to see what you are working on, and (3) a "memory" which accepts files and programs.

Part of the memory is permanent programs that are built into the computer. The rest of the memory, with its storage capabilities, holds programs and data that you enter, generally on *hard disk drives* or *floppy disk drives,* and preferably on a two-disk system. Hard disk drives have been greatly improved in recent years to speed your work and enlarge the computer's storage capacity. One expert makes this recommendation: "Buying a less expensive computer and

---

[1] Paul Andereck, "Desktop Publishing Is Next Step," *Genealogical Computing,* Vol 7, No 3 (Jan–Mar 1988), 26.

spending your money on hard disk storage is preferable to buying a more expensive computer."[2]

In order to print what you have stored on the computer's memory, you need a printer. Printers employ a handful of different methods, which vary in speed, quality, price, and adaptability. The *dot matrix* printers are relatively fast but give you reports and charts that have the "computer-print" look. A *letter-quality* printer is comparatively slow but, as its name implies, gives you sharp images in a type-style such as "Letter Gothic" or "Prestige" from a *print-wheel* or *daisy-wheel,* much like that on electronic typewriters. *Laser printers* represent newer technology, are very fast and still rather expensive, and probably are instruments of the future for most computer hobbyists.

In order to use the computer, you need *software:* system software that controls and coordinates the operation of the hardware, and programs which let you play games, file genealogical data, create letters, and keep track of personal finances.

A *data base* is a compilation of information, such as your address book, with names, addresses, Zip Codes, phone numbers, perhaps birthdays and children's names. The data can be sorted in a number of helpful ways: chronologically by birthdays, alphabetically by surnames, in Zip Code order, etc. A general *data base management program* can allow you to file your research notes, but some programs of this kind limit what you can file, the quantity you can enter, and how you print out your data. If you have been a genealogist for some time, it will be very time-consuming to enter all your information, and your notes may be too numerous and complex to warrant the expense of a program capable of managing such a large data base. Still, it is worth investigating such a program.

Writing letters, family history chapters, outlines, biographies, or research reports is easier and quicker than ever before with a good *word processing program.* Once texts or notes are typed in, they can be edited, corrected, rearranged, indexed, and stored or printed. When entering long place names or personal names in your text, you may be able to use an abbreviation or initials instead of typing out a long name

many times. For example, "Ferdinand Glen Coleman, son of Elliott G. Coleman" could be entered originally as *FGC* or any other designation. When you finish writing the text, you use the *global search and replace* function in the word processing program to change all occurrences of *FGC* to the man's full name and identification.

When you prepare to print such texts, you have a number of options, depending on the program, for centering, **boldface** or *italics,* underlining, indenting, right margin justification, indexing, page headings, automatic page numbering, footnoting, column sizes, and spacing. You can even create your own blank form and merge it with data; or you can write a letter to your first cousins and merge the text with their names to "personalize" each letter. There are some advanced programs which combine data base and text organization to allow you the capabilities of both.

The authors of *Computer Genealogy* developed a checklist for choosing an adequate word processing program:[3] be sure it is compatible with your computer's make and model, disk operating system (DOS), memory size, number of disk drives, screen size and display speed, and printer features; look for capabilities you want, such as global search and replace; merge; automatic page heading and/or numbering; user control of margins, page lengths, spacing; automatic centering, italics, or right-margin justification; easy-to-use editing, insertion, deletion, and moving procedures and cursor movement. An advanced type of word processing software is a *desktop publishing program* which allows you to control and customize the format of charts and reports and to integrate text with charts and graphics.[4]

Special genealogy programs are data base programs designed to link family members together, to alphabetize, to register vital statistics for family members, and to print out pedigree and family group charts. No program can do everything that is desirable; you perhaps will want or need separate word-processing, data base, or graphics software. Not all programs are written to operate on all computers. In choosing genealogy software, like word processing programs, be sure the program you buy is compatible with your computer system (make and model,

[2]Paul A. Andereck and Richard A. Pence, *Computer Genealogy: A Guide to Research Through High Technology* (Salt Lake City: Ancestry, Inc., 1985), 48.

[3]*Ibid.,* 79–83.

[4]Andereck, "Desktop Publishing Is Next Step," *Genealogical Computing,* Jan–Mar 1988, 2, 26.

memory, disk drives, and DOS) and your word processing program requirements. Find out if the genealogy software has the capabilities and features you want: room for many, many names, even thousands or tens of thousands; clear and understandable instructions; support, help, and updates from the vendor; chart and report formats that please you; word processing functions, especially editing and/or integration with your word processing program; broad search capabilities; sorting by date, place, name, or event; charting of ancestors or descendants or any given person on file.[5]

Dozens of genealogy software programs are available commercially. The one that has been considered top-of-the-line for several years by a number of genealogists is ROOTS II, by Commsoft, 2257 Old Middlefield Way, Mountain View, CA 94043, telephone 415-967-1900 or 1-800-32-ROOTS, and in California, 1-800-53-ROOTS. ROOTS II is used on an IBM-compatible personal computer, has many desirable features with certain extras, including automatic book indexing, a picture and map storage capability, automatic double-dating for appropriate dates under the Old Style calendar, and book printing capabilities.

Another very fine program is *Family Roots,* by Quinsept, Inc., PO Box 216, Lexington, MA 02173, telephone 617-641-2930. The program is available for certain Apple II, Macintosh, TRS80 (Tandy Radio Shack), IBM PC, Commodore 64, and other computers. *Family Roots* also has many useful features, including a number of word processing functions, extensive search and indexing capabilities, and book printing.

Less expensive, and often less adequate, genealogy software falls into a category called *shareware* or *user supported* software. The author makes it available free, and satisfied users are asked to send him a registration fee, usually in the neighborhood of $35-$60.

Once you have chosen a computer and/or genealogy software, you will probably find valuable help and support from a *user group.* Most groups are formed by and for users of specific hardware or software. Within the user groups for owners of particular hardware systems, there will be *SIGs,* or Special Interest Groups, including genealogists. Although there may be annual dues or fees for membership, user groups offer many benefits, including rosters of

users, newsletters and program updates, classes, software libraries, manufacturer discounts on equipment, support, and lots of answers as you learn and use your computer. Some of these groups are affiliated with local, county, and state genealogical societies, including those in San Diego, Santa Barbara, Seattle; Champaign County, Illinois; Orange County, California; Collin County, Texas; Southern California, Colorado, Minnesota; and South King County, Kent, Washington.[6] The National Genealogical Society (NGS) has a large computer interest group (CIG), which can be contacted at the NGC Office, 4527 17th Street N, Arlington, VA 22207, telephone 703-525-0050. Other user groups relate to a particular genealogy software:

1. ROOTS User Group (RUG), (ROOTS/M, ROOTS/89, ROOTS II), c/o 7304 Mariposa, Manassas, VA 22111.

2. Quinsept User Group, (*Lineages* and *Family Roots*), c/o 102 Broadfield Lane, Spotsylvania, VA 22553.

3. Dollarhide Users Group (DUG), (*Family Research Manager*), c/o PO Box 1790, Ames, IA 50010 and c/o PO Box 970, Leadville, CO 80461.

4. PAF Users Group, (Personal Ancestral File of the Genealogical Society of Utah and the Mormon Church), c/o 7371 Rue Michael, La Jolla, CA 92037.

5. Apple Corps of Dallas, Genealogy SIG, c/o PO Box 821103, Dallas, TX 75231.

6. *Family Roots* User Group (FRUG), (from Quinsept), c/o 2504 Banner Elk Circle, Plano, TX 75023.

Telecommunications

The genealogist who is advanced in computer skills and who wants to exchange information with another person's computer by telephone will need special equipment: (1) communications software or "terminal program" such as *ProComm* or *Q-Modem,* and (2) a modem. In sending files from one computer to another, there are ways to prevent errors, additions, and deletions due to telephone line interference. To accomplish accurate transfer of data, both computers must use the same transfer process, or *protocol.* Good communications software will include several *file transfer protocols,* such as XMODEM (and

---

[5] Andereck and Pence, *Computer Genealogy,* 91-98.

[6] "Interest Group Directory," *Genealogical Computing,* Jan-Mar 1988, 21-25

its variations YMODEM, MODEM7, WXMODEM, and TELELINK), KERMIT, COMPUSERVE B, and ASCII (American Standard Code for Information Exchange), although the latter is vulnerable to telephone line interference.[7] The Genealogical Society of Utah, operated by the Mormon Church, is developing a standard format for importing and exporting data from one computer to another. Called GEDCOM, GEnealogical Data COMmunications, it generates a standard version of the data filed by many different genealogy software programs so that the data can be transferred to computers using different programs.

A *modem* is the hardware device or accessory which allows inter-computer communication. If its cables and connectors are compatible with the computer's *modem port* or outlet, it plugs directly into the computer. If the two units are not compatible, they may be connected with an intermediary device called an *interface.* The accepted standard in modem connections is designated *RS-232,* and modems with this standard RS-232 port are compatible with most computers except Commodores.[8]

The speed at which the modem sends data over the telephone lines is designated by the term *baud rate.* A 1200-baud modem transmits data 4 times as fast as a 300-baud modem. The 1200-baud unit is more expensive to purchase than the slower one but it can save you money on long-distance charges because it is faster. Of course, if your call is local, you are not charged long-distance rates.

At present, 1200-baud and 300-baud operations are in use among the relatively few genealogists who have modems; but purchasing a modem that can handle 2400 baud will allow you to use the slower rates and, at the same time, be prepared for the faster capabilities that are becoming more widespread.[9]

Telecommunications is a field still in its infancy. Currently, most computer-to-computer linkages take place between individuals or between individuals and bulletin boards. The transfer of information or messages can go either direction. Receiving a program, file, or message from another computer is called *downloading;* sending the program, file, or message is called *uploading.* When you contact a local or national bulletin board via your modem and computer, you can download software programs that are "public domain" (not copyright-protected) and therefore available free. You can also arrange the exchange of genealogical data with other genealogists, leave and receive queries or messages, and meet with other genealogists for "live" conferences. Some bulletin boards have a registration or membership fee; some also have hourly charges based on the length of time you use the system.

If you plan to spend a great deal of time on long-distance telecomputing, you may want to contact your long-distance telephone company to learn of their flat-rates to which you can subscribe and save on long-distance charges. One service called *PC Pursuit* is available through U.S. Sprint's Telenet; another is AT&T's *Reach Out America* plan.[10]

One of the genealogy bulletin boards available is Genealogy Roundtable within GEnie (*General Electric Network for Information Exchange*). GEnie has an annual registration fee and is available via a local phone call in more than 550 cities. For specific information about joining, call 1-800-638-9636.

The National Genealogical Conference (NGC) is coordinated by Howard Nurse of Commsoft; for information, call 1-800-32-ROOTS (in California: 1-800-53-ROOTS). The NGC is a network of bulletin boards available for genealogists across the country. Each bulletin board has an area and time available for use by the NGC network. Local genealogists can leave messages and queries, and the network sends them to all other systems in the NGC.

The VINE Genealogical Bulletin Board System is provided at no charge to owners of the Genealogical Data Base Systems (GDBS) program by Data Base Systems (DBS), PO Box 7263, Huntsville, AL 35807. DBS's business phone number is 205-881-6957.

Two other large subscriber information services are The Source and CompuServe. Contact a local computer interest group for availability and registration information.

The technology of the future for computer genealogists is the searching of online data bases using

[7] Paul Andereck, "Exploring File Transfer Protocols," *Genealogical Computing,* Jan–Mar, 1988, 4; Todd Heimarck, "How to Buy a Modem for Your Commodore," *Compute!'s Gazette,* Vol 6, No 1 (January 1988), 20.
[8] Todd Heimarck, "How to Buy a Modem for Your Commodore," *Compute!'s Gazette,* Vol 6, No 1 (January 1988), 20.
[9] John and Carolyn Cosgriff, *Turbo Genealogy* (Christiansburg, VA: Progenesys Press, 1987), 34.
[10] Tom Netsel, "Going Online," *Compute!'s Gazette,* Vol 6, No 1 (January 1988), 32.

computers and modems. One data base which now includes some historical materials is called *Knowledge Index*, available through a commercial company, Dialog, at 1-800-3-DIALOG. The *Index* includes Marquis' *Who's Who*, local history from the United States, Canada, and other areas, and abstracts of doctoral dissertations in many fields from many universities in the United States and Canada.

No online genealogical data bases are yet available. The Center of Immigration Research at Temple University, Philadelphia, Pennsylvania, is developing a computerized project from the 1820–1924 passenger lists held by the National Archives. Let us hope that this type of project will be available for online searching in the coming years.

Bibliography

Andereck, Paul A. and Richard A. Pence. *Computer Genealogy: A Guide to Research through High Technology*. Salt Lake City: Ancestry Incorporated, 1985.

Cosgriff, John C., Jr., and Carolyn H. Cosgriff. *Turbo Genealogy*. Christiansburg, VA: Progenesys Press, 1987.

Posey, Joanna W. *Tracing Your Roots by Computer*. Orem, UT: Posey International, 1986.

Genealogical Computing. Salt Lake City: Ancestry Incorporated. (A quarterly journal.)

The Genealogical Computer Pioneer. Orem, UT: Posey International. (Bimonthly)

Sharing Your Family History

Once you have gathered as much information as you want or as much as is available, you will probably want to share the results with the family at large. Notebooks and clippings may fascinate those who gathered them, but they do not entertain those who have not shared in the search. What then?

Writing a Family History

One approach is to write in narrative form all the information on one family, from its earliest proven ancestor to the present generations. Each chapter is a biography of an ancestor, from birth to death, including his marriage and family. Each chapter also includes the general history of the area and period in which he lived. This material you can find in county, state, and regional histories. Social histories and reprints of contemporary books and articles can tell you about the customs, clothing, and everyday life of the period in which the ancestor lived.

You can set the stage for your ancestor's arrival by describing the family that he was born into: the number and ages of older children, the ages of his parents and other adults in the household, the house the family lived in, and what you have learned about their living conditions or community, etc.

So often we tend to think of all people of the past living in one large generation at the same time, or we tend to consider those who became famous as always being famous. We forget that they began life more or less as the rest of us did. It is fun to find some of those famous individuals who were contemporaries of your ancestor, some who were adults when he was born and some who were children. Mentioning them adds some perspective and interest to your stage-setting. Information of this kind can be found in such books as the *Dictionary of American Biography* (Dumas Malone, et al. [eds], 13 vol, New York: Charles Scribner's Sons, 1928–1974) and the *Encyclopedia of American History* (Richard B. Morris [ed.], New York: Harper and Row, 1965). These books and other standard reference books can give

you information about events which took place in the community or nation at the time when your ancestor was born. Perhaps he was born during the Civil War in Vicksburg, Mississippi. Do a little extra research to find out whether he was born during the seige of Vicksburg. If he was, he and his family probably had a rough time. A number of primary sources exist which tell the experiences of many of the city residents at that time. You may not find your family mentioned in these sources; but you can relate in your account what their fellow citizens experienced and suggest that your family may have had similar experiences. Word your account carefully so that you don't claim as fact something that is only an educated guess.

Here is one way of introducing an ancestor's biography; it was an effort to add some perspective on the year of his birth and on the family at the time of his birth. The facts were used to suggest what could have happened in the family as the new baby arrived on the scene.

In 1829, Andrew Jackson was serving his first year as President of the 24 United States. Sam Houston was governor of Tennessee, and U.S. Grant was an Ohio 7-year-old. Robert E. Lee graduated from West Point that year, and 20-year-old Abe Lincoln lived on his family's farm in Indiana. That year Stephen Foster was a Pennsylvania 3-year-old, and Charles Goodyear was going bankrupt in his hardware business in Connecticut. Daniel Boone, Thomas Jefferson, and John Adams were now names of the past; James Madison and James Monroe were retired elder statesmen; and Samuel Clemens, Andrew Carnegie, and Joel Chandler Harris were still names of the future.

November 22 of 1829 was a Sunday, and possibly a cold one, in Caldwell County, Kentucky. If Hiram and Celestine Brelsford were regular churchgoers, they probably did not go that day; for during the day Celestine gave birth to their fourth child and third son, whom they named Samuel Black Brelsford, after Celestine's father. Grandparents Samuel and Keturah Black probably admired their new grandson that day

SAMPLE FAMILY GROUP SHEET

Family of Elliott G. Coleman I

Elliott G. Coleman - born by 1764, Cumberland Co., Virginia, married 23 November
    1789, died 1822, Cumberland Co., Va.

Elizabeth W. Daniel - born c. 1773, died c. 1853, daughter of William and Patty
    Field (Allen) Daniel. Born and died in Cumberland Co., Va.

Children:

1. Newton H. Coleman
    probably eldest son since he was first executor of his father's estate.
    Died September, 1829, unmarried.

2. Ferdinand Glen Coleman
    born c. 1794, Cumberland Co., married c. 3 January 1822, Elizabeth A.
    Phillips, daughter of Peter Talbot and Elizabeth A. (Allen) Phillips. 14
    children.

3. Mary D. Coleman
    married John A. Allen, 14 January 1817; died by 1825. Children: Cary Allen;
    Archer Allen, who married Caroline _____, and had son Cary. Archer died in
    July, 1852.

4. Elliot R. Coleman
    died between 1841 and 1850, apparently. No evidence of marriage found.

5. Archer Allen Coleman
    died October, 1829, unmarried. Under 21 in 1818.

6. Creed D. Coleman
    born c. 1800-1810, under 21 in 1818; elected delegate to Virginia House of
    Delegates, 1859-1860; living in 1860.

7. John Henry Coleman
    born c. 1810, living in 1860.

8. William Pride Coleman
    under 21 in 1818, died November, 1829, unmarried.

9. Martha Coleman

10. Susan E. Coleman
    married February, 1848, William P. Miller, moved to Hollysprings,
    Mississippi. Son Daniel Miller, born 1849.

Information gathered from Cumberland County wills, census records, family
records and letters, marriage records, deeds.

along with his big sister, Mary Jane, who would be 4 the next Friday, and brothers Marjoram (2½) and William (1½).

Grandmother Keturah must have worked in double time that week. She still had five children at home. The youngest, John Thomas, was just a toddler. Dorcas was 18 now, and may have had to baby-sit with John and Mary Jane, Marjoram, and William. Keturah may have sent her to Celestine's house to help out for a while. It was customary for grand-mother to go or for the new mother and baby to be at grandmother's house; but Keturah had only four days left to finish preparations for Mary Katherine's wedding, next Thursday.

At the close of each biographical chapter, it is helpful to include a family group outline or family group sheet listing the subject, his children, and per-haps grandchildren, similar to the one in Figure 16. Other sheets can be added to update each branch of the family.

Some genealogists compile an extensive outline which lists each descendant of the common ancestor with an individual identification number. This sys-tem has merit, but if family history is to mean any-thing, it must be more than just lists of names and dates. A narrative is perhaps the best way to share the stories and letters, or to set the family into the society in which they lived.

Many family histories are written using letters or diaries as a foundation. They are tied together with editorial comments and explanations by the research-er. In this case, the searcher has preserved the flavor of the original but has interpreted it for the present and future generations.

Perhaps you do not consider yourself "a writer," but still you want to share the history you have found. Compile copies of the actual documents that have taught you about your ancestors and add a little ex-planation here and there as well as copies of your charts.

When your presentation is in its final form, you may want to consider these options:

    a. If the local or state library or historical society or university library in your research area has a file of area family genealogies, send them a copy of yours, especially if you used their ma-terials in your search.

    b. The Genealogical Society Library in Salt Lake City collects family histories from everywhere. Send them a copy of yours.

    c. Present your gift in honor of or in memory of special relatives. I prefer to give something "in honor of" the person while he or she is living as a way of saying "Thank you" or "You are special to me."

Outline for a Family History Project

Even while you are working on the more complete family history, you can collect, preserve, and organize valuable and interesting family data. This project is an exciting way to share the more recent family history of three to five generations. It makes great Christmas, birthday, or anniversary gifts for other family mem-bers and may stimulate interest in your larger gene-alogy effort. Grandparents can prepare it for children and grandchildren; aunts can give it to nieces and nephews; brothers or sisters can share it with parents and siblings.

The items suggested in the outline are ideas; the collection certainly can contain whatever you want to include. Once the pages are arranged, you can photo-copy them and bind each set into booklets or folders for family members. You can also use plastic sheet protectors for inserting any original documents, photos, or double-sided keepsakes you include.

Contents are listed in a random order; arrange yours however you wish.

1. **Title Page.** List title, your name as compiler, date, perhaps your address, any dedication statement.

2. **Table of Contents.** Items can be grouped by topic, generation, surname, decades, any way you think best. You may want to leave blank sheets at the end for notes and additions.

3. **Foreword.** Write a note or letter to your family, preferably in your own handwriting, or at least signed, explaining what the collection is and why you want to share it, or what you hope it will mean to the family in years to come...whatever you want to say.

4. One or more **five-generation charts**, filled with whatever information you have, from personal ex-perience, documents in your possession, research that represents facts that can be proved. You can begin the chart with your children or grandchildren or with yourself.

5. **Family Group Sheets,** which list parents and children of each generation: (1) you, your spouse, and your children, (2) your parents and their chil-dren, (3) your spouse's parents and their children, (4) your child, his/her spouse, their children (one

sheet for each of your children), (5) your grand-parents and their children (one sheet for each set of grandparents), (6) your spouse's grandparents and their children (again, two sets of grandparents), (7) great-grandparents and their children if you have that information, (8) your brothers and sisters with their spouses and children (one sheet for each couple).

6. **Names and addresses** of living relatives who may be on the family group charts, especially any who have worked on family history or have information on the family's past.

7. **Biographical sketches** or outlines, one person to a page. See Form #3, Appendix F. You should include yourself, your spouse, one or both parents, your spouse's parents, etc. It might be helpful to include the residence of the subject in the census years: 1920, 1910, 1900, 1880, etc.

8. **Interesting Tidbits** which you have available. The idea here is not to make a complete, comprehensive history, but that certainly can be your ultimate goal. This is a collection of "spice" that adds interest and personality to all the names and dates on the charts. These items might be arranged topically and may not take more than a few lines each.

a. *Church history:* who belonged to what denominations or congregations.

b. *Occupational history:* any working women in the family history, occupations of the men. Who were the farmers? teachers? ministers? any doctors? salesmen? elected officials? craftsmen? etc.

c. *Medical history:* causes of death, diseases or physical problems which have repeated themselves, longevity, occurrence of twins or triplets (One family identified 14 sets of twins!), physical characteristics which "run in the family," predominant hair color or other physical features.

d. *Educational history:* who went where, especially college attendance and degrees.

e. *Military history:* who fought where in which war, peacetime service, any family members who are members of DAR, SAR, UDC, etc.

f. *Talents or outstanding characteristics* of family members: musical ability, authors, artists, terrific cooks, seamstresses; sense of humor, gentleness, meanness; beauties, those who excel in sports, etc.

g. *How we got our names:* who was named for whom, nicknames and real names, anything unusual about the surnames represented.

h. *Special traditions and customs:* Christmas traditions, birthday celebration traditions, vacations the family have taken; oral traditions about family history—where we came from, why they immigrated to this country, why they settled where they did (relatives there, job there, stationed there, etc.).

i. *Hobbies* and pastimes of family members, especially of previous generations; pets.

j. *Favorites,* especially of previous generations: favorite foods, sports, books, movies, authors, teams, music, performers, places to visit, cars, pets, color, hymn, scripture, friend, etc. Interesting habits of family members, especially previous generations. Sayings or expressions that family members use(d).

9. **Keepsakes and collectibles** (originals or copies):

a. *Documents:* birth certificates, marriage licenses, diplomas, degrees, awards, report cards, transcripts, driver's licenses, poll tax receipts, voter registration cards, ration books, newspaper clippings, funeral cards and anouncements, etc.

b. *Photographs,* labeled with name(s), approximate date, place.

c. *Letters* and cards from those who have gone before as well as from present family members, especially those in their own handwriting. A note from each living family member. One in my own family very characteristically wrote: "I've always wondered why I'm not rich since I'm so smart."

d. *Recipes* (favorites), especially in the cook's own handwriting.

e. *Handwriting samples,* especially signatures, from letters and cards, from wills and other documents. These can be arranged in the form of a five-generation chart or as shown in Figure 17, page 110.

f. Photos of *houses* in which family generations have lived. Sketches of the floor plans of family homes of the past, especially those which are no longer standing.

g. Samples of *creativity* from family members: poetry, music, drawing, short story, parody, photos of items which cannot be included (furniture, paintings, sculpture, doll houses, etc.).

10. **Memories,** a paragraph or one-page recollection or story handed down. Topics could include a *memorable* Christmas, vacation, wedding, storm, fire, job, friendship, pet, relative, experience, anything *unusual* or *comical* that happened, stories of the Depression or war or college years; *childhood* memories. *Bits of information* which could help someone in researching family history later: your

great-grandmother lived in Oklahoma City when she died; your great-grandmother was married 5 times and outlived all her husbands; towns the family lived in; great-grandfather was one of 15 children. *Interviews* such as the one in Figure 6, page 36. Separate *biographical cassette tape* to give along with the booklet. Memories of *firsts:* first car, first movie, first television, first date, first apartment, first home, first day of school, first telephone, first baby, first solo, first job, etc.

11. **Map** of state or United States (Form #7). See Figure 10, page 49, showing residences of family in certain years, or movement of one family over the years.

Tape interviews with grandparents and great-grandparents about their childhood, their own parents and grandparents, family stories, and their memories, using the questions suggested in chapters 7, 8, and 9. Such tapes preserve the history as well as special memories of the subject for those who will hear the tapes in the future. One year when I was teaching American history, I invited an 80-year-old family friend to be our guest in class and talk with us about his growing-up in the 1890s. I taped the session and have a delightful memento of the visit. After his death several years later, I sent a copy of the tape to his son. He was thrilled and was making copies for everyone in the family because everybody wanted one! They now have not only his voice but many family stories and a few vital statistics as well.

Another way of sharing family mementos and history is to have a "show-and-tell" reunion, to which everybody brings their old family pictures, family Bible, or other objects for display. Such an occasion is a good opportunity to identify unlabeled pictures,

to share and tape-record stories about common ancestors or the "good old days," to take group pictures, to make video tapes, to collect autographs or recipes, to serve food made from old family recipes, to furnish updated vital statistics on each part of the family, and to renew old acquaintances.

Family history makes special gifts:

a. Give a book to the local history or genealogy library in the name of a friend or relative.

b. Give friends or relatives some of their own family history that you or someone else has gathered: a book by or about an ancestor, tapes of interviews with or about an ancestor, photographs, antiques, or collectibles that have been in the family.

c. Give a book on the history or genealogy of the county where their ancestor lived, or the family church, university, hometown, etc.

d. Give a subscription to a family association newsletter or membership in such an organization.

e. Give a subscription to a genealogical periodical, especially one from their favorite research locale.

f. Especially for a genealogist, consider giving a genealogy resource book, such as a guide to research in a particular state, or the holdings of a particular collection that could be helpful in their search.

g. For a beginning family history searcher, a copy of *Unpuzzling Your Past*.

Regardless of how your material is shared, it can have meaning for the family only when it is shared. Whether done formally or informally, published or mimeographed, or only typed, it holds insight and fascination for the whole family for years to come.

CHILDREN

Thomas Blalock King

Sarah Elizabeth King

PARENTS

Alfred Thomas King III

Judith Louise Croom King

GRANDPARENTS

Audrey Lee King

Alfred Thomas King

Pitser Blalock Croom

Fletcher Metcalfe Croom

GREAT-GRANDPARENTS

Jewell. B. Thornton

Arthur Thornton

Albert Sidney J. Croom

Hunter Metcalfe

Fletcher Elizabeth Metcalfe Warren

GREAT-GREAT-GRANDPARENTS

Mrs. Mattie E. Metcalfe

great-grandmother Maggie.

Mrs. M. McKennon

Catharine M. Coleman

P.G. Coleman

Appendix

This section includes basic references and blank forms to help you begin your own family record. There is even a map of the United States which you can use to trace your family's movements within the country.

Any of these forms may be reproduced easily and inexpensively at your local photocopy center. Many banks and libraries also have a photocopy machine for use by their customers.

Contents of Appendix

GLOSSARY

Abstract—summary of important points of a given text, especially deeds and wills.

Administrator (of an estate)—person appointed to manage or divide the estate of a deceased person.

Administratrix—a female administrator.

Alien—foreigner.

American Revolution—U.S. war for independence from Great Britain, 1775–83.

Ancestor—person from whom you are descended; a forefather.

Ante—Latin prefix meaning *before*, as in *antebellum* South, "the South before the war."

Archives—records of a government, organization, institution; the place where such records are stored.

Attest—to affirm; to certify by signature or oath.

Banns—public announcement of an intended marriage.

Bequeath—to give property to a person in a will. Noun: *bequest.*

Bond—written, signed, witnessed agreement requiring payment of a specified amount of money on or before a given date.

Bounty Land Warrant—a right to obtain land, specific number of acres of unallocated public land, granted for military service.

Census—official enumeration, listing, or counting of citizens.

Civil War—War between the States; war between North & South, 1861–65.

Codicil—addition to a will.

Common ancestor—one shared by any two people.

Confederate—pertaining to the Southern states which seceded from the U.S. in 1860–61, their government and their citizens.

Consort—usually, a wife whose husband is living.

Cousin—relative descended from a common ancestor, but not a brother or sister.

Daughter-in-law—wife of one's son.

Deceased—dead.

Declaration of Intention—first paper, sworn to and filed in court, by an alien stating that he wants to become a citizen.

Deed—transfer of ownership of property.

Devisee—one to whom property is given in a will.

Devisor—one who gives property in a will.

Dissenter—one who did not belong to the established church, especially the Church of England in the American colonies.

Dower—legal right or share which a wife acquired by marriage in the real estate of her husband, allotted to her after his death for her lifetime.

Emigrant—one leaving a country and moving to another.

Enumeration—listing or counting, such as a census.

Estate—all property and debts belonging to a person.

Executor—one appointed in a will to carry out its provisions.

Father-in-law—father of one's spouse.

Fraternity—group of men (or women) sharing a common purpose or interest.

Friend—member of the Religious Society of Friends; a Quaker.

Genealogy—study of family history and descent.

Given name—name given to a person at birth or baptism, one's first and middle names.

Grantee—one who buys property or receives a grant.

Grantor—one who sells property or makes a grant.

Great-aunt—sister of one's grandparent.

Great-uncle—brother of one's grandparent.

Guardian—person appointed to care for and manage property of a minor orphan or an adult incompetent of managing his own affairs.

Half-brother (Half-sister)—child by another marriage of one's mother or father; the relationship of two people who have only one parent in common.

Heirs—those entitled by law or by the terms of a will to inherit property from another.

Homestead Act—law passed by Congress in 1862 allowing a head of a family to obtain title to 160 acres of public land after clearing and improving it and living on it for 5 years.

Illegitimate—born to a mother who was not married to the child's father.

Immigrant—one moving into a country from another.

Indentured servant—one who bound himself into service of another person for a specified number of years, often in return for transportation to this country.

Instant—(calendar) of the current month; of this month.

Intestate—one who dies without a will. Used as an adjective—*dying without a will.*

Issue—offspring; children.

Late—recently deceased; now deceased.

Legacy—property or money left to someone in a will.

Legislature—lawmaking branch of state or national government; elected group of lawmakers.

Lineage—ancestry; direct descent from a specific ancestor. Adjective form: *lineal.*

Lodge—chapter or meeting hall of a fraternal organization.

Loyalist—Tory, an American colonist who supported the British side during the American Revolution.

Maiden name—a girl's last name, or surname, before she marries.

Maternal—related through one's mother. Maternal grandmother is the mother's mother.

Microfilm—reproduction of documents on film at reduced size.

Microfiche—sheet of microfilm with greatly reduced images of pages of documents.

Migrant—person who moves from place to place, usually in search of work.

Migrate—to move from one country or state or region to another. Noun: *migration.*

Militia—citizens of a state who are not part of the national military forces but who can be called into military service in an emergency; a citizen army, apart from the regular military forces.

Minor—one who is under legal age; not yet a legal adult.

Mortality—death; death rate.

Mortality schedules—enumeration of persons who died during the year prior to June 1 of 1850, 1860, 1870, and 1880 in each state of the United States, conducted by the Bureau of the Census (e.g., deaths occuring between June 1, 1849, and June 1, 1850, were reported on the 1850 Mortality Schedules).

Mother-in-law—mother of one's spouse.

Namesake—person named after another person.

Necrology—listing or record of persons who have died recently.

Nee—used to identify a woman's maiden name: *Mrs. Susan Jones, nee Smith.*

Nephew—son of one's brother or sister.

Niece—daughter of one's brother or sister.

Orphan—child whose parents are dead; sometimes, a child who has lost one parent by death.

Patent—grant of land from a government to an individual.

Paternal—related through one's father. Paternal grandmother is the father's mother.

Patriot—one who loves his country and supports its interests.

Pedigree—family tree; ancestry.

Pension—money paid regularly to an individual, especially by a government as reward for military service during wartime or upon retirement from government service.

Pensioner—one who receives a pension.

Poll—list or record of persons, especially for taxing or voting.

Post—Latin prefix meaning *after,* as in *post-war economy.*

Posterity—descendants; those who come after.

Pre—Latin prefix meaning *before*, as in *pre-war military build-up.*

Probate—having to do with wills and the administration of estates.

Progenitor—a direct ancestor.

Proximo—in the following month, in the month after the present one.

Public Domain—land owned by the government.

Quaker—member of the Religious Society of Friends.

Relict—widow.

Republic—government in which supreme authority lies with the people or their elected representatives.

Revolutionary War—U.S. war for independence from Great Britain, 1775–83.

Shaker—member of a religious group formed in 1747 which practiced communal living and celibacy.

Sibling—person having one or both parents in common with another; a brother or sister.

Sic—Latin meaning *thus*; copied exactly as the original reads. Often suggests a mistake or surprise in the original.

Son-in-law—husband of one's daughter.

Spouse—husband or wife.

Statute—law.

Step-brother (Step-sister)—child of one's step-father or step-mother.

Step-child—child of one's husband or wife from a previous marriage.

Step-father—husband of one's mother by a later marriage.

Step-mother—wife of one's father by a later marriage.

Surname—family name or last name.

Territory—area of land owned by the United States, not a state, but having its own legislature and governor.

Testator—person who makes a valid will before his death.

Tithable—taxable.

Tithe—formerly, money due as a tax for support of the clergy or church.

Tory—Loyalist; one who supported the British side in the American Revolution.

Township—division of U.S. public land that contained 36 sections, or 36 square miles. Also a subdivision of the county in many Northeastern and Midwestern states of the U.S.

Ultimo—in the month before this one.

Union—the United States; also the "North" during the Civil War, the states which did not secede.

Vital records—records of birth, death, marriage, divorce.

Vital statistics—data dealing with birth, death, marriage, divorce.

War Between the States—U.S. Civil War, 1861–65.

Will—document declaring how a person wants his property divided after his death.

Witness—one who is present at a transaction, such as a sale of land or signing of a will, who can testify or affirm that it actually took place.

ABBREVIATIONS
(commonly used in genealogy or in documents)

b—born.

B—black; Negro.

c, ca—about, approximately; from Latin *circa*.

co—county, or company.

col—"colored;" black; Negro.

CSA—Confederate States of America, the association of Southern states which seceded from the U.S. in 1860–61.

d—died.

dau—daughter.

dea—deacon.

decd—deceased.

et al—Latin *et alii*, meaning "and others."

etc—Latin *et cetera*, meaning "and other things."

F—female.

fmc—free man of color.

fwc—free woman of color.

govt—government.

ibid—Latin *ibidem*, meaning "in the same place." Used in footnotes to mean the same work as just cited.

IOOF—Independent Order of Odd Fellows, fraternal organization.

IS—Interim Supply, meaning that a minister is appointed as full-time minister to the congregation but on an interim or temporary basis.

JP—Justice of the Peace.

LDS—The Church of Jesus Christ of Latter-Day Saints, the Mormons.

LE—Local Elder.

LS—Latin *locus sigilli;* on documents, the place where man's seal is placed.

m—married.

M—male.

m1—married first.

m2—married second.

MG—Minister of the Gospel.

Mu—Mulatto, person with one Caucasian parent and one Negro parent.

nd—no date given.

n m—never married.

np—no page or publisher given.

NS—New Style, referring to the Gregorian calendar.

OM—Ordained Minister.

OS—Old Style, referring to the Julian calendar.

OS—Occasional Supply, referring to a minister appointed to serve when needed, not on a regular basis.

pp—pages.

SS—Stated Supply, referring to a minister appointed as regular minister of a congregation.

unm—unmarried.

VDM—Latin *Verbi Domini Ministerium*, minister of the Word of God.

W—white; Caucasian.

(w) or wit—witness.

RELATIONSHIP CHART

Instructions for using the chart on page 115 to identify the relationship between any two people.

1. Identify the common ancestor of the two people. Locate the box in the upper left corner for the common ancestor.
2. Across the top row of the chart, find the relationship of one of the two people to their common ancestor.
3. Down the left edge of the chart, find the relationship of the second person to their common ancestor.
4. Read down the column of the first person and across the chart on the row of the second person. Where the two rows intersect is the box which identifies their relationship.

Example:

1. The common ancestor is Elliott Coleman.
2. Judith is the great-great-granddaughter of Elliott, four generations away from him. Read down column #4.
3. Word is the grandson of Elliott, two generations away from him. Read across row #2.
4. Column #4 and row #2 intersect at the box which reads "1 cou 2 R," or first cousin two generations removed. Judith and Word are first cousins twice removed.

RELATIONSHIP CHART

	1	2	3	4	5	6	7	8	9
	COMMON ANCESTOR	SON / DAU.	GRAND-SON	GREAT GRAND-SON	G-G GRAND-SON	G-G-G GRAND-SON	4G GRAND-SON	5G GRAND-SON	6G GRAND-SON	7G GRAND-SON
1	SON / DAU.	BRO / SIS.	NEPHEW / NIECE	GRAND NEPHEW	GREAT GRAND-NEPHEW	G-G GRAND-NEPHEW	G-G-G GRAND-NEPHEW	4G GRAND-NEPHEW	5G GRAND-NEPHEW	6G GRAND-NEPHEW
2	GRAND-SON	NEPHEW / NIECE	1ST COUSIN	1 COU 1 R	1 COU 2 R	1 COU 3 R	1 COU 4 R	1 COU 5 R	1 COU 6 R	1 COU 7 R
3	GREAT GRAND-SON	GRAND NEPHEW	1 COU 1 R	2ND COUSIN	2 COU 1 R	2 COU 2 R	2 COU 3 R	2 COU 4 R	2 COU 5 R	2 COU 6 R
4	G-G GRAND-SON	GREAT GRAND-NEPHEW	1 COU 2 R	2 COU 1 R	3RD COUSIN	3 COU 1 R	3 COU 2 R	3 COU 3 R	3 COU 4 R	3 COU 5 R
5	G-G-G GRAND-SON	G-G GRAND-NEPHEW	1 COU 3 R	2 COU 2 R	3 COU 1 R	4TH COUSIN	4 COU 1 R	4 COU 2 R	4 COU 3 R	4 COU 4 R
6	4G GRAND-SON	3G GRAND-NEPHEW	1 COU 4 R	2 COU 3 R	3 COU 2 R	4 COU 1 R	5TH COUSIN	5 COU 1 R	5 COU 2 R	5 COU 3 R
7	5G GRAND-SON	4G GRAND-NEPHEW	1 COU 5 R	2 COU 4 R	3 COU 3 R	4 COU 2 R	5 COU 1 R	6TH COUSIN	6 COU 1 R	6 COU 2 R
8	6G GRAND-SON	5G GRAND-NEPHEW	1 COU 6 R	2 COU 5 R	3 COU 4 R	4 COU 3 R	5 COU 2 R	6 COU 1 R	7TH COUSIN	7 COU 1 R
9	7G GRAND-SON	6G GRAND-NEPHEW	1 COU 7 R	2 COU 6 R	3 COU 5 R	4 COU 4 R	5 COU 3 R	6 COU 2 R	7 COU 1 R	8TH COUSIN

ABBREVIATIONS

BRO = brother
SIS = sister
DAU = daughter
COU = cousin
R = removed (generations removed)

G-G = great-great
GRANDSON = grandson or granddaughter
SON = son or daughter
NEPHEW = nephew or niece

The chart may be extended in either direction for identifying more distant relationships.

BIBLIOGRAPHY

CHAPTER 5

Bardsley, Charles W., *A Dictionary of English and Welsh Surnames with Special American Instances*. Baltimore: Genealogical Publishing Company, 1980 reprint of 1901 edition.

Benson, Morton, (ed.), *Dictionary of Russian Personal Names*. Philadelphia: University of Pennsylvania Press, 1964.

Black, George F., *Surnames of Scotland: Their Origin, Meaning, and History*. New York: New York Public Library, 1986 reprint of 1946 edition.

Chuks–Orji, Ogonna, *Names from Africa*. Chicago: Johnson Publishing Co., 1972.

Coghlan, Ronan, *Pocket Guide to Irish First Names*. St. Paul, MN: Irish Books and Media, 1985.

Ewen, Cecil, *A History of Surnames of the British Isles*. New York: Gordon Press.

——, *A Guide to the Origins of British Surnames*. New York: Gordon Press.

Foreign Versions of English Names: And Foreign Equivalents of U.S. Military and Civilian Titles. Document No. M-131. Detroit: Gale Research Co., 1980 reprint of 1973 edition.

Grehan, Ida, *Pocket Guide to Irish Family Names*. St. Paul, MN: Irish Books and Media, 1985.

Gruffudd, Haini, *Welsh Personal Names*. Willits, CA: British American Books, not dated.

Hook, J.N., *Family Names: How Our Surnames Came to America*. New York: Macmillan, 1982.

Kolatch, Alfred J., *The Complete Dictionary of English and Hebrew First Names*. Middle Village, NY: Jonathan David Publishers, 1984.

Lower, Mark A., *English Surnames*. 2 Vol, 4th ed. Detroit: Gale Research Co., 1968 reprint of 1875 edition.

O'Corrain, Donnchadh, and Fidelma Maguire, *Gaelic Personal Names*. Wolfeboro, NH: Longwood Publishing Group, 1981.

Room, Adrian, *Dictionary of Translated Names and Titles*. New York: Methuen, Inc., 1985.

Shankle, George E., *American Nicknames*. 2nd ed. Bronx, NY: H.W. Wilson, 1955.

Stewart, George R., *American Given Names: Their Origin and History in the Context of the English Language*. New York: Oxford University Press, 1979.

White, C. Pawley, *A Handbook of Cornish Surnames*. New York: State Mutual Books, 1985.

Woods, Richard C. (comp.), *Hispanic First Names: A Comprehensive Dictionary of 250 Years of Mexican-American Usage*. Westport, CT: Greenwood, 1984.

CHAPTER 10

Akey, Denise S. (ed.), *Encyclopedia of Associations: A Guide to National and International Organizations*. Detroit: Gale Research Co., latest edition.

Beattie, Jerome Francis (ed.), *The Hereditary Register of the United States*. The Hereditary Register Publications, Inc., latest edition.

Chambers, Valerie N., *The Genealogical Helper*. Logan, UT: The Everton Publishers, Inc., 6 issues per year.

McDonald, Donna (comp.), *A Directory of Historical Societies and Agencies in the United States and Canada*. Nashville: American Association for State and Local History, latest edition.

CHAPTER 11

Brown, Mary J. (comp.), *Handy Index to the Holdings of the Genealogical Society of Utah.* Logan, UT: The Everton Publishers, Inc., 1971.

Moore, John Hammond (comp.), *Research Material in South Carolina: A Guide.* Columbia: University of South Carolina Press, 1967.

Press, Jacques Cattell (ed.), *American Library Dictionary.* New York: R. R. Bowker Co., latest edition.

Stemmons, John D. and E. Diane Stemmons (comp.), *The Vital Record Compendium.* Logan, UT: The Everton Publishers, Inc., 1979.

United States Department of Health and Human Services, *Where to Write for Vital Records: Births, Deaths, Marriages, and Divorces.* Hyattsville, MD, 1982. Available at $3.25 (1982 price) from Superintendent of Documents, U.S. Government Printing Office, Washington, DC 20402, or from a U.S. Government Bookstore.

CHAPTER 12

Lancour, Harold (comp.), *A Bibliography of Ship Passenger Lists, 1538–1825.* Third Edition. Revised by Richard J. Wolfe. New York: New York Public Library, 1963.

National Genealogical Society, *Index to Revolutionary War Pension Applications in the National Archives.* Washington, 1976.

Neagles, James C. and Lila Lee Neagles, *Locating Your Immigrant Ancestor.* Logan, UT: The Everton Publishers, Inc., 1975.

United States Department of Commerce, Bureau of the Census, *Twenty Censuses: Population and Housing Questions, 1790–1980.* Washington, 1979. Available from Superintendent of Documents, Government Printing Office, Washington, DC 20402, or from a U.S. Government Bookstore.

United States Senate Document 514, 23 Congress, 1st Session, *Report from the Secretary of War in Relation to the Pension Establishment of the United States.* Washington, 1835. Reprint. Baltimore: Genealogical Publishing Co., 1968. Short Title: *Pension Roll of 1835,* 3 vols.

United States Senate Executive Document 84, 47 Congress, 2nd Session, *List of Pensioners on the Roll January 1, 1883.* Washington.

CHAPTER 13

United States Department of Commerce, Bureau of the Census, *Age Search Information.* Washington, 1981. Available from Superintendent of Documents, Government Printing Office, Washington, DC 20402, or from a U.S. Government Bookstore. $4.25 (1982 price).

United States Department of Health and Human Services, *Where to Write for Vital Records: Births, Deaths, Marriages, and Divorces.* See under Chapter 11.

CHAPTER 16

Kirkham, E. Kay, *How to Read the Handwriting and Records of Early America.* Salt Lake City: Deseret Book Co., 1961.

CHAPTER 18

Malone, Dumas, Allen Johnson, Harris T. Starr, Robert Livingston Schuyler, Edward T. James, and John A. Garraty (eds.), *Dictionary of American Biography,* 13 vols., including Supplements. New York: Charles Scribner's Sons, 1928–1974.

Morris, Richard B. (ed.), *Encyclopedia of American History.* New York: Harper and Row, 1965.

ADDITIONAL SOURCES

Askin, Jayne, *Search: A Handbook for Adoptees and Birthparents*. New York: Harper and Row, 1982. Includes help-groups, agencies. Discusses 20th century U.S. sources.

Beard, Timothy Field, with Denise Demong, *How to Find Your Family Roots*. New York: McGraw–Hill, 1977. Comprehensive. Suggests sources in many foreign countries.

DePlatt, Lyman, *Genealogical Historical Guide to Latin America*. Detroit: Gale Research Co., 1978. Gale Genealogy and Local History Series. Surveys records in Mexico, Central and South America, Cuba, Dominican Republic, Puerto Rico; church records, public records; helpful discussion of calendar and dating documents; frequently used terms and English equivalents.

Doane, Gilbert, *Searching for Your Ancestors*. Minneapolis: University of Minnesota Press, 1948. Especially helpful for New England records.

Eakle, Arlene and Johni Cerny (eds.), *The Source: A Guidebook of American Genealogy*. Salt Lake City: Ancestry, Inc., 1984.

Everton, George B., Sr., and Gunnar Rasmuson, *Handy Book for Genealogists*. Logan, UT: The Everton Publishers, Inc., latest edition. Very handy book for U.S. and Europe, Canada, South Africa searches.

Fletcher, William, *Recording Your Family History*. New York: Dodd, Mead and Co., 1986.

Groene, Bertram Hawthorne, *Tracing Your Civil War Ancestor*. Winston–Salem: John F. Blair, 1973. State-by-state bibliography of sources for regimental histories, rosters, identifying weapons, uniforms. National and state archives sources.

Helmbold, F. Wilbur, *Tracing Your Ancestry*. Birmingham: Oxmoor House, Inc., 1976. Thorough discussion of public records, especially land and military records; extensive bibliography.

Heraldic Artists, Ltd., *Handbook on Irish Genealogy: How to Trace Your Ancestors and Reletives in Ireland*. Dublin, 1970.

Kemp, Thomas J., *Vital Records Handbook*. Baltimore: Genealogical Publishing Co., 1988.

Kirkham, E. Kay, *Research in American Genealogy*. Salt Lake City: Deseret Book Co., 1962.

Law, Hugh T., *How to Trace Your Ancestors to Europe: 117 Stories, Procedures, and Sources to Use for 24 Countries*. Cottonwood Books, 1987.

Miller, Olga K., *Genealogical Research for Czech and Slovak Americans*. Detroit: Gale Research Co., 1978. Sources and archives in Czechoslovakia; surnames and given names with English and German versions; translation of Catholic feast days, calendar terms, family relationships, occupations, terms used in documents.

Pine, L.G., *The Genealogists' Encyclopedia*. New York: Macmillan, 1969. Excellent presentation of British Isles and Continental sources, including Jewish records. Some Latin American and Oriental sources; heraldry.

Punch, Terrence M., *Genealogical Research in Nova Scotia*. Halifax: Petheric Press, Ltd., 1978. Sources in N.S. archives, public records, newspapers, county histories; lists printed N.S. genealogies.

Stevenson, Noel C., *Search and Research*. Salt Lake City: Deseret Book Co., 1959. State-by-state survey of courses.

Valentine, John F. (ed.), *Handbook for Genealogical Correspondence*. Logan, UT: Cache Genealogical Library, 1963.

Wellauer, Maralyn A., *A Guide to Foreign Genealogical Research*. Milwaukee, 1976. Bibliography of books on surnames; glossary in genealogy terms in Danish, Dutch, Norwegian, German, Swiss, Austrian, French.

Westin, Jeane Eddy, *Finding Your Roots*. New York: Ballantine Books, 1978.

Wright, Norman E. and David H. Pratt, *Genealogical Research Essentials*. Salt Lake City: Bookcraft Co., 1967.

MAJOR PUBLISHERS OF GENEALOGICAL MATERIALS

Accelerated Indexing Systems International, Inc., 40 North Highway 89, North Salt Lake, UT 84054. Tel.: 1-800-444-0098; 801-298-8444.

AMS Press, Inc., 56 East 13th St., New York, NY 10003. Tel.: 212-777-4700.

Ancestry, Inc., Box 476, Salt Lake City, UT 84110. Tel.: 1-800-531-1790.

Congaree Publications, Box 11874, Capitol Station, Columbia, SC 29211. Tel.: 803-356-1860.

Cook Publications, 3318 Wimberg Ave., Evansville, IN 47712.

The Everton Publishers, Inc., Box 368, Logan, UT 84321. Tel.: 801-752-6022.

Gale Research Company, subsidiary of International Thomson Publishing, Inc., Book Tower, Detroit, MI 48226. Tel.: 313-961-2242 or 1-800-223-4253.

Genealogical Publishing Company and Gateway Press, 1001 N. Calvert St., Baltimore, MD 21202. Tel.: 301-837-8271.

Heritage Books, Inc., 1540 E. Pointer Ridge Pl., Suite 201, Bowie, MD 20716.

Irvington Publishers, 740 Broadway, Suite 905, New York, NY 10003. Tel.: 212-777-4100.

Southern Historical Press, Inc., P.O. Box 738, Easley, SC 29641-0738. Tel.: 803-859-2346.

The Thaxton Company, P.O. Box 886, Americus, GA 31709-0886. Tel.: 912-924-4038.

Westland Publications, P.O. Box 117, McNeal, AZ 85617. Tel.: 602-642-3500.

In addition, many university presses, public libraries, historical and genealogical societies publish books. Most publishers will make their catalogs available on request.

SOME LARGER SUPPLIERS OF GENEALOGICAL MATERIALS

In addition to the publishers themselves, many companies around the country sell books and supplies of interest to genealogists. The two listed here are by no means the only two, but they have extensive catalogs.

Genealogy Unlimited, Inc., 789 S. Buffalo Grove Rd., Buffalo Grove, IL 60089. Tel.: 312-541-3175.

Tuttle Antiquarian Books, Inc., P.O. Box 541, Rutland, VT 05701-0541.

SELECTED LIBRARIES AND ARCHIVES

The location of the largest genealogical collections varies from state to state. In some states, such as Virginia and South Carolina, the state library and archives have excellent collections of primary and secondary sources for genealogical research. In other states, such as Rhode Island and Washington, the state libraries are not really genealogical centers.

Many public libraries and local historical societies have some local genealogical materials, and hundreds have a local or regional history collection. Many of the university libraries have special documents or manuscript collections which are helpful in researching area history and, to some degree, genealogy. In your research area, ask librarians about their collections and others nearby.

The libraries listed here are, by no means, all the libraries which have genealogy collections, and the ones listed vary considerably in size and scope. The libraries chosen are among the larger ones in their state or have special collections which may interest genealogists working in that area. In states such as Pennsylvania, Virginia, Massachusetts, New York, Louisiana, and North Carolina, so many city and county libraries and county historical societies have local history and genealogy materials that they cannot all be listed here.

To learn of libraries and societies and their holdings, you may find the following references helpful:

A Directory of Historical Societies and Agencies in the United States and Canada (Donna McDonald, comp.), Nashville: American Association for State and Local History, latest edition.

A Preliminary Guide to Church Records Repositories (Aug. R. Suelflow, comp.), Society of American Archivists, 1969.

American Library Directory (Jacques Cattell Press, ed.), New York: R. R. Bowker Co., latest edition.

Directory of Archives and Manuscript Repositories in the United States, Washington, D.C.: National Historical Publications and Records Commission, National Archives and Records Service, General Services Administration, latest edition.

Encyclopedia of Associations: A Guide to National and International Organizations (Denise S. Akey, ed.), Detroit: Gale Research Co., latest edition.

The Genealogical Helper, Logan, UT: The Everton Publishers, Inc. Each July–August issue carries a directory of genealogical societies, libraries, and periodicals.

The Official Museum Directory, Washington, DC: American Association of Museums, latest edition.

ALABAMA

A number of libraries have local history collections; others with genealogy collections include Camden, Cullman, Demopolis, Evergreen, Fayette, Grove Hill, Guntersville, Oneonta, Opelika, Sheffield, Sylacauga, and Valley.

Anniston—Cheaha Regional Library, 108 East Tenth St., Box 308, 36201. Tel.: 205-238-1581.
   —Public Library of Anniston and Calhoun County, 108 East Tenth St., 36202. Tel.: 205-237-8501.

Auburn—Auburn University Library, Auburn, 36849-3501. Tel.: 205-826-4500.

Birmingham—Birmingham Public and Jefferson County Free Library, 2 Park Place, 35203. Tel.: 205-226-3600.
   —Birmingham–Southern College Library, 800 Eighth Avenue W., P.O. Box A-20, 35254. Tel.: 205-226-4740, x 244. (Alabama Methodism)
   —Samford University Library, 800 Lakeshore Drive, 35229. Tel.: 205-870-2846. (Genealogy and Baptist history)

Decatur—Wheeler Basin Regional Library, Decatur Public Library, 504 Cherry St. NE, Box 1766, 35602. Tel.: 205-353-2993.

Enterprise—Enterprise State Junior College Library, Dothan Highway, Box 1300, 36331. Tel.: 205-347-2623, x 300.

Florence—Florence–Lauderdale Public Library, 218 North Wood Ave., P.O. Box 160, 35631. Tel.: 205-764-6563.

Gadsden—Gadsden–Etowah County Library, 254 College St., 35999-3101. Tel.: 205-547-1611.

Huntsville — Huntsville–Madison County Public Library, 108 Fountain, P.O. Box 443, 35804. Tel.: 205-536-0021.

Mobile — Mobile Public Library, 701 Government St., 36602. Tel.: 205-438-7073.

Montgomery — Alabama Department of Archives and History, 624 Washington Ave., 36130. Tel.: 205-261-4361. (Newspapers, state documents).
— Huntingdon College Library, 1500 E. Fairview Ave., 36194. Tel.: 205-265-0511, x 421. (United Methodist history — Ala/W. Florida)

Scottsboro — Scottsboro Public Library, 1002 S. Broad St., 35768. Tel.: 205-574-4335.

Selma — Public Library of Selma and Dallas County, 1103 Selma Ave., 205, 36701. Tel.: 205-875-3535.

ALASKA

A number of libraries have local history collections; Kenai also has a genealogy collection.

Anchorage — Anchorage Museum of History and Art, Archives, 121 West 7th Ave., 99501. Tel.: 907-264-4326.

Fairbanks — Fairbanks North Star Borough Public Library and Regional Center, 1215 Cowles St., 99701. Tel.: 907-452-5177.

Juneau — Alaska Historical Library and Museum, State Office Building, P.O. Box G, 99811. Tel.: 907-264-4326.
— Alaska State Library, P.O. Box G, State Office Building, 99811. Tel.: 907-465-2910.

ARIZONA

A number of libraries have local history and Indian collections; Bisbee (museum library) and Payson also have genealogy collections.

Kingman — Mohave County Historical Society, Mohave Museum of History and Arts Library, 400 W. Beale St., 86401. Tel.: 602-753-3195.

Mesa — LDS Branch Library, 464 E. First Ave., 85204. Tel.: 602-964-1200.

Phoenix — Arizona State Library, Archives and Public Records, State Capitol, 1700 W. Washington, 85007. Tel.: 602-255-4035.

Prescott — Prescott Historical Society Library, 415 W. Gurley St., 86301. Tel.: 602-445-3122. (Indian and early state history)

Tucson — Arizona Daily Star Library, 4850 South Park Ave., P.O. Box 26807, 85726. Tel.: 602-294-4433. (Daily Star newspaper from 1877, city directories)
— Arizona Historical Society Research Library, 949 E. Second St., 85719. Tel.: 602-628-5774.
— Tucson Public Library Annex, Southern Arizona Genealogy Society Collection, 111 E. Pennington, P.O. Box 27470, 85726. Tel.: 602-791-4391.

ARKANSAS

A number of libraries have local history collections; those with genealogy collections include Arkadelphia, Bentonville, Hamburg, Harrison, Helena, Lake Village, and Malvern.

Conway — Hendrix College Library, Washington and Front Sts., 72032. Tel.: 501-450-1303. (Arkansas Methodism)

El Dorado — Union County Libraries, Barton Library, East 5th and N. Jefferson Sts., 71730. Tel.: 501-863-5447.

Fayetteville — Ozarks Regional Library, 217 E. Dickson St., 72701. Tel.: 501-442-6253.

Fort Smith — Fort Smith Public Library, 61 South 8th St., 72901. Tel.: 501-783-0229.

Hot Springs — Tri-Lakes Regional Library, 125 B Albert Pike, 71913. Tel.: 501-623-3943.

Jonesboro — Craighead County and Jonesboro Public Library, 315 West Oak, 72401. Tel.: 501-935-5133.

Little Rock — Arkansas Gazette News Library, 112 West Third, P.O. Box 1821, 72203. Tel.: 501-371-3740. (Gazette issues from 1819)
— Arkansas History Commission Archives, Branch of State Library, One Capitol Mall, 72201. Tel.: 501-371-2141.

—Arkansas State Library, One Capitol Mall, 72201. Tel.: 501-371-1526. (History and documents)
—Central Arkansas Library System, 700 Louisiana St., 72201. Tel.: 501-370-5954.

North Little Rock—Laman Public Library, 2800 Orange St., 72114-2296. Tel.: 501-758-1720.

Pine Bluff—Pine Bluff and Jefferson County Library System, 200 East Eighth Ave., 71601. Tel.: 501-534-4802. (Southern genealogy)

Texarkana—Texarkana Public Library, 600 West 3rd St., TX 75501. Tel.: 214-794-2149.

CALIFORNIA

A number of libraries have local history collections; some of those with genealogy collections are Coalinga, La Verne (university library), Napa and San Rafael (historical society libraries), Santa Maria, Sonora (genealogy society library), Tiburon (HMS Bounty Society Library), Tulare, Ukiah, and Yreka.

Berkeley—Western Jewish History Center, 2911 Russell St., 94705. Tel.: 415-849-2710, x5. (Western Jewish Americana)

Carmichael—See under Sacramento.

Claremont—School of Theology at Claremont Library, 1325 N. College Ave., 91711. Tel.: 714-626-3521, x265. (Methodist and Protestant Episcopal history)

Colma—Archdiocese of San Francisco, 1500 Old Mission Rd., 94014. Tel.: 415-994-5211. Write to Chancery Archives, P.O. Box 1799, Colma, 94014. (Catholic history in San Francisco area)

Huntington Beach—Huntington Beach Public Library, 7111 Talbert Ave., 92648. Tel.: 714-842-4481. (Orange County Genealogical Society collection)

Long Beach—Long Beach Jewish Community Center Library, 3801 E. Willow, 90815. Tel.: 213-426-7601. (Southwest Jewish history)

Los Angeles—Los Angeles Public Library, 630 West 5th St., 90071. Tel.: 213-612-3200.
—Archdiocese of Los Angeles, Chancery Office, 1531 West 9th St., 90015.
—Hebrew Union College Library, 3077 University Ave., 90007, Tel.: 213-749-3424. (West Coast Jewish archives)
—Jewish Federation Council of Greater Los Angeles, Library, 6505 Wilshire Blvd., 90048. Tel.: 213-852-1234, x3202. (Los Angeles area Jewish history and archives)

Modesto—Stanislaus County Free Library, 1500 I St., 95334. Tel.: 209-571-6821.

Riverside—Riverside Public Library, 3871 Seventh St., Box 468, 92502. Tel.: 714-787-7211.

Sacramento—California State Archives Library, 1020 O St., 95814. Tel.: 916-445-4293. (state history & government)
—California State Library, 914 Capitol Mall, Library–Courts Building, P.O. Box 942837, 94237-0001. Tel.: 916-445-2585.

—Sacramento Public Library, Genealogy collection at Carmichael Regional Library, 5605 Marconi Ave., Carmichael, CA 95608. Tel.: 916-483-6055.

San Carlos—Ragusan Press, Yugoslav Immigration Library, also Croatian Serbian Slovene Genealogical Society, 2527 San Carlos Ave., 94070. Tel.: 415-592-1190.

San Francisco—American Indian Historical Society Library and Archives, 1451 Masonic Ave., 94117. Tel.: 415-626-5235. Open by appointment.
—California Historical Society Library, 2099 Pacific Ave., 94109. Tel.: 415-567-1848.
—San Francisco African–American Historical and Cultural Society, Inc., Library, Ft. Mason Center Building C, No. 165, 94123. Tel.: 415-441-0640. (Black history and African descendants)
—San Francisco Public Library, Civic Center, 94102. Tel.: 415-558-4235.
—Society of California Pioneers Library, 456 McAllister St., 94102. Tel.: 415-861-5278.
—Sutro Library, Branch of California State Library, 480 Winston Dr., 94132. Tel.: 415-731-4477.
—Holocaust Library and Research Center, 601 14th Ave., 94118. Tel.: 415-751-6040.

Santa Barbara—Santa Barbara Genealogical Society Library, Box 1303, 93116.

—Santa Barbara Historical Society Library, 136 East De La Guerra St., P.O. Box 578, 93102. Tel.: 805-966-1601.

—Santa Barbara Mission Archives Library, Old Mission, 2201 Laguna St., 93105. Tel.: 805-682-4713. (Catholic diocese archives)

Stockton—United Methodist Church Research Library, University of the Pacific, 3601 Pacific Ave., 95211. Tel.: 209-946-2269. Open by appointment. (West Coast Methodist history and genealogy)

—Stockton–San Joaquin County Public Library, 605 N. El Dorado St., 95202. Tel.: 209-944-8415.

Thousand Oaks—Thousand Oaks Public Library, 1401 E. Janss Rd., 91362. Tel.: 805-497-6282.

Whittier—Whittier College, Wardman Library, 7031 Founders Hill Rd., 90608. Tel.: 213-693-0771. (Quaker collection)

COLORADO

Denver—Colorado Historical Society Library, 1300 Broadway, 80203. Tel.: 303-866-2305.

—Denver Public Library, 1357 Broadway, 80203. Tel.: 303-571-2000. (Consult Social Science–Genealogy branch)

—Iliff School of Theology Library, 2201 South University Blvd., 80210. Tel.: 303-744-1287. (Archives of the Rocky Mountain Conference of the United Methodist Church)

—Stagecoach Library for Genealogical Research, 1840 South Wolcott Ct., 80219. Tel.: 303-936-0118.

Greeley—Greeley Public Library, 919 7th St., 80631. Tel.: 303-353-6123, x 393. (Genealogy and German–Russian collection)

Pueblo—Pueblo Library Dictrict, 100 East Abriendo Ave., 81004. Tel.: 303-544-1942.

Steamboat Springs—Tread of Pioneers Museum Library, 1289 Lincoln Ave., P.O. Box 770786, 80477. Tel.: 303-879-0240.

CONNECTICUT

Many local public libraries have local history collections. Town libraries with genealogy collections include Cos Cob (historical society), Granby (historical society), Haddam, New Canaan, Putnam, Seymour, Southport, Stonington, Watertown (historical society), and West Willington (historical society).

Bloomfield—St. Thomas Seminary Library, 467 Bloomfield Ave., 06002. Tel.: 203-242-5573. (early Catholic Americana)

Darien—Darien Historical Society Library, 45 Old King's Highway North, 06820. Tel.: 203-655-9233.

—Darien Library, 35 Leroy Ave., 06820. Tel.: 203-655-2568.

Enfield—Enfield Central Library, 104 Middle Rd., 06082. Tel.: 203-749-0766. (Shaker history)

Fairfield—Fairfield Historical Society Library, 636 Old Post Rd., 06430. Tel.: 203-259-1598.

Groton—Groton Public Library, Route 117, Newton Rd., 06340. Tel.: 203-448-1552.

Guilford—Guilford Free Library, 67 Park St., 06437. Tel.: 203-453-6561.

Hartford—Connecticut Historical Society Library, One Elizabeth St., 06105. Tel.: 203-236-5621.

—Connecticut State Library, 231 Capitol Ave., 06106. Tel.: 203-566-4301.

—Episcopal Diocese of Connecticut, 1335 Asylum Ave., 06105. (Connecticut Episcopalian church archives)

Middletown—Middlesex County Historical Society Library, 151 Main St., 06457. Tel.: 203-346-0746.

—Godfrey Memorial Library, 134 Newfield St., 06457. Tel.: 203-346-4375.

Milford—Milford Public Library, 57 New Haven Ave., 06460. Tel.: 203-783-3290.

New Haven—New Haven Colony Historical Society Library, 114 Whitney Ave., 06510. Tel.: 203-562-4183.

—Yale University Library, 120 High St., P.O. Box 1603 A, Yale Station, 06510. Tel.: 203-432-1775. (Family history, New England history, etc.)

Norwich—Otis Library, 261 Main St., 06360. Tel.: 203-889-2365.

Rocky Hill—French-Canadian Genealogical Society of Connecticut Library, P.O. Box 262, 06067. Tel.: 203-529-9040.

Stamford—Stamford Genealogical Society, Inc., and Public Library, One Public Library Plaza, 06904. Tel.: 203-964-1000.

Torrington—Torrington Historical Society Library, 192 Main St., 06790. Tel.: 203-482-8260.

West Hartford—Connecticut Society of Genealogy, Inc., 16 Royal Oak Dr., 06107.

Windsor—Windsor Historical Society Library, 96 Palisado Ave., 06095. Tel.: 203-688-3813.

DELAWARE

A number of public libraries have local history collections.

Georgetown—Georgetown Public Library, 10 West Pine St., 19947. Tel.: 302-856-7958.

Smyrna—Smyrna Public Library, 107 South Main St., 19977. Tel.: 302-653-4579.

Wilmington—Historical Society of Delaware Library, 505 Market Street Mall, 19801. Tel.: 302-655-7161.
—Holy Trinity (Old Swedes) Church Foundation Library, 606 Church St., 19801. Tel.: 302-652-5629. (Swedish and Delaware history and genealogy).
—Widener University, Delaware Campus Library, Concord Pike, P.O. Box 7139, 19803. Tel.: 302-478-3000. (Brandywine Valley history)
—Wilmington Institute Library, 10th and Market St., 19801. Tel.: 302-571-7400. (Delawareana)

DISTRICT OF COLUMBIA

Library of Congress, Independence Avenue at First St. East, 20540. Tel.: 202-287-5000.
National Archives, Pennsylvania Avenue at Eighth St. NW, 20408. Tel.: 202-523-3134.
National Society, Colonial Dames XVII Century, Library, 1300 New Hampshire Ave. NW, 20036. Tel.: 202-293-1700.
National Society, Daughters of American Colonists Library, 2205 Massachusetts Ave. NW, 20008. Tel.: 202-667-3076.
National Society, Daughters of the American Revolution Library, 1776 D St. NW, 20006. Tel.: 202-879-3229 or 202-628-1776.
Wesley Theological Seminary Library, 4500 Massachusetts Ave. NW, 20016. Tel.: 202-885-8691. (early American Methodist history)

FLORIDA

Bartow—Polk County Historical/Genealogical Library, 495 North Hendry, P.O. Box 1719, 33830. Tel.: 813-533-5146.

Boca Raton—Branch Genealogical Library, P.O. Box 2350, 33427. Tel.: 305-395-6644.

Bradenton—Manatee County Public Library System, Central Library, 1301 Barcarrota Blvd. W., 33505. Tel.: 813-748-5555.

Dunedin—Dunedin Public Library, 223 Douglas Ave., 33528. Tel.: 813-733-4115.

Ft. Myers—Ft. Myers-Lee County Library, 2050 Lee St., 33901. Tel.: 813-334-3992.

Ft. Pierce—St. Lucie County Library System, 124 N. Indian River Dr., 33450. Tel.: 305-461-5708.

Gainesville—Alachua County Public Library, Gainesville Public Library Headquarters, 222 East University Ave., 32601. Tel.: 904-374-2091.
—Yonge Library of Florida History, University of Florida, 441 Library West, 32611. Tel.: 904-392-0319.

Jacksonville—Jacksonville Public Library, 122 North Ocean St., 32202, Tel.: 904-633-2107.

Orlando—Orlando Public Library, 101 East Central Blvd., 32801. Tel.: 305-425-4694.

Pensacola—Pensacola Historical Society Library, 405 South Adams St., 32501. Tel.: 904-433-1559.
   —West Florida Regional Library, Pensacola Public Library, 200 West Gregory, 32501. Tel.: 904-435-1760.

St. Augustine—St. Augustine Historical Society Library, 271 Charlotte St., 32084. Tel.: 904-824-2872.

St. Petersburg—St. Petersburg Public Library, 3745 Ninth Ave. N., 33713. Tel.: 813-893-7724.

Sarasota—Selby Public Library, 1001 Blvd. of the Arts, 33577. Tel.: 814-366-7303.

Tallahassee—Florida State Library, R. A. Gray Building, 32301. Tel.: 904-487-2651.

Tampa—Tampa-Hillsborough County Public Library System, 900 North Ashley Dr., 33602. Tel.: 813-223-8945.
   —Hillsborough County Historical Commission Museum Library, Second Floor, County Courthouse, 401 Pierce St., 33602. Tel.: 813-272-5919.

Vero Beach—Indian River County Library, 1028 20th Pl., 32960. Tel.: 305-567-4111.

GEORGIA

Public and regional libraries in these towns have genealogy collections: Americus, Athens, Bainbridge, Cochran (Middle Georgia College Library), Cuthbert, Douglas, Gainesville, Lafayette, Madison, Manchester, Moultrie, Newnan, Quitman, and Vidalia. Others have local history collections.

Atlanta—Atlanta Public Library, One Margaret Mitchell Square NW, 30303. Tel.: 404-688-4636.
   —Emory University Library, Central Library, 1364 Clifton Rd. NE, 30322. Tel.: 404-727-6861. (Family papers, Methodist history)
   —Genealogical Center Library, with special services for the blind, 15 Dunwoody Park Rd., Suite 130, 30338; P.O. Box 88100, 30356-8100. Tel.: 404-242-2076.
   —Georgia Department of Archives and History, 330 Capitol Ave. SE, 30334. Tel.: 404-656-2393.

Columbus—Chattahoochee Valley Regional Library, 1120 Bradley Dr., 31995. Tel.: 404-327-0211.

Decatur—Columbia Theological Seminary, Campbell Library, 701 Columbia Dr., 30031. Tel.: 404-378-8821. (Presbyterian history)

Macon—Middle Georgia Regional Library, 1180 Washington Ave., P.O. Box 6334, 31208. Tel.: 912-744-0800.

Rome—Shorter College Library, Box 5, 30161. Tel.: 404-291-2121. (Georgia Baptist history)

Savannah—Georgia Historical Society Library, 501 Whitaker St., 31499. Tel.: 912-651-2128.

Smyrna—Smyrna Public Library, 2873 King St., 30080-3597. Tel.: 404-436-2370.

Statesboro—Statesboro Regional Library, 124 South Main St. and Grady, 30458. Tel.: 912-764-7573.

Swainsboro—Emanuel County Junior College Library, 30401. Tel.: 912-237-7831.

Thomasville—Thomas College Library, 1501 Millpond Rd., 31792. Tel.: 912-226-1621. (Southern history and church histories)

Waycross—Okefenokee Regional Library, 401 Lee Ave., P.O. Box 1669, 31502. Tel.: 912-283-3216.

HAWAII

Honolulu—Hawaiian Historical Society Library, 560 Kawaiahao St., 96813. Tel.: 808-537-6271.
   —Hawaii Chinese History Center Library, 111 North King St., Rm. 410, 96817. Tel.: 808-521-5948.
   —D.A.R. Clubhouse Library, 1914 Makiki Heights Dr., 96822.
   —Hawaii State Archives, Iolani Palace Ground, 96813. Tel.: 808-548-2355.

IDAHO

Boise—Idaho Historical Society Library, Library and Archives Building, 325 West State St., 83702. Tel.: 208-334-3356. Genealogy Library Tel.: 334-2305.
   —Idaho State Library, 325 West State St., 83702. Tel.: 208-334-2150. (Idaho and Northwest U.S. history)

Grangeville—Grangeville Centennial Library, 215 West North, 83530-1729. Tel.: 208-983-0951.

Hayden Lake — Hayden Lake Area Free District Library, 838 N. Government Way, 83835-0872. Tel.: 208-772-5612. (North Idaho genealogy)

Lewiston — Lewiston City Library, 428 Thain Rd., 83501-5399. Tel.: 208-743-6519.

Moscow — Moscow–Latah County Library System, 110 S. Jefferson, 83843. Tel.: 208-882-3925.

Murphy — Owyhee County Historical Society, Library Complex, 83650-0067. Tel.: 208-495-2319.

Rexburg — Ricks College Library, 83440. Tel.: 208-356-2351.

Salmon — Salmon Public Library, 204 Main St., 83467. Tel.: 208-756-2311.

ILLINOIS

Many towns and cities have local history and genealogy materials in their public libraries; only the larger ones are listed here.

Arlington Heights — Arlington Heights Memorial Library, 500 N. Dunton Ave., 60004. Tel.: 312-392-0100.

Belleville — Belleville Public Library, 121 E. Washington St., 62220. Tel.: 618-234-0441.

Berwyn — Czechoslovak Heritage Museum Library, 2701 South Harlem Ave., 60402. Tel.: 312-795-5800, x354.

Bloomington — McLean County Historical Society Library, 201 East Grove St., 61701. Tel.: 309-827-0428.
— United Methodist Church Central Illinois Conference Library, P.O. Box 515, 61702. Tel.: 309-828-5092, x45. (Methodist history; staff genealogist/historian)

Chicago — Balzekas Museum of Lithuanian Culture, Library, 6500 South Pulaski Rd., 60629. Tel.: 312-582-6500. (Lithuanian genealogy, history)
— Chicago Historical Society Library, North Ave. and Clark St., 60614. Tel.: 312-642-4600.
— Chicago Public Library, 425 North Michigan Ave., 60611. Tel.: 312-269-2900.
— Chicago Public Library, Special Collections Dept., 78 East Washington St., 60602. Tel.: 312-269-2926.
— Jesuit–Krauss–McCormick Library, 1100 E. 55th St., 60615. Tel.: 312-667-3500. (Merged collections of McCormick Theological Seminary, Lutheran School of Theology; Presbyterian and Lutheran church history, archives)
— Lithuanian Research and Studies Center, Inc., 5620 S. Claremont Ave., 60636. Tel.: 312-434-4545. (Lithuanian Historical Society)
— Naes College Library, 2838 W. Peterson, 60659. Tel.: 312-761-5000. (American Indian tribal histories)
— National Huguenot Society, 9027 S. Damen Ave., 60620.
— Newberry Library, 60 West Walton St., 60610. Tel.: 312-943-9090. (Genealogy; American Indian collection)
— Polish Genealogical Society, 984 N. Milwaukee Ave., 60622. Tel.: 312-384-3352. (Polish Museum of America Library)
— Spertus College of Judaica, Library, 618 S. Michigan Ave., 60605. Tel.: 312-922-9012, x249. (Chicago Jewish history)
— Swedish–American Historical Society, Swedish–American Archives, 5120 N. Spaulding Ave., 60625. Tel.: 312-583-5722. (Chicago Swedes, Swedish immigration history)
— University of Chicago Library, 1100 East 57th St., 60637. Tel.: 312-962-7874. (Kentucky–Ohio River Valley history, English manorial records of Norfolk, Suffolk)
— University of Illinois at Chicago, Special Collections Library, 801 S. Morgan St., P.O. Box 8198, 60680. Tel.: 312-996-2716. (Pre-fire Chicago manuscripts, Hull House papers, Immigrants' Protective League and other organization collections)

Collinsville — Collinsville Memorial Public Library, 408 W. Main, 62234. Tel.: 618-344-1112.

Danville — Danville Public Library, 307 N. Vermilion St., 61832. Tel.: 217-446-7420.

Deerfield — Trinity Evangelical Divinity School, Library, 2065 Half Day Rd., 60015. Tel.: 312-945-8800, x317. (Evangelical Free Church of America archives)

Dixon — Dixon Public Library, 221 Hennepin Ave., 61021. Tel.: 815-284-7261.

Edwardsville—Edwardsville Public Library, 112 S. Kansas, 62025. Tel.: 618-656-4594.
　　　　—Madison County Historical Society Museum Library, 715 N. Main, 62025. Tel.: 618-656-7562.

Elgin—Church of the Brethren General Board, Brethren Historical Library and Archives, 1451 Dundee Ave., 60120. Tel.: 312-742-5100, x 294. (Brethren history, archives)

Elmwood Park—Ed Sadowski PM, Masonic Historical Library, 1924 N. 74th Ct., 60635. Tel.: 312-456-0091. (Masonic history, records)

　　　　—Eureka College Library, 300 College Ave., 61530. Tel.: 309-467-3721, x 219. (local archives, Disciples of Christ church archives)

Glenview—Glenview Public Library, 1930 Glenview Rd., 60025. Tel.: 312-7297500.

Kankakee—Kankakee Public Library, 304 S. Indiana Ave., 60901. Tel.: 815-939-4564.
　　　　—Kankakee County Historical Society Museum, 8th and Water St., 60901. Tel.: 815-932-5279.

Moline—Moline Public Library, 504 17th St., 61265. Tel.: 309-762-6883.

Oak Forest—Slovak Catholic Culture Center Library, 5900 W. 147th St., 60452. Tel.: 312-687-2877.

Peoria—Peoria Public Library, 107 NE Monroe St., 61602. Tel.: 309-672-8835.

Quincy—Quincy Public Library, 526 Jersey St., 62301. Tel.: 217-223-1309.

Rockford—Rockford Public Library, 215 N Wyman St., 61101. Tel.: 815-965-6731.

Rock Island—Swenson Swedish Immigration Research Center Library, Augustana Collection, Box 175, 61201. Tel.: 309-794-7204.

South Holland—South Suburban Genealogical and Historical Society Library, 320 E. 161st Pl., P.O. Box 96, 60473. Tel.: 312-333-9474.

Springfield—Daughters of Union Veterans of the Civil War, 503 S Walnut St., 62704. Tel.: 217-544-0616.
　　　　—Illinois State Archives, Archives Building, 62756. Tel.: 217-782-4682.
　　　　—Illinois State Historical Library, Old State Capitol, 501 South Second, 62701. Tel.: 217-782-4836.

Urbana—Urbana Free Library, 201 South Race St., 61801. Tel.: 217-367-4057.

Wheaton—Wheaton Public Library, 225 N Cross St., 60187. Tel.: 312-668-1374.

INDIANA

Many public libraries have local history and genealogy collections.

Anderson—Anderson and Stony Creek Township Public Library, 32 W Tenth, 46016. Tel.: 317-644-0938.

Bloomington—Indiana University Library, Tenth St. and Jordan Ave., 47405. Tel.: 812-335-3403.

Evansville—Willard Library of Evansville, 21 First Ave., 47710. Tel.: 812-425-4309.

Ft. Wayne—Allen County–Ft. Wayne Historical Society Library, 302 E Berry, 46802. Tel.: 219-426-2882.
　　　　—Allen County–Ft. Wayne Public Library, 900 Webster St., P.O. Box 2270, 46801. Tel.: 219-424-7241.

Franklin—College of Indiana Library, 46131. Tel.: 317-736-8441. (Indiana Baptist collection)

Gary—Public Library of Gary, 220 W Fifth Ave., 46402. Tel.: 219-886-2484.
　　　　—Roman Catholic Diocese of Gary, 668 Pierce St., 46402. (Catholic archives, NW Indiana)

Greencastle—DePauw University Library, Box 137, 46135. Tel.: 317-658-4512. (Indiana United Methodism archives)

Hanover—Hanover College Library, Box 287, 47243. Tel.: 813-866-2151, x 333. (Indiana Presbyterian archives)

Indianapolis—American Legion National Headquarters Library, 700 N Pennsylvania St., 46206. Tel.: 317-635-8411. (Local, state, national American Legion archives)
　　　　—Indiana State Historical Society, 315 West Ohio St., 46202. Tel.: 317-232-1879.
　　　　—Indiana State Library, Genealogy Division, 140 N Senate Ave., 46204. Tel.: 317-232-3675. (Houses state historical society library)

—Society of Indiana Pioneers, State Library and Historical Building, 315 W Ohio St., 46202. Tel.: 317-232-3675.

Kokomo—Kokomo Howard County Public Library, 220 N Union St., 46901. Tel.: 317-457-3242.

Lafayette—Tippecanoe County Historical and Genealogical Associations, Library, 909 South St., 47901. Tel.: 317-142-8411.

—Tippecanoe County Public Library, 638 North St., 47901. Tel.: 317-423-2602. (Local newspaper collection from 1831)

Marion—Marion Public Library, 600 South Washington St., 46953. Tel.: 317-664-7363.

Michigan City—Michigan City Public Library, 100 E Fourth St., 46360. Tel.: 219-879-4561.

New Albany—New Albany Floyd County Public Library, 180 W Spring St., 47150. Tel.: 812-944-8464.

Plainfield—Western Yearly Meeting of Friends, Library, 203 South East St., P.O. Box 70, 46168. Tel.: 317-839-2789. (W. Indiana–E. Illinois Quaker records)

Richmond—Earlham College Library, 47374. Tel.: 317-983-1360. (Quaker archives and genealogy)

—First Friends Meeting House, E. Main and 15th St., 47374. (Ohio, Michigan, Indiana Quaker records; open by appointment)

—Wayne County, Indiana Historical Museum Library, 1150 North A St., 47374. Tel.: 317-962-5756.

South Bend—South Bend Public Library, 122 W Wayne St., 46601. Tel.: 219-282-4600.

—Northern Indiana Historical Society Library, 112 S Lafayette St., 46601. Tel.: 219-284-9664.

Vincennes—Vincennes University, Lewis Historical Collection Library, 1002 N First St., 47591. Tel.: 812-885-4330.

IOWA

A number of public libraries have local history collections; some of those with genealogical collections are Amana, Audubon, Bedford, Boone, Carroll, Chariton, Charles City, Clarinda (community college library), Conrad, Creston, Dallas Center, Eldon, Ft. Madison, Greenfield, Hampton, Jamaica, Keosauqua, Mount Ayr, Sioux Center, Webster City, and Winterset.

Davenport—Davenport Public Library, 321 Main St., 52801. Tel.: 319-326-7832.

Decorah—Norwegian–American Historical Museum, 502 W Water St., 52101. Tel.: 319-382-9681.

Des Moines—Episcopal Diocese of Iowa, 225 37th St., 50312. (Iowa Episcopal archives, vital records)

—Iowa Genealogical Society Library, 6000 Douglas Ave., Suite 145, P.O. Box 7735, 50322. Tel.: 515-276-0287.

—Iowa State Historical Department Library, East 12th and Grand Ave., 50319. Tel.: 515-281-5472.

Dubuque—Schools of Theology in Dubuque, Library, 2000 University, 333 Wartburg Pl., 52001. Tel.: 319-589-3215 and 589-0266. (American Lutheran Church archives)

Iowa City—State Historical Dept. of Iowa Library, 402 Iowa Ave., 52240. Tel.: 319-338-5471.

LeMars—Westmar College Library, 51031. Tel.: 712-546-7081. (United Methodism collection)

Marshalltown—Marshalltown Public Library, 36 N Center St., 50158. Tel.: 515-754-5738. (Central Iowa Genealogical Society)

Mt. Pleasant—Iowa Wesleyan College Library, 52641. Tel.: 319-385-8021.

Oskaloosa—Wilcox Library, William Penn College, N Market St., 52577. Tel.: 515-673-8311, x 291. (Quaker collection)

Pella—Central College Library, 812 Peace St., 50219. Tel.: 515-628-5219. (Collection on Dutch in America and Iowa)

Sioux City—Catholic Diocese of Sioux City, 1821 Jackson St., 51105. (20th century vital records from all its parishes; parish histories)

Waterloo—Grout Museum of History and Science, Library, 503 South St., 50701. Tel.: 319-234-6357.

KANSAS

These Kansas public libraries have genealogy and local history collections: Anthony, Arkansas City, Bonner Spring, Chanute, Coffeyville, Columbus, Coolidge, Ellsworth, Emporia, Galena, Haysville, Hillsboro (Tabor College), Iola, Jetmore, Ness City, Newton, Osborne, Ottawa, Phillipsburg, Pratt, Saint Joan, Ulysses, and Winfield.

Kansas City—Kansas City Public Library, 625 Minnesota Ave., 66101. Tel.: 913-621-3073. (Wyandotte Indian collection)
—Archdiocese of Kansas City, 2220 Central Ave., 66102. (Vital records of diocese parishes)

Lawrence—Kansas and Special Collections, Kenneth Spencer Research Library, University of Kansas, 66045. Tel.: 913-684-4334.

Leavenworth—Leavenworth Public Library, Fifth and Walnut Sts., 66048. Tel.: 913-682-5666.

Manhattan—Riley County, Kansas Genealogical Society Library, 2005 Claflin, 66502. Tel.: 913-537-2205.

North Newton—Bethel College, Mennonite Library and Archives, Drawer A, 67117. Tel.: 316-283-2500, x 213. (German, Dutch genealogy; Mennonite & Anabaptist history)

Shawnee Mission—Johnson County Library, 8700 W 63rd St., Box 2901, 66201. Tel.: 913-831-1550.

Topeka—Kansas State Historical Society Library, Memorial Building, 120 W Tenth, 66612. Tel.: 913-296-4776.
—Topeka Genealogical Society Library, 2717 Indiana St., 66604.

Wichita—Friends University Library, 2100 University Ave., 67213. Tel.: 316-261-5880. (Quaker collection)
—Wichita Public Library, 223 South Main, 67202. Tel.: 316-262-0611.
—Wichita State University Library, Box 68, 67208. Tel.: 316-689-3586. (local and state history)
—Midwest Historical and Genealogical Society, Inc., Library, 1203 N Main, P.O. Box 1121, 67201. Tel.: 316-264-3611.

KENTUCKY

A number of city and county public libraries have local history and genealogy collections.

Ashland—Boyd County Public Library, 1740 Central Ave., 41101. Tel.: 606-329-0090.

Bowling Green—Bowling Green Public Library, 1225 State St., 42101. Tel.: 502-781-4882.
—Western Kentucky University, Kentucky Library, 42101. Tel.: 502-745-6263.

Covington—Kenton County Public Library, 502 Scott St., 41011. Tel.: 606-491-7610.

Frankfort—Kentucky Department for Libraries and Archives, 300 Coffee Tree Rd., Box 537, 40602. Tel.: 502-875-7000.
—Kentucky Historical Society Library, Old Capitol Annex, Box H, 40602. Tel.: 502-564-3016.
—Kentucky Genealogical Society, Box 153, 40601.

Hopkinsville—Hopkinsville Christian County Public Library, 1101 Bethel Street, 42240. Tel.: 502-887-4263.

Lexington—Lexington Public Library, 251 West Second St., 40507. Tel.: 606-231-5500.
—Lexington Theological Seminary Library, 631 S Limestone St., 40508. Tel.: 606-252-0361. (Disciples of Christ collection)
—Transylvania University Library, 300 N Broadway, 40508. Tel.: 606-233-8225. (Kentucky collection)
Lexington—University of Kentucky Library, 40506. Tel.: 606-257-3801. (Kentucky and Appalachia collection)

Louisville—Filson Club, 1310 S Third St., 40208. Tel.: 502-635-5083.
—Louisville Free Public Library, Fourth at York St., 40203. Tel.: 502-561-8600.
—Louisville Presbyterian Theological Seminary Library, 1044 Alta Vista Rd., 40205. Tel.: 502-895-3411. (Presbyterian history)
—National Society, Sons of the American Revolution, Genealogical Library, 1000 South Fourth, 40203. Tel.: 502-589-1776.

Murray—Murray State University Library, 42071. Tel.: 502-762-2291.

Owensboro—Kentucky Wesleyan College Library, 3000 Frederica St., Box 1039, 42302. Tel.: 502-926-3111, x 131. (Kentucky Methodism)

—Owensboro Davies County Public Library, 450 Griffith Ave., 42301. Tel.: 502-684-0211.

Midway—Midway College Library, 40347. Tel.: 606-846-4421. (Disciples of Christ collection)

LOUISIANA

A number of parish libraries have genealogy and local history collections; smaller towns which have genealogy collections are Amite, Arcadia, Bastrop, Buras, Chalmette, DeRidder, Eunice, Franklin, Laplace, Marrero, Napoleonville, Opelousas, St. Martinsville, Thibodaux, and Winnfield.

Alexandria—Louisiana State University at Alexandria, Library, 71302. Tel.: 318-473-6438.
   —Alexandria Historical and Genealogical Library, 503 Washington, 71301.

Baton Rouge—Louisiana State Library, Box 131, 760 Riverside N, 70821. Tel.: 504-342-4922. (state history and documents)
   —Southern University Library, Southern Branch Post Office, 70813. Tel.: 504-771-4990. (Black history and archives)

Lake Charles—Calcasieu Parish Public Library, 411 Pujo St., 70601. Tel.: 318-437-3485.

Metairie—Jefferson Parish Library Dept., Lobby Branch, 3420 N. Causeway Blvd., 70002. (Main Library Tel.: 504-834-5850)

Monroe—Ouachita Parish Public Library, 1800 Stubbs Ave., 71201. Tel.: 318-255-1920.

New Orleans—Louisiana State Museum, Library, Mailing address: 751 Chartres St., 70116. Tel.: 504-568-8215. (Louisiana history)
   —New Orleans Public Library, 219 Loyola Ave., 70140. Tel.: 504-596-2550. (City archives, state documents)
   —Southern Historical Association and Howard Tilton Library, Map and Genealogy Room. Tulane University, 6823 St. Charles Ave., 70118. Tel.: 504-865-5131.

Ruston—Lincoln Parish Library, 509 W. Alabama, 71270. Tel.: 318-255-1920.

Shreveport—Ark–La–Tex Genealogical Association, P.O. Box 4462, 71134. Tel.: 318-425-7513.
   —Shreve Memorial Library, 424 Texas, Box 21523, 71120. Tel.: 318-221-5871.

Thibodaux—Nicholls State University Library, 70301. Tel.: 504-446-8111, x401. (Local history, including papers from area sugar plantations.)

MAINE

Town libraries with genealogy collections include Bar Mills, Bath, Belfast, Calais, Chebeaque, Dover, Eliot, Farmington, Islesboro, Madawaska, North Berwick, Searsport, Springvale, Waterville, and Yarmouth.

Auburn—Auburn Public Library, 49 Spring St., 04210. Tel.: 207-782-3191.

Augusta—Maine State Library and Archives, State House Station 64, LMA Building, 04333. Tel.: 207-289-5600.

Bangor—Bangor Public Library, 145 Harlow St., 04401. Tel.: 207-947-8336.

New Gloucester—Shaker Library, Sabbathday Lake, Rt. 26, 04274. Tel.: 207-926-4597. (Quaker collection)

Portland—Maine Historical Society Library, 485 Congress St., 04101. Tel.: 207-774-1822.
   —Portland Public Library, Baxter Library, 5 Monument Square, 04101. Tel.: 207-773-4761.

York—York Public Library, 172 York St., 03909. Tel.: 207-363-2818.
   —York Historical Society Library, York St., Box 312, 03909. Tel.: 207-363-3872.

MARYLAND

Smaller towns with genealogy and local history collections include Cambridge, Middletown, Oakland, Saint Mary's City (college library), and Westminster.

Annapolis—Maryland State Archives Library, 361 Rowe Blvd., 21404. Tel.: 301-269-3914.
   —Maryland State Law Library, Court of Appeals Building, 361 Rowe Blvd., 21401. Tel.: 301-974-3345. (Maryland newspapers from 1745)

Baltimore—Jewish Historical Society of Maryland, Inc., 15 Lloyd St., 21202. Tel.: 301-732-6400.
　　—Maryland Historical Society Library, 201 West Monument St., 21201. Tel.: 301-685-3750.
　　—Ner Israel Rabbinical College Library, 400 Mt. Wilson Land, 21208. Tel.: 301-484-7200. (Collections of Hebrew newspapers of Europe, 1820–1937.)
　　—Archdiocese of Baltimore, Catholic Center, 320 Cathedral St., 21202. (Diocese archives)
　　—Saint Mary's Seminary and University, School of Theology Library, 5400 Roland Ave., 21210. Tel.: 301-323-3200, x 64. (Early Catholic Americana)
　　—Sojourner-Douglass College Library, 500 North Carolina St., 21205. Tel.: 301-276-0306. (African and African-American history)
　　—United Methodist Historical Society, Lovely Lane United Methodist Church Museum Library, 2200 St. Paul St., 21218. Tel.: 301-889-4458. (Methodist history, archives of Baltimore Conference, United Methodist Church)

Bowie—Bowie State College Library, Jericho Park, 20715. Tel.: 301-464-3237. (Afro-American experience, slave documents)

Cumberland—Alleghany County Library, 31 Washington St., 21502. Tel.: 301-777-1200.

Emmitsburg—Mount Saint Mary's College and Seminary Library, 21727. Tel.: 301-447-6122, x 243. (Early Catholic Americana)

Frederick—Frederick County Public Library, 110 East Patrick, 21701. Tel.: 301-694-1613.

Hagerstown—Washington County Free Library, 100 S. Potomac St., 21740. Tel.: 301-739-3250.

Leonardtown—Saint Mary's County Historical Society Library, Box 212, 20650. Tel.: 301-475-2467.

Rockville—Montgomery County Historical Society Library, 103 West Montgomery Ave., 20850. Tel.: 301-762-1492.

Worton—National Society, United States Daughters of 1812, Library, c/o President, Green Point, Rt. 1, Box 358, 21678.

MASSACHUSETTS

Numerous town libraries have genealogical and historical collections; some of those with genealogical collections are Amherst, Barnstable, Braintree, Chatham, Chelsea, Deerfield, Dracut, Great Barrington, Hinsdale, Ipswich, Kingston, Lancaster, Lawrence, Leominster, Lynnfield, Marshfield, Melrose, Newburyport, North Reading, Oxford, Palmer, Plymouth, Rockland, Salisbury, Scituate (historical society), Shrewsbury, Sudbury, Swansea, Watertown, Wenham, Westborough, Westford, and Woburn.

Beverly—Beverly Historical Society Library, 117 Cabot St., 01915. Tel.: 617-922-1186.

Boston—Boston Public Library, Copley Square, 02116. Tel.: 617-536-5400.
　　—American Congregational Association, Congregational Library, 14 Beacon St., 02108. Tel.: 617-523-0470. (Congregational church history, archives)
　　—Episcopal Diocese of Massachusetts Library and Archives, One Joy St., 02108. Tel.: 617-742-4720, x 40.
　　—Massachusetts Historical Society, 1154 Boylston St., 02215. Tel.: 617-536-1608, x 1609.
　　—Massachusetts State Archives, State House, Beacon Hill, 02133.
　　—New England Conference Historical Depository, Boston University School of Theology Library, 745 Commonwealth Ave., 02215. Tel.: 617-353-3034. (New England United Methodist records)
　　—New England Historic Genealogical Society Library, 101 Newbury St., 02116. Tel.: 617-536-5740.
　　—State Library of Massachusetts, State House, Beacon Hill, 02133. Tel.: 617-727-2590.

Brighton—Roman Catholic Archdiocese of Boston, 2121 Commonwealth Ave., 12135. Tel.: 617-254-0100, x 142. (Diocese archives & registers)

Haverhill—Haverhill Public Library, 99 Main St., 01830. Tel.: 617-373-1586 and 373-1588.

Lynn—Lynn Historical Society Museum Library, 125 Green St., 01902. Tel.: 617-592-2465.
　　—Lynn Public Library, 5 N. Common St., 01902. Tel.: 617-595-0567.

New Bedford—New Bedford Free Public Library, 613 Pleasant St., 02740. Tel.: 617-999-6291.
— Institute of Family History and Genealogy, 99 Ash St., 02740. Tel.: 617-994-4616. (Irish Genealogical Society, Italian family history, New England Family History Society)

Newton Centre—Andover Newton Theological School Library, 169 Herrick Rd., 02159. Tel.: 617-964-1100. (New England Baptist history)

Pittsfield—Berkshire Athenaeum, Pittsfield Public Library, One Wendell Ave., 01201. Tel.: 413-499-9480.

Springfield—City Library, 220 State St., 01103. Tel.: 413-739-3871. (New England and French-Canadian genealogy)
— Connecticut Valley Historical Museum Library, 194 State St., 01103. Tel.: 413-732-3080.

Taunton—Old Colony Historical Society Library, 66 Church Green, 02780. Tel.: 617-822-1622.

Waltham—American Jewish Historical Society Library, 2 Thornton Rd., 02154. Tel.: 617-891-8110.

Worcester—American Antiquarian Society Library, 185 Salisbury St., 01609. Tel.: 617-755-5221.

MICHIGAN

A number of public libraries have local history collections; some of those with genealogy collections are Belding, Carson City, Chesaning, Decatur, Deckerville, Frankenmuth, Ludington, Mayville, Mount Clemens, Ortonville, Pittsford, Sturgis, and Tawas City.

Albion—Albion College Library, 602 E Cass St., 49224. Tel.: 517-629-5511, x 285. (Western Michigan Conference, United Methodist Church Archives)

Ann Arbor—University of Michigan, Clements Library, 909 S. University Ave., 48109. Tel.: 313-764-2347.
— University of Michigan Historical Collection, Bentley Historical Library, 1150 Beal Ave., 48109. Tel.: 313-764-3482.

Detroit—Detroit Public Library, 5201 Woodward Ave., 48202. Tel.: 313-833-1000. (Michigan, Northwest Territories history and genealogy)

Flint—Genesee District Library, G-4195 West Pasadena Ave., 48504. Tel.: 313-732-0110.

Grand Rapids—Grand Rapids Public Library, 60 Library Plaza NE, 49503. Tel.: 616-456-3600.

Hancock—Finnish-American Historical Archives, Suomi College, 49930. Tel.: 906-482-5300, x 273.

Holland—Herrick Public Library, 300 River Ave., 49423. Tel.: 616-394-1400. (Dutch and local genealogy)
— Western Theological Seminary Library, 85 East 13th, 49423. Tel.: 616-392-8555. (History, Reformed Church in America)

Kalamazoo—Kalamazoo College Library, Thompson and Academy Sts., 49007. Tel.: 616-383-8499. (Michigan Baptist history)

Lansing—French-Canadian Heritage Society Library, P.O. Box 30007, 48909. Tel.: 517-485-5576.

Marquette—Marquette County Historical Society Library, 213 North Front St., 49855. Tel.: 906-226-3571.

Midland—Dow Memorial Library, 1710 W Saint Andrews Dr., 48640. Tel.: 517-835-7151.

Monroe—Monroe County Library System, 3700 S Custer Rd., 48161. Tel.: 313-241-5277.

Saginaw—Public Library of Saginaw, 505 James St., 48605. Tel.: 517-755-0904.

MINNESOTA

Other libraries with genealogy collections include Alexandria, Bovey, and historical society libraries in Anoka, Glenwood, and International Falls.

Arden Hills—Bethel Theological Seminary Library, 3949 Bethel Dr., 55112. Tel.: 612-638-6184.

Albert Lea—Freeborn County Historical Society Library, 1031 N Bridge Ave., Box 105, 56007. Tel.: 507-373-8003.

Chisholm—Iron Range Research Center, Highway 169W, P.O. Box 392, 55719. Tel.: 218-254-5733.

Hibbing—Hibbing Public Library, 2020 E. Fifth Ave., 55746. Tel.: 218-262-1038 and 262-1039.

Minneapolis—American–Swedish Institute Library, 2600 Park Ave., 55407. Tel.: 612-871-4907.
   —Minneapolis Public Library, 300 Nicollet Mall, 55401. Tel.: 612-372-6500.
   —United Methodist Church Archives and Historical Library, 122 West Franklin Ave., Room 400, 55404. Tel.: 612-870-3657.
   —University of Minnesota Library, Immigration History Research Center and Manuscript Collection, 826 Berry St., 55454. Tel.: 612-376-7271.

Northfield—St. Olaf College Library, 55057. Tel.: 507-663-3224. (Norwegian–American Historical Association collection)

Saint Cloud—Stearns County Historical Society Library, 235 33rd Ave. South, Box 702, 56302. Tel.: 612-253-8424.

St. Paul—Catholic Historical Society of St. Paul, College of St. Thomas, School of Divinity Library, 2260 Summit Ave., 55105. Tel.: 612-690-4355. (Catholicism in Minnesota and Dakotas)
   —Luther Northwestern Seminary Library, American Lutheran Church, 2375 Como Ave. W, 55108. Tel.: 612-641-3225. (Norwegian Lutheran records)
   —Minnesota Historical Society, Division of Archives and Manuscripts, 1500 Mississippi St., 55101. Tel.: 612-296-6980. (state archives)
   —Minnesota State Historical Society, 690 Cedar St., 55101. Tel.: 612-296-2150.
   —St. Paul Public Library, 90 West Fourth St., 55102. Tel.: 612-292-6311.

Winona—Winona County Historical Society Library, 160 Johnson St., 55987. Tel.: 507-454-2723.

MISSISSIPPI

A number of town libraries have local collections; some of those with genealogy collections are Cleveland, Columbia, Corinth, Greenwood, Marks, McComb, New Albany, Philadelphia, Picayune, Pontotoc, Union, and Water Valley.

Biloxi—Biloxi Public Library, 217 Lameuse St., 39530. Tel.: 601-374-0330.

Clarksdale—Carnegie Public Library, 114 Delta Ave., Box 280, 38614. Tel.: 601-624-4461.

Clinton—Mississippi College Library, Box 127, 39056. Tel.: 601-924-5131. (Mississippi Baptist Convention archives, history)
   —Mississippi Baptist Convention Board, Mississippi Baptist Historical Commission, Box 51, 39056. Tel.: 601-925-3434. (Mississippi Baptist history)

Columbus—Columbus Public Library, 314 N Seventh St., 39701. Tel.: 601-328-1056.

Gulfport—Harrison County Library System, 14th St. and 21st Ave., Box 4018, 39502. Tel.: 601-868-1383.

Hattiesburg—Hattiesburg Public Library, 723 N Main, 39401. Tel.: 601-582-4461.

Jackson—Mississippi State Department of Archives and History, 100 South State St., Box 571, 39205. Tel.: 601-359-1424, x34.
   —Reformed Theological Seminary Library, 5422 Clinton Blvd., 39209. Tel.: 601-922-4988, x252. (Southern Presbyterianism)

Meridian—Meridian Public Library, 2517 Seventh St., 39301. Tel.: 601-693-6771 and 693-4913.

Mississippi State—Mississippi State University Library, P.O. Drawer 5408, 39762. Tel.: 601-325-3060.

Pascagoula—Jackson–George Regional Library, 3214 Pascagoula St., 39567. Tel.: 601-769-3060.

Tupelo—Lee County Library, 219 Madison, 38801. Tel.: 601-841-9029.

Vicksburg—Warren County–Vicksburg Public Library, corner of Veto and Walnut, Box 511, 39180. Tel.: 601-636-6411. (Area history)

MISSOURI

A number of libraries have local history collections. Some of those with genealogy collections are Brookfield, Caruthersville, Gallatin, Harrisonville, Ironton, Jackson, Kennett, Macon, Maryville, Memphis, Mexico (historical society), Princeton, Rock Port, Salem, Shelbina, Stanberry, Troy, Unionville, and Van Buren.

Canton—Culver–Stockton College Library, College Hill, 63435. Tel.: 314-288-5221, x321. (Disciples of Christ church history)

Cape Girandeau—Cape Girandeau Public Library, 711 N Clark, 63701. Tel.: 314-334-5279.

Columbia—State Historical Society of Missouri, University Library Building, 1020 Lowry St., 65201. Tel.: 314-882-7083.

Conception—Conception Abbey and Seminary College Library, 64433. Tel.: 816-944-2211. (American Catholic history and area Catholic archives)

Fayette—Central Methodist College Library, 65248. Tel.: 816-248-3391, x271. (Missouri Methodist history)

Independence—Mid-Continent Public Library, 15616 E 24 Highway, 64050. Tel.: 816-836-5200.

Jefferson City—Missouri State Library, 2002 Missouri Blvd., Box 387, 65102.
      —Missouri State Archives, 1001 Industrial Dr., 65101; P.O. Box 778, 65102.

Kansas City—Kansas City Public Library, 311 East 12th St., 64106. Tel.: 816-221-2685.
      —Heart of America Genealogical Society Library, 311 East 12th, 64106. Tel.: 816-221-2685, x71.

Liberty—Missouri Baptist Historical Society, William Jewell College, Curry Library, 64068. Tel.: 816-781-3806. (Missouri Baptist history)

Marshall—Missouri Valley College Library, 500 E College, 65340. Tel.: 816-886-6924, x123. (Archives, Cumberland Presbyterian Church)

Springfield—Springfield–Green County Library, 397 E Central, Box 737, 65801. Tel.: 417-869-4621.

St. Louis—Christian Board of Publication, Stevenson Library, 1316 Convention Plaza, Box 179, 63166. Tel.: 314-231-8500, x254. (Disciples of Christ church history, biographies)
      —Concordia Historical Institute Library, Missouri Synod of the Lutheran Church, 801 DeMun Ave., 63105. Tel.: 314-721-5934, x320.
      —Missouri Historical Society, Jefferson Memorial Building, 63112. Tel.: 314-361-1424.
      —St. Louis Public Library, 1301 Olive St., 63103. Tel.: 314-241-2288.
      —Diocese of Missouri Archives, Episcopal Church, 1210 Locust St., 63103. Tel.: 314-231-1220.

MONTANA

A number of towns have local history and Indian history collections; Chester also has a genealogy collection.

Billings—Parmly Billings Library, 510 N Broadway, 59101. Tel.: 406-657-8257.

Bozeman—Montana State University Library, 59717. Tel.: 406-657-8257.

Glendive—Glendive Public Library, 106 S Kendrick, 59330. Tel.: 406-365-3633. (German–Russian Immigrations)

Great Falls—Great Falls Genealogical Society Library, 1400 First Ave. N, Paris Gibson Square, Room 30, 59401.

Helena—Montana Historical Society Library, 225 North Roberts, 59620. Tel.: 406-444-2681. (State archives and genealogy)
      —Montana State Library, 1515 East 6th Ave., 59620. Tel.: 406-444-3004.

Missoula—University of Montana, Mansfield Library, 59812. Tel.: 406-243-6800. (Montana history)

NEBRASKA

Other towns with genealogy collections include Broken Bow (public library and county historical society), Central City, Curtis, Minden, and Potter.

Grand Island—Grand Island Public Library, 211 N Washington, 68801. Tel.: 308-381-5333.
      —Stuhr Museum of the Prairie Pioneer, Research Library, 3133 W Highway 34, 68801. Tel.: 308-384-1380.

Hastings—Adams County Historical Society Archives, 1330 N Burlington Ave., Box 102, 68901. Tel.: 402-463-5838.

Lincoln—Historical Center of the United Methodist Church Library, Nebraska Wesleyan University, 5000 St. Paul Ave., 68504. Tel.: 402-465-2175. (United Methodist clergy and history)
—American Historical Society of Germans from Russia, Library, 615 D St., 68502. Tel.: 402-474-3363.
—Nebraska State Historical Society Library, 1500 R St., Box 82554, 68501. Tel.: 402-471-3270.

McCook—McCook Community College Library, 1205 East 3rd, 69001. Tel.: 402-345-6303.

Norfolk—Norfolk Public Library, 308 Prospect, 68701. Tel.: 402-644-8711.

NEVADA

Carson City—Nevada State Library, 401 N Carson St., Capitol Complex, 89710. Tel.: 702-885-5130.

Elko—Northeastern Nevada Historical Society Museum Research Library, 1515 Idaho St., Box 2550, 89801. Tel.: 702-738-3418. (Local history)

Las Vegas—LDS Branch Genealogy Library, 509 South 9th, 89101. Tel.: 702-382-9695.

Reno—Nevada Historical Society Museum–Research Library, 1650 N Virginia St., 89503. Tel.: 702-789-0190.
—University of Nevada Library, 89557. Tel.: 702-784-6533. (State history)

NEW HAMPSHIRE

Other libraries in the state with genealogy collections include Antrim, East Swanzey, New Castle, Plymouth, and Tilton.

Claremont—Fiske Free Library, 108 Broad St., 03743. Tel.: 603-542-4393.

Concord—New Hampshire Historical Society, 30 Park St., 03301. Tel.: 603-225-3381.
—New Hampshire State Library, 20 Park St., 03301. Tel.: 603-271-2394.

Dover—Dover Public Library, 73 Locust St., 03820. Tel.: 603-742-3513.

Hanover—Dartmouth College, Baker Memorial Library, 03755. Tel.: 603-646-2235. (State and Congregational Church history)

Keene—Keene Public Library, 60 Winter St., 03431. Tel.: 603-352-0157.

Manchester—American–Canadian Genealogical Society, Box 668, 03105. Tel.: 603-622-2883.
—City Library, Carpenter Memorial Building, 405 Pine St., 03124. Tel.: 603-624-6550.

NEW JERSEY

A number of public libraries have local history collections; some of the towns with genealogy collections are Mount Holly (county and city libraries), Glassboro (college library), and historical society libraries in Burlington, Freehold, Matawan, Salem, and Somers.

Atlantic City—Atlantic City Free Public Library, One North Tennessee Ave., 08401. Tel.: 609-345-2269.

Bridgeton—Bridgeton Free Public Library, 150 E Commerce St., 08302. Tel.: 609-455-0080.

Camden—Camden County Historical Society Library, Park Blvd. at Euclid Ave., 08103. Tel.: 609-964-3333.

Elizabeth—New Jersey Society, Sons of the American Revolution, Library, 1045 E Jersey St., 07201. Tel.: 201-355-1776.

Morristown—Joint Free Public Library of Morristown and Morris Township, New Jersey History and Genealogy Department, One Miller Rd., 07960. Tel.: 201-538-6161.

Newark—New Jersey Historical Society Library, 230 Broadway, 07140. Tel.: 201-483-3939.

New Brunswick—New Brunswick Free Public Library, 60 Livingston Ave., 08901. Tel.: 201-745-5108.
—New Brunswick Theological Seminary, Library, 21 Seminary Pl., 08901. Tel.: 201-247-5243. (Archives of Reformed Church in America)

Princeton—Historical Society of Princeton Library, 158 Nassau St., 08542. Tel.: 609-921-6748.

Trenton—New Jersey State Library, 185 West State St., 08625. Tel.: 609-292-6200.

Vineland—Historical and Antiquarian Society Library, 108 South 7th St., P.O. Box 35, 08360. Tel.: 609-691-1111.

Westfield—Westfield Memorial Library, 425 East Broad St., 07090. Tel.: 201-233-1515.

Woodbury—Gloucester County Historical Society Library, 17 Hunter St., P.O. Box 409, 08096. Tel.: 609-845-4771.

NEW MEXICO

Albuquerque—Albuquerque Public Library, 501 Copper Ave. NW, 87102. Tel.: 505-766-5100.

Carlsbad—Carlsbad Public Library, 101 S Halagueno, 88220. Tel.: 505-885-6776.

Lovington—Lovington Public Library, 103 N First, 88260. Tel.: 505-396-3144.

Portales—Portales Public Library, 218 S Avenue B, 88130. Tel.: 505-356-3940.

Roswell—Roswell Public Library, 301 N Pennsylvania Ave., 88201. Tel.: 505-622-7101.

Santa Fe—Library of the Museum of New Mexico, 110 Washington Ave., Box 2087, 87503. Tel.: 505-827-6470.
—New Mexico State Library, 325 Don Gaspar, 87503-1629. Tel.: 505-827-3800.
—New Mexico State Commission of Public Records and Archives, 404 Montezuma St., 87503. Tel.: 505-827-8860.

NEW YORK

Many public libraries and county historical societies have local history collections.

Albany—Albany Institute of History and Art, McKinney Library, 125 Washington Ave., 12210. Tel.: 518-463-4478. (Dutch in New York history, family papers)
—New York State Library, Cultural Education Center, Empire State Plaza, 12230. Tel.: 518-474-5930. (Dutch colonial records, Shaker collection, U.S. and state documents)

Auburn—Foundation Historical Association, Inc., Library, Seward House, 33 South St., 13021. Tel.: 315-252-1283.

Brooklyn—Long Island Historical Society Library, 128 Pierrepont and Clinton St., 11201. Tel.: 212-624-0890.
—World Jewish Genealogy Organization, 1533 60th St., 11219. Tel.: 718-435-7878.

Buffalo—Buffalo and Erie County Historical Society Library, 25 Nottingham Ct., 14216. Tel.: 716-873-9644.

Huntington—Huntington Historical Society Library, 209 Main St., 11743. Tel.: 516-427-7045.

New Paltz—Huguenot Historical Society Library, 88 Huguenot St., 12561. Tel.: 914-255-8445.

New York City—American Federation of Jews from Central Europe, Research Foundation for Jewish Immigration, Library, 570 Seventh Ave., 16th Floor, 10018. Tel.: 212-921-3871.
—American–Irish Historical Society Library, 991 Fifth Ave., 10028. Tel.: 212-288-2263. (Irish & Scotch–Irish in N.Y. & colonies)
—General Society, Sons of the (American) Revolution, c/o Fraunces Tavern Museum, 54 Pearl St., 10004. Tel.: 212-425-1776.
—Holland Society of New York, Library, 122 East 58th St., 10022. Tel.: 212-758-1675. (Genealogy in Dutch settlements)
—Military Ordinariate, 30 E 51st St., 10022. (vital records sent in by military Catholic chaplains, worldwide, including World War I)
—New York Genealogical and Biographical Society, 122 E 58th St., 10022. Tel.: 212-755-8532. (Also Huguenot Society, tel.: 755-0592.)
—New York Historical Society Library, 170 Central Park West, 10024. Tel.: 212-873-3400.
—Huguenot Society of America Library, 122 E 58th St., 10022. Tel.: 212-755-0592.
—New York Public Library, Genealogy Division, Fifth Ave. and 42nd St., 10018. Tel.: 212-930-0829.
—Society of Friends, New York Yearly Meeting, Haviland Records Room, 222 E 16th St., 10003. Write to 15 Rutherford Pl., New York, NY 10003.

Rochester—American Baptist Historical Society Library, 1106 South Goodman St., 14620. Tel.: 716-473-1740. (Archives of the American Baptist Convention, English Baptist history)
  —Rochester Pulic Library, 115 South Ave., 14604. Tel.: 716-428-7300.

Utica—Utica Public Library, 303 Genesee St., 13501. Tel.: 315-735-2279.

Valhalla—Westchester County Historical Society Library, 75 Grasslands Rd., 10595. Tel.: 914-592-4338.

NORTH CAROLINA

Many North Carolina county libraries have local history and genealogy collections.

Asheville—Asheville–Buncombe Library System, 67 Haywood St., 28801. Tel.: 704-252-8701.

Chapel Hill—University of North Carolina at Chapel Hill Library, 27514. Tel.: 919-962-1301.

Durham—Duke University, Perkins Library, 27706. Tel.: 919-684-2034. (Newspapers, U.S. Documents, Methodist collection)

Elon—Elon College Library, Box 187, 27244-2256. Tel.: 919-584-2338. (United Church of Christ history)

Greensboro—Greensboro Public Library, 201 N Greene St., P.O. Box X-4, 27402. Tel.: 919-373-2474.
  —Guilford College Library, 5800 West Friendly Ave., 27410. Tel.: 919-292-5511. (Genealogy, Quaker collection)

Lake Junaluska—Commission on Archives and History of the United Methodist Church, Box 488, 49 North Lakeshore Dr., 28745. (United Methodist and Evangelical United Brethren archives)

Montreat—Historical Foundation of the Presbyterian and Reformed Churches Library, Assembly Dr., P.O. Box 847, 28757. Tel.: 704-669-7061. (Presbyterian records)

Raleigh—North Carolina Division of State Library, 109 East Jones St., 27611. Tel.: 919-733-2570. (State and U.S. documents)

Wake Forest—Southeastern Baptist Theological Seminary Library, P.O. Box 752, 27587. Tel.: 919-556-3101, x 250. (Baptist history)

Winston–Salem—Moravian Church in America, Southern Province Archives and Research Library, 4 East Bank St., 27101. Tel.: 919-722-1742.
  —Forsyth County Public Library, 660 West Fifth St., 27101. Tel.: 919-727-2556.
  —Wake Forest University, Reynolds Library, P.O. Box 7777, 27109. Tel.: 919-761-5480. (Baptist history)

NORTH DAKOTA

Bismarck—State Historical Society of North Dakota, North Dakota Heritage Center, 58505. Tel.: 701-224-2668.

Fargo—North Dakota State University Library, 58105. Tel.: 701-237-8888. (North Dakota biographies and pioneer reminiscences)

Grand Forks—Grand Forks Public Library, 2110 Library Cir., 58201. Tel.: 701-772-8116.
  —University of North Dakota, Chester Fritz Library, 58202. Tel.: 701-777-2617. (North Dakota and western history)

Minot—Minot Public Library, 516 Second Ave. SW, 58701. Tel.: 701-852-1045.
  —Minot State College, Memorial Library, 58701. Tel.: 701-857-3200. (Indians of North Central states, Dakota Territory and state history)

Fort Yates—Standing Rock College Library, 58538. Tel.: 701-854-3861. (Sioux Indian collection)

OHIO

Smaller Ohio towns with library genealogical collections include Bryan, Cambridge, Bucyrus, Eaton, Gallipolis, Greenville, Jackson, Jefferson, Kenton, Lebanon (historical society), Madison, Marysville, Minerva, Norwalk, Painesville, Sidney, Tiffin, Upper Sandusky, Washington Court House, Westlake, Wooster; a number of others have local history collections.

Bluffton—Mennonite Historical Library, Musselman Library, Bluffton College, 45817. Tel.: 419-358-8015. (Mennonite & Amish history)

Canton—Malone College, Cattell Library, 515 25th St. NW, 44709. Tel.: 216-489-7393. (Quaker collection. Write the library about the availability of records to researchers.)
   —Stark County District Library, 715 Market Ave. N, 44702. Tel.: 216-452-0665.

Cincinnati—American Jewish Archives, Hebrew Union College, 3101 Clifton Ave., 45220. Tel.: 513-221-1875.
   —Public Library of Cincinnati and Hamilton County, 800 Vine St., 45202. Tel.: 513-369-6000.
   —University of Cincinnati Library, Central Library, University at Woodside, 45221. Tel.: 513-475-2218. (German–Americana & U.S. Documents)

Cleveland—Cleveland State University Library, 1860 East 22nd St., 44115. Tel.: 216-687-2486. (City and county history)
   —International Society for British Genealogy and Family History, Box 20425, 44120.
   —Western Reserve Historical Society Library, 10825 East Boulevard, 44106. Tel.: 216-721-5722. (Genealogy, Shaker history)

Columbus—Ohio Historical Society Library, I-71 & 17th Ave., 43211. Tel.: 614-297-2510.
   —State Library of Ohio, State Office Building, 65 South Front St., 43266. Tel.: 614-644-6966. (Genealogy Section)

Dayton—Wright State University Library, 7751 Col. Glenn Highway, 45435. Tel.: 513-873-2380. (Family & business papers, early records from a number of counties, includes Miami Valley Genealogical Soc. library)

Delaware—Ohio Wesleyan University Library, Beeghly Library, 43 University Ave., 43015. Tel.: 614-369-4431. (Western Ohio Methodist records)
   —Methodist Theological Seminary in Ohio Library, 3081 Columbus Pike, P.O. Box 1204, 43015. Tel.: 614-363-1146, x242. (United Methodist Church history)

Findlay—Findlay Hancock County Public Library, 206 Broadway, 45840. Tel.: 419-422-1712.

Lima—Allen County Historical Society Library, 620 W Market St., 45801. Tel.: 419-222-9426.

Mansfield—Ohio Genealogical Society Library, 419 West Third St., P.O. Box 2625, 44906. Tel.: 419-522-9077.

Marietta—Ohio Historical Society Library, Campus Martius Museum Library, 601 Second St., 45750. Tel.: 614-373-3750.
   —Washington County Public Library, 615 Fifth St., 45750. Tel.: 614-373-1057.

Massillon—Massillon Public Library, 208 Lincoln Way East, 44646. Tel.: 216-832-9831. (Early Ohio and Quaker history)

Mentor—Lake County Historical Society Library, 8610 King Memorial Rd., 44060. Tel.: 216-255-8979.
   —Library of Henry J. Grund, 4987 Corduroy Rd., Mentor Headlands, 44060. Tel.: 216-257-7490.

Middletown—Middletown Public Library, 1255 Broad St., 45044. Tel.: 513-424-1251.

Sandusky—Sandusky Library Association, 114 W Adams, 44870. Tel.: 419-625-3834.

Springfield—Clark County Historical Society Library, Box 2157, 45501. Tel.: 513-324-0657.

Toledo—Toledo Public Library, 325 Michigan St., 43624. Tel.: 419-255-7055.

Wilmington—S. Arthur Watson Library, Wilmington College, 45177. Tel.: 513-382-6661. (Quaker collection)

Youngstown—Public Library of Youngstown and Mahoning County, 305 Wick Ave., 44503. Tel.: 216-744-8636.

OKLAHOMA

Other libraries have genealogy, local history, and American Indian collections; some of those with genealogy collections are Alva, Altus (historical society), Blackwell, Cherokee, Claremore, Cushing, Hobart, Miami, Pawhuska, Poteau, Sapulpa, and Watonga.

Ardmore—Ardmore Public Library, 73401. Tel.: 405-223-8290.

Bartlesville—Bartlesville Public Library, 6th and Johnstone, 74003. Tel.: 918-337-5210.

Duncan—Duncan Public Library, 815 Ash, 73533. Tel.: 405-255-0636.

Lawton—Lawton Public Library, 110 SW Fourth St., 73501. Tel.: 405-248-6287.

Oklahoma City—Oklahoma Historical Society, Historical Building, 2100 N Lincoln Blvd., 73105. Tel.: 405-521-2491. (The major genealogy collection in the state)

Shawnee—Oklahoma Baptist University Library, 74801. Tel.: 405-275-2850, x 2256. (State Baptist history, archives)

Stillwater—Stillwater Public Library, 206 W 6th Ave. at Husband, 74074. Tel.: 405-372-3633. (Local records, county genealogical society)

Tahlequah—Cherokee National Historical Society, Inc., Library, Cherokee National Museum, TSA-LA-GI, Box 515, 74465. Tel.: 918-456-6007.

Tulsa—Rudisill North Regional Library, 1520 N Hartford, 74106. Tel.: 918-582-8654.

OREGON

Eugene—Northwest Christian College Library, 828 East 11th and Alder, 97401. Tel.: 503-343-1641.(Disciples of Christ Church history)

Klamath Falls—Klamath County Library, 126 South Third St., 97601. Tel.: 503-882-8894.

Lake Oswego—Lake Oswego Public Library, 706 Fourth St., 97034. Tel.: 503-636-7628.

Newburg—George Fox College, Shambaugh Library, 97132. Tel.: 503-538-8383. (Archives, Northwest Yearly Meeting, Society of Friends)

Portland—Oregon Historical Society Museum & Library, 1230 SW Park Ave., 97205. Tel.: 503-222-1741.
—Genealogical Forum of Oregon Library, 1410 SW Morrison St., Suite 812, 97205. Tel.: 503-227-2398.
—Western Conservative Baptist Seminary Library, 5511 SE Hawthorne.

Salem—Oregon State Library, Summer and Court Sts., 97310-0640. Tel.: 503-378-4243.
—Willamette University Library, 900 State St., 97301. Tel.: 503-370-6312. (Northwest and Methodist history)

PENNSYLVANIA

Many of the county libraries and historical societies have genealogy and local history collections.

Annville—Lebanon Valley College Library, 17003. Tel.: 717-867-6120. (Pennsylvania German collection)

Bethlehem—The Archives of the Moravian Church, 41 W Locust St., 18018. Tel.: 215-866-3255.

Birdsboro—Pennsylvania German Society Library, P.O. Box 397, 19508. Tel.: 215-582-1441.

Chester—Delaware County Historical Society Library, Widener University, 19013. Tel.: 215-874-6444.

Easton—Easton Area Public Library, 6th and Church Sts., 18042. Tel.: 215-258-2917.

Erie—Erie City and County Library, 3 South Perry Square, 16501. Tel.: 814-452-2333.

Gettysburg—Lutheran Theological Seminary Library, 66 W Confederate Ave., 17325. Tel.: 717-334-6286.

Harrisburg—Historical Society of Dauphin County, 219 S Front St., 17104. Tel.: 717-233-3462.
—Pennsylvania Historical and Museum Commission, Reference Library, 3rd and North Sts., P.O. Box 1026, 17108. Tel.: 717-783-9898.
—Pennsylvania State Library, P.O. Box 1601, Walnut St. and Commonwealth Ave., 17105. Tel.: 717-787-2646.

Haverford—Friends Historical Association, Haverford College Library, 19041. Tel.: 215-896-1175. (Quaker collection)

Indiana—Historical and Genealogical Society of Indiana County, South 6th and Wayne Ave., 15701. Tel.: 412-463-9600.

Lancaster—Archives of the Evangelical and Reformed Historical Society and of the United Church of Christ, Lancaster Theological Seminary, 555 West James St., 17603. Tel.: 717-393-0654. (Pennsylvania and nearby states)

—Lancaster Mennonite Historical Society Library, 2215 Mill Stream Rd., 17602. Tel.: 717-393-9745. (S.E. Pennsylvania, Mennonite, Amish history, genealogy)
—Lancaster County Historical Society Library, 230 N. President Ave., 17603. Tel.: 717-392-4633.

Lansdale—Mennonite Library and Archives of Eastern Pennsylvania, 1000 Forty Foot Rd., 19446. Tel.: 215-362-0304.

Lebanon—Lebanon County Historical Society, 924 Cumberland St., 17042. Tel.: 717-272-1473.

Montrose—Susquehanna County Historical Society and Free Library Association, Monument Square, 18801. Tel.: 717-278-1881 and 278-1622.

Nazareth—Moravian Historical Society, Inc., Library, 214 East Center St., mailing address: 331 East Center St., 18064. Tel.: 215-759-1530. (Moravian church records)

Philadelphia—American–Swedish Historical Museum Library, 1900 Pattison Ave., 19145. Tel.: 215-389-1776.
—Archives of the American Catholic Historical Society of Philadelphia, 263 South 4th St., P.O. Box 84, 19105. Tel.: 215-839-3760.
—Balch Institute for Ethnic Studies, Library, 18 S Seventh St., 19106. Tel.: 215-925-8090. (Archives of Scotch–Irish Society of the U.S.A.; Philadelphia Jewish archives; immigration & ethnic history)
—Genealogical Society and Historical Society of Pennsylvania, Library, 1300 Locust St., 19107. Tel.: 215-545-0391 or 732-6200.
—Germantown Historical Society Library, 5214 Germantown Ave., 19144. Tel.: 215-844-0514.
—Lutheran Theological Seminary Library, 7301 Germantown Ave., 19119. Tel.: 215-248-4616. (New Jersey, Pennsylvania Lutheran records)
—Methodist Historical Center, 326 New St., 19106. (Historical Society of Pennsylvania Annual Conference, archives, biographies)
—Philadelphia City Archives, 523 City Hall Annex, 19107. Tel.: 215-686-2249.
—United Presbyterian Church in the U.S.A., Presbyterian Historical Society Library, 425 Lombard St., 19147. Tel.: 215-627-1852. (Some archives of the United Presbyterian Church and the Library of the Scotch–Irish Society)

Pittsburgh—Carnegie Library of Pittsburgh, 4400 Forbes Ave., 15213. Tel.: 412-622-3100.
—Mount Lebanon Public Library, 16 Castle Shannon Blvd., 15228. Tel.: 412-531-1912.
—Reformed Presbyterian Theological Seminary Library, 7418 Pennsylvania Ave., 15208. Tel.: 412-731-8690. (Covenanter history)
—Western Pennsylvania Historical and Genealogical Societies, Library, 4338 Bigelow Blvd., 15213. Tel.: 412-681-5533.

Reading—Historical Society of Berks County, Library, 940 Centre Ave., 19061. Tel.: 215-375-4375.

Scranton—Lackawanna Historical Society Library, 232 Monroe Ave., 18510. Tel.: 717-344-3841.

Swarthmore—Friends Historical Library of Swarthmore College, 19081. Tel.: 215-328-8496. (Quaker meeting records, archives)

University Park—Pennsylvania State University Library, 16802. Tel.: 814-865-0401. (Some family papers, archives from area labor unions)

West Chester—Chester County Historical Society Library, 225 N High St., 19380. Tel.: 215-692-4800.

York—York County Historical Society Library, 250 E Market St., 17403. Tel.: 717-848-1587, x 25.

RHODE ISLAND

A number of libraries have local history collections; some of those with genealogy collections are Central Falls, Coventry, Foster, Johnston, Middletown, Narragansett, North Kingstown, and North Scituate.

East Greenwich—East Greenwich Free Library, 82 Pierce St., 02818. Tel.: 401-884-9511.

Kingston—University of Rhode Island, Library, 02881. Tel.: 401-792-2666. (Records of Episcopal Diocese of Rhode Island, state history, documents)

Newport—Newport Historical Society, 82 Touro St., 02840. Tel.: 401-846-0813.

Pawtucket — American-French Genealogical Society, Box 2113, 02861. Tel.: 401-769-8079.
— Pawtucket Public Library and Regional Library Center, 13 Summer St., 02860. Tel.: 401-725-3714. (Polish collection, local & state history)

Providence — Brown University, University Library (Tel.: 401-863-2167) and John Carter Brown Library (Tel.: 401-863-2725), P.O. Box 1894, 02912.
— Providence Public Library, 150 Empire St., 02903. Tel.: 401-521-7722.
— Rhode Island Historical Society Library, 121 Hope St., 02906. Tel.: 401-331-8575. (New England genealogy, archives of New England Yearly Meeting, Society of Friends)
— Rhode Island Jewish Historical Association, 130 Sessions St., 02906. Tel.: 401-331-1360. (Jewish history of Rhode Island)
— Rhode Island State Archives, State Capitol, 02903. Tel.: 401-277-2353.
— Rhode Island State Library, State House, 82 Smith St., 02903. Tel.: 401-277-2473.

Tiverton — Tiverton Library Services, 238 Highland Rd., 02878. Tel.: 401-624-8079.

Westerly — Westerly Public Library, Broad St., Box 356, 02891. Tel.: 401-596-2877.

SOUTH CAROLINA

Many city and county libraries have genealogy collections.

Charleston — Charleston County Library, 404 King St., 29403. Tel.: 803-723-1645.
— Charleston Diocese Archives, 119 Broad St., 29401. (South Carolina Catholic history, archives)
— Charleston Library Society, 164 King St., 29401. Tel.: 803-723-9912. (State history; South Carolina Jewish collection)
— South Carolina Historical Society Library, Fireproof Building, 100 Meeting St., 29401. Tel.: 803-723-3225.
— Huguenot Society of South Carolina, 94 Church St., 29401.

Columbia — South Caroliniana Library, University of South Carolina, 29208. Tel.: 803-777-3131.
— South Carolina State Library, 1500 Senate St., 29201, or P.O. Box 11469, 29211. Tel.: 803-734-8666.
— South Carolina Department of Archives and History, Capitol Station, Box 11669, 29211. Tel.: 803-734-8577.

Greenville — Furman University Library, Duke Building, Poinsett Highway, 29613. Tel.: 803-294-2191. (South Carolina Baptist archives, history)
— Greenville County Library, 300 College St., 29601. Tel.: 803-242-5000.

Greenwood — Abbeville-Greenwood Regional Library, 106 North Main St., 29646. Tel.: 803-223-4515.

Lancaster — Lancaster County Library, 313 S White St., 29720. Tel.: 803-285-1502.

Richburg — Chester District Genealogical Society Library, P.O. Box 336, 29729. Open by appointment.

Rock Hill — York County Library-Rock Hill Public Library, 138 E Black St., P.O. Box 10032. 29731. Tel.: 803-324-3055.

Spartanburg — Wofford College Library, 429 North Church St., 29301. Tel.: 803-585-4821. (South Carolina Conference of the United Methodist Church)
— Spartanburg Public Library, 333 South Pine St., P.O. Box 2409, 29302. Tel.: 803-596-3507.

SOUTH DAKOTA

Aberdeen — Aberdeen Public Library, 519 S Kline St., 57401. Tel.: 605-225-4186.

Belle Fourche — Belle Fourche Public Library, 185 E Third St., Box 237, 57717. Tel.: 605-892-4407.

Freeman — Freeman Public Library, 185 E Third St., Box 237, 57209. Tel.: 605-925-7127. (Germans in South Dakota)

Pierre — South Dakota Historical Society, Archives Resource Center, Memorial Building, 500 E. Capitol, 57501. Tel.: 605-773-3616.
— South Dakota State Library, State Library Building, 800 N Illinois, 57501. Tel.: 605-773-3131.

Sioux Falls—Augustana College Library, 57197. Tel.: 605-336-4921. (Dakota and Norwegian collections)
—North American Baptist Seminary Library, 1321 West 22nd St., 57105. Tel.: 605-336-6588. (North American Baptist Archives)

Vermillion—University of South Dakota, Weeks Library, 57069. Tel.: 605-677-5371.

TENNESSEE

Many public libraries in the state have local history & genealogy collections.

Chattanooga—Chattanooga–Hamilton County Library, 1001 Broad St., 37402. Tel.: 615-757-5310.

Columbia—Columbia State Community College, Finney Library, P.O. Box 1315, 38401. Tel.: 615-388-0120, x 234.

Johnson City—Emmanuel School of Religion Library, Route 6, P.O. Box 500, 37601. Tel.: 615-926-1186. (Church of Christ and Disciples of Christ archives, history)

Knoxville—Knoxville–Knox County Public Library, 500 West Church Ave., 37902. Tel.: 615-523-0781.

Memphis—Memphis–Shelby County Public Library, 1850 Peabody Ave., 38104. Tel.: 901-725-8855
—Memphis State University Library, Southern Ave., 38152. Tel.: 901-454-2201. (Family papers; history of lower Mississippi Valley)
—Memphis Theological Seminary Library, 168 E Parkway S, 38104. Tel.: 901-458-8232. (Cumberland Presbyterian history, archives)

Nashville—Historical Commission, SBC, Southern Baptist Historical Library & Archives, 901 Commerce, Suite 400, 37203. Tel.: 615-244-0344. (Southern Baptist history & archives)
—Public Library of Nashville and Davidson County, 8th Avenue N and Union, 37203. Tel.: 615-244-4700.
—Disciples of Christ Historical Society Library, 1101 19th Avenue S, 37212. Tel.: 615-327-1444. (Archives, history)
—Archives of the Jewish Federation of Nashville and Middle Tennessee, 801 Percy Warner Blvd., 37205. Tel.: 615-356-7170.
—Tennessee Historical Society, Tennessee State Library Building, 403 Seventh Ave. N, 37219. Tel.: 615-741-2660.
—Tennessee State Library and Archives, Tennessee State Library Building, 403 Seventh Ave. N, 37219. Tel.: 615-741-2451.

Sewanee—University of the South Library, 37375. Tel.: 615-598-5931. (Protestant Episcopal Church, Southern diocese history)

TEXAS

Many of the public libraries have local history & genealogy collections.

Austin—Texas Catholic Historical Society, Catholic Archives of Texas Library, West 16th at N Congress, P.O. Box 13327, Capitol Station, 78711. Tel.: 512-476-4888. (Texas Catholic archives, history)
—Texas State Library and Archives, 1200 Brazos St., P.O. Box 12927, Capitol Station, 78711. Tel.: 512-463-5460.
—University of Texas, Barker Texas History Center, 78712. Tel.: 512-471-5961. (Family papers, archives)
—Library and Archives of the Episcopal Church Historical Society, 606 Rathervue Pl., 78768. Tel.: 512-472-4134.

Beaumont—Beaumont Public Library, Tyrrell History Library, 695 Pearl St., 77701. Tel.: 409-838-0780.

Dallas—Bishop College Library, 3837 Simpson–Stuart Rd., 75241. Tel.: 214-372-8734. (Black Baptist church archives)
—Dallas Public Library, 1515 Young St., 75201. Tel.: 214-670-1400.
—Dallas Historical Society Research Center, Hall of State, Fair Park Station, P.O. Box 26038, 75226. Tel.: 214-421-5136.
—Methodist Historical Society, Southern Methodist University, Fondren Library, 75275. Tel.: 214-692-2323.

El Paso—El Paso Public Library, 501 N Oregon, 79901. Tel.: 915-541-4864.

Fort Worth—Fort Worth Public Library, 300 Taylor St., 76102. Tel.: 817-870-7700.
—Southwestern Baptist Theological Seminary Library, 2001 West Seminary Dr., 76115, or P.O. Box 22000-2E, 76122. Tel.: 817-923-1921. (Texas Baptist history)

Houston—Clayton Center for Genealogical Research, 5300 Caroline, 77004. Tel.: 713-524-0101.
—William Marsh Rice University, Fondren Library, 6100 Main, 77005, or P.O. Box 1892, 77251. Tel.: 713-527-8101.

Lubbock—Lubbock City–County Library, 1306 Ninth St., 79401. Tel.: 806-762-6411.

San Antonio—San Antonio Public Library, History, Social Sciences, and Genealogy Reference Division, 203 S St. Mary's, 78205. Tel.: 512-299-7813.
—Daughters of the Republic of Texas Library, Box 2599, 78299. Tel.: 512-225-1071 or 225-8155.
—San Antonio College Library, 1001 Howard St., 78284. Tel.: 512-733-2480. (Southwestern Genealogical Society)
—Episcopal Diocese of West Texas, Cathedral Library, 111 Torcido, Box 6885, 78209. Tel.: 512-824-5387.

Texarkana—See under Arkansas.

Waco—Masonic Grand Lodge of Texas AF & AM Library, 715 Columbus, P.O. Box 446, 76703. Tel.: 817-753-7395.
—Baylor University, CSB 356, 76798-0356. Tel.: 817-755-3590.
—Waco–McLennan County Library, 1717 Austin Ave., 76701. Tel.: 817-754-4694.

UTAH

Provo—Family History and Genealogical Research Center, Brigham Young University, 4500 University Hill, 84602. Tel.: 801-378-2905.

Salt Lake City—Genealogical Society of the Church of Jesus Christ of Latter-day Saints, 50 East North Temple, 84150. Tel.: 801-531-2323.
—Utah State Library, 2150 South 300 West, 84115. Tel.: 801-533-5875.
—Utah State Historical Society Library, 300 Rio Grande, 84101. Tel.: 801-533-5808.

VERMONT

A number of public libraries have local history collections.

Bennington—Bennington Museum, Genealogical Library, 05201. Tel.: 802-447-1571.

Brattleboro—Brooks Memorial Library, 224 Main St., 05301. Tel.: 802-254-5290.

Montpelier—Vermont Historical Society Library, Pavilion Building, 109 State St., 05602. Tel.: 802-828-2291. (Center for genealogical research in Vermont)

VIRGINIA

A number of public libraries and local museums have local history and genealogy collections.

Arlington—National Genealogical Society Library, 4527 17th St. N, 22207. Tel.: 703-525-0050.

Ashland—Randolph Macon College Library, Virginia Conference of the United Methodist Church Historical Society, 23005. Tel.: 804-752-7257. (Virginia Methodist records, bibliography)

Charlottesville—University of Virginia Library, 22903. Tel.: 804-924-3026. (Virginia collection and personal papers)

Harrisonburg—Eastern Mennonite College and Seminary Library, 22801-2462. Tel.: 703-433-2771. (Anabaptist/Mennonite history, genealogy, archives)

Radford—Radford University Library, 24142. Tel.: 703-831-5471. (Southwest Virginia history, archives)

Richmond—Museum of the Confederacy Library, 1201 East Clay St., 23219. Tel.: 804-649-1861. (Primary sources of the Confederacy and the South)

Richmond—Museum of the Confederacy Library, 1201 East Clay St., 23219. Tel.: 804-649-1861. (Primary sources of the Confederacy and the South)

—United Daughters of the Confederacy Library, 328 North Blvd., 23220. Tel.: 804-355-1636. (Family papers, documents)

—University of Richmond Library, 23173. Tel.: 804-289-8454. (Virginia Baptist history)

—Virginia Historical Society Library, 428 North Blvd., P.O. Box 7311, 23221. Tel.: 804-358-4901.

Williamsburg—College of William and Mary in Virginia, Swem Library, 23185. Tel.: 804-253-4408. (Fine collection of Virginia history)

Wise—Clinch Valley College of the University of Virginia, Library, 24293. Tel.: 703-328-2431, x 233. (SW Virginia archives, family papers, business papers, U.S. and state documents)

WASHINGTON

Olympia—Washington State Library, Capitol Campus, 98504. Tel.: 206-753-5590. (Its genealogical materials are in the Seattle Public Library.)

—Washington Division of Archives and Record Management, 12th and Washington, P.O. Box 9000, 98504. Tel.: 206-753-5485.

Seattle—Seattle Public Library, 1000 Fourth Avenue, 98104. Tel.: 206-386-4636.

—Seattle Genealogical Society Library, 215 Jones Bldg., 1331 Third, P.O. Box 549, 98111. Tel.: 206-682-1410.

—University of Washington Library, FM-25, 98195. Tel.: 206-543-9153. (Northwest history, manuscripts)

Spokane—Spokane Public Library, West 906 Main Ave., 99201. Tel.: 509-838-3361.

Tacoma—Tacoma Public Library, 1102 Tacoma Avenue S, 98402-2098. Tel.: 206-591-5666. (City and regional archives)

—Washington State Historical Society Library, 315 North Stadium Way, 98403. Tel.: 206-593-2830.

WEST VIRGINIA

Bethany—Bethany College Library, 26032. Tel.: 304-829-7321. (Disciples of Christ Church archives)

Buckhannon—West Virginia Wesleyan College Library, 26201. Tel.: 306-473-8000. (West Virginia Methodist history)

Charleston—West Virginia Historical Society, Cultural Center, Capitol Complex, 25305. Tel.: 304-348-0230.

—West Virginia Department of Culture and History, Archives and History Library, Science and Culture Center, State Capitol Complex, 25305. Tel.: 304-348-0230.

Fairmont—Marion County Public Library, 321 Monroe St., 26554. Tel.: 304-366-1210.

Madison—Boone-Madison Public Library, 375 Main St., 25130. Tel.: 304-369-4675. (Southern West Virginia genealogy)

Moorefield—Hardy County Public Library, 26836. Tel.: 804-538-6560.

New Martinsville—New Martinsville Public Library, 160 Washington St., 26155. Tel.: 304-485-4545.

Parkersburg—Parkersburg and Wood County Public Library, 3100 Emerson Ave., 26101. Tel.: 304-485-6564.

Princeton—Princeton Public Library, 205 Center St., 24740. Tel.: 304-425-3324.

Ripley—Jackson County Public Library, 208 N Church St., 25271. Tel.: 304-372-5343.

Wheeling—Ohio County Public Library, 52 Sixteenth St., 26003-3696. Tel.: 304-232-0244.

WISCONSIN

Beloit—Beloit Public Library, 409 Pleasant St., 53511-6279. Tel.: 608-364-6715.

Eau Claire—University of Wisconsin at Eau Claire, Library, 105 Garfield Ave., 54702. Tel.: 715-836-3715. (Native American collection, lumbering company papers, state and U.S. documents)

Green Bay—Brown County Library, 515 Pine St., 54301. Tel.: 414-497-3452.

—University of Wisconsin at Green Bay, Library, 2420 Nicolet Dr., 54301-7001. Tel.: 414-465-2333. (Area history research center, Belgian–American ethnic collection)

Janesville—Rock County Historical Society, Research Library, Ten South High, P.O. Box 896, 53547. Tel.: 608-756-4509. (Local family and business papers)

   —Seventh Day Baptist Historical Society Library, 3120 Kennedy Rd., P.O. Box 1678, 53547. Tel.: 608-752-5055. (Open by appointment)

Madison—State Historical Society of Wisconsin, Library, 816 State St., 53706. Tel.: 608-262-3421.

   —University of Wisconsin at Madison, Memorial Library, 728 State Street, 53706. Tel.: 608-262-2600. (Local history and Norwegian–American collection)

   —Vesterheim Genealogical Center, 4909 Sherwood Rd., 53711. Tel.: 608-271-8826. (Norwegian–American records)

Milwaukee—Milwaukee Public Library, Local History Room, 814 West Wisconsin Ave., 53233-2385. Tel.: 414-278-3000.

   —University of Wisconsin at Milwaukee, Library, 2311 East Hartford Ave., P.O. Box 604, 53201. Tel.: 414-963-4785. (Area research center for Wisconsin history)

Oshkosh—Oshkosh Public Library, 106 Washington Ave., 54901. Tel.: 414-236-5200.

Platteville—University of Wisconsin at Platteville Library, 725 West Main St., 53818-9989. Tel.: 608-342-1688. (Southwest Wisconsin area research center, archives)

Racine—Racine County Historical Society and Museum, Reference Library of Local History and Genealogy, 701 Main St., P.O. Box 1527, 53401. Tel.: 414-637-8585.

Superior—University of Wisconsin at Superior, Hill Library, 18th and Grand Ave., 54880. Tel.: 715-394-8343. (Regional history research center)

Whitewater—University of Wisconsin at Whitewater Library, 800 West Main St., 53190. Tel.: 414-472-1000. (Regional history research center)

WYOMING

Cheyenne—Laramie County Library System, 2800 Central Ave., 82001. Tel.: 307-634-3561.

   —Wyoming State Archives and Historical Department, Barrett Building, 22nd and Central Ave., 82002. Tel.: 307-777-7519.

   —Wyoming State Library, Supreme Court–Library Building, 82002. Tel.: 307-777-7281. (Area history and documents)

Yellowstone National Park—Yellowstone Library and Museum Association, P.O. Box 168, 82190. Tel.: 307-344-7381. (Montana Historical Society Collection)

CANADIAN LIBRARIES AND ARCHIVES

ALBERTA

Edmonton—Alberta Genealogical Society, Box 12015, Edmonton, Alberta, Canada T5J 3L2. (Branches in Brooks, Edmonton, Grande Prairie, Lethbridge, Medicine Hat, Red Deer, and Wetaskiwin.)

   —Alberta Department of Culture, History Resources Library, 12845 102nd Ave., Edmonton, Alberta, Canada, T5N 0M6.

   —Social Services and Community Health, Division of Vital Statistics, Texaco Building, 10130 112th St., Edmonton...T5K 2P2. (Provincial vital statistics)

   —The Alberta Genealogical Society, Box 3151, Station A, Edmonton...T5J 2G7.

   —The Public Archives of Alberta, 12845 102nd Ave., Edmonton...T5N 0M6.

   —City of Edmonton Archives and Library, 10105 112th Ave., Edmonton...T5J 0H1.

BRITISH COLUMBIA

Chilliwack—Chilliwack Historical Society Library, 9291 Corbould St., Chilliwack, British Columbia, Canada
     V2P 4A6.

Nanaimo—Vancouver Island Regional Library, Box 3333, Nanaimo, BC. . .V9R 5N3.

New Westminster—New Westminster Public Library, 716 Sixth Ave., New Westminster, BC. . .V3M 2B3.

Prince George—Prince George Public Library, 887 Dominion St., Prince George. . .V2L 5L1.

Richmond—The British Columbia Genealogical Society, Box 94371, Richmond. . .V6Y 1A8.

Surrey—Surrey Public Library, 14245 56th Ave., Surrey. . .V3W 1J2.

Vancouver—British Columbia Genealogical Society Library, 4397 West 2nd Ave., P.O. Box 94371, Richmond
     . . .V6Y 2A8.

Victoria—Victoria Genealogical Society, P.O. Box 4171, Station A, Victoria. . .V8X 3X8.
     —Provincial Archives of British Columbia, Northwest Collection Library, 655 Belleville, Victoria. . .
        V8V 1X4.
     —Division of Vital Statistics, British Columbia Ministry of Health, 1515 Blanshard St., Victoria. . .
        V8W 3C8.

MANITOBA

Winnipeg—Manitoba Genealogical Society Library, 420-167 Lombard Ave., Winnipeg, Manitoba, Canada
     R3B 0T6.
     —The Public Archives of Manitoba, 20 Vaughan St., Winnipeg. . .R3C 0P8.
     —Manitoba Community Services, Vital Statistics, Norquay Building, Room 104, 401 York Ave.,
        Winnipeg. . .R3C 0P8.
     —Manitoba Department of Culture, Heritage, and Recreation, Public Library Services Branch, 139
        Hamelin St., Winnipeg. . .R3T 4H4.
     —Legislative Library of Manitoba, 200 Vaughan Street, Winnipeg. . .R3C 1T5.

NEW BRUNSWICK

Fredericton—Public Archives of New Brunswick, Box 6000, Fredericton, New Brunswick, Canada E3B 5H1.
     —New Brunswick Legislative Library, Legislative Building, Box 6000, Fredericton. . .E3B 5H5.
     —The Registrar General, Department of Health, Fredericton. . .E3B 5H5.
     —University of New Brunswick Library, Box 7500, Fredericton. . .E3B 5H5.
     —York Regional Library, 4 Carleton St., Fredericton. . .E3B 5P4.

Moncton—Société Historique Acadienne, P.O. Box 2363, Station A, Moncton. . .E1C 8J3.

Newcastle—Old Manse Library, 225 Mary Street, Newcastle. . .E1V 1Z3.

St. John—New Brunswick Museum Library and Archives, 277 Douglas Ave., St. John. . .E2K 1E5.

NEWFOUNDLAND

St. John's—Newfoundland Public Library Services, Arts and Culture Center, Provincial Reference and Research
     Division, Allandale Rd., St. John's, Newfoundland, Canada A1B 3A3.
     —Public Archives of Newfoundland and Labrador, Colonial Building, Military Road, St. John's. . .
        A1C 5E2.
     —Newfoundland and Labrador Genealogical Society, Colonial Building, St. John's. . .A1C 3C7.
     —Registrar of Vital Statistics, Department of Health, Confederation Building, St. John's. . .A1C 5T7.

NORTHWEST TERRITORIES

Yellowknife—Northwest Territories Archives Branch, Government of Northwest Territories, Prince of Wales
     Building, Yellowknife, Northwest Territories, Canada X1A 2L9.
     —Registrar-General of Vital Statistics for the Northwest Territories, Box 1320, Yellowknife. . .
        X1A 2L9.

NOVA SCOTIA

Armdale—Nova Scotia Historical Society, Genealogy Committee, Box 895, Armdale, Nova Scotia, Canada B0S 1P0.

Halifax—Legislative Library of Nova Scotia, Province House, Hollis St., Halifax...B3J 2P8.
—Public Archives of Nova Scotia, 6016 University Ave., Halifax...B3H 1W4.
—The Deputy Registrar, Department of Health, Province Building, Box 157, Halifax...B3J 2M9.

Sydney—Cape Breton Regional Library, 110 Townsend, Sydney...B1P 5E1.
—College University of Cape Breton, Beaton Institute, George St., Box 5300, Sydney...B1P 6J1.

Wolfville—Acadia University Library, Acadia Street, Box D, Wolfville...B0P 1X0. (Acadia archives, Baptist history)

ONTARIO

Some of the towns with local history and/or genealogy collections are Barrie, Bradford, Chatham, Goderich, Hawkesbury, Lindsay, Owen Sound, Pt. Hope, Richmond Hill, Saint Thomas, Simcoe (Museum and Public Library), Trenton, Waterford, and Welland.

Brampton—Brampton Public Library, 65 Queen St. E, Brampton, Ontario, Canada, L6W 3L6.

Brantford—Brantford Public Library, 73 George St., Brantford...N3T 2Y3.

Cambridge—Cambridge Public Library, 20 Grand Ave. N, Cambridge...N1S 2K6.

Guelph—Guelph Public Library, 100 Norfolk St., Guelph...N1H 4J6.

Hamilton—Hamilton Public Library, 55 Main St. W, Hamilton...L8R 3K1.
—Canadian Baptist Archives, McMaster Divinity College, Hamilton...L8S 4K1.

Kingston—Archives of the Anglican Diocese of Ontario, 90 Johnson St., Kingston...K7L 1X7.
—Kingston Public Library, 130 Johnson St., Kingston...K7L 1X8.

London—London Public Libraries and Museums, 305 Queens Ave., London...N6B 3L7.
—University of Western Ontario Library, 1151 Richmond St. N, London...N6A 3K7.

Mississauga—Mississauga Public Library, 165 Dundas St. W, Suite 801, Mississauga...L5B 2N6.

Niagara Falls—Niagara Falls Public Library, 4848 Victoria Ave., Niagara Falls...L2E 4C5.

North York—North York Public Library, 35 Fairview Mall Dr., North York...M2J 4S4.

Oakville—Oakville Public Library, 120 Navy St., Oakville...L6J 2Z4.

Oshawa—Oshawa Public Library, 65 Bagot St., Oshawa...L1H 1N2.

Ottawa—Ottawa Public Library, 120 Metcalfe St., Ottawa...K1P 5M2.
—Canadian Historical Association, National Library of Canada, and Public Archives of Canada (all three institutions), 395 Wellington St., Ottawa...K1A 0N3.

Peterborough—Peterborough Public Library, 345 Aylmer St. N, Peterborough ...K9H 3V7.

St. Catharine's—St. Catharine's Historical Museum, Library and Archives, 343 Merritt St., St. Catharine's... L2T 1K7.

Toronto—Office of Registrar General, MacDonald Block, Parliament Building, Toronto...M7A 1Y5.
—Archives of Ontario Library, 77 Grenville St., Queen's Park, Toronto...M7A 2R9.
—United Empire Loyalists' Association of Canada, Library, 23 Prince Arthur Ave., Toronto...M5R 1B2.
—The United Church of Canada Archives, Victoria University, 73 Queens Park Crescent East, Toronto ...M5S 1K7.

Willowdale—Ontario Genealogical Society Library, Box 66, Station Q, Willowdale...M4T 2L7.
—Toronto Jewish Congress, Jewish Public Library, 4600 Bathurst St., Willowdale...M2R 3V3.

PRINCE EDWARD ISLAND

Charlottetown — The Prince Edward Genealogical Society, Box 902, 2 Kent St., Charlottetown, Prince Edward Island, Canada, C1A 7M4.
— Confederation Centre Public Library, Charlottetown Public Library, P.O. Box 7000, Charlotte-town...C1A 8G8.
— Director of Vital Statistics, Department of Health, Box 2000, Charlottetown...C1A 7N8.
— The Public Archives of Prince Edward, Box 1000, Charlottetown...C1A 7M4.
— Prince Edward Island Provincial Library, Enman Cres., Box 7500, Charlottetown...C1A 8T8.
— Prince Edward Island Museum and Heritage Foundation Library, 2 Kent St., Charlottetown ...C1A 1M6.

QUEBEC

Among towns which have local history and/or genealogical collections are Aylmer, Boucherville, Brossard, Lachine, Saint-Jean-Sur-Richelieu, Sept Îles, Sherbrooke, and Victoriaville.

Longueil — Bibliothèque Municipale de Longueil, 100 "O" St., Laurent, CP 5000, Longueil, Quebec, Canada, J4K 4Y7. Consult also the Grignon Branch of the Longueil Library, 1660 Bourassa, Longeuil... J7J 3A5.

Montreal — Canadian Jewish Congress, Archives, 1590 Doctor Penfield, Montreal...H3G 1C5.
Bibliothèque Publique Juive, Jewish Public Library, 5151 Ste. Catherine Rd., Montreal...H3W 1M6.

Quebec — Director of Vital Statistics, Department of Health, Demography Branch, Quebec. (Provincial vital records)

Sainte Foy — Bibliothèque des Archives Nationales du Quebec, 1210, Avenue Du Séminaire, Sainte Foy... G1V 4N1.
— Archives Nationales de Quebec, Section de Généalogie, CP 10450, Sainte Foy...G1V 4N1. (located at 1210 Avenue Du Séminaire)

SASKATCHEWAN

Moose Jaw — Palliser Regional Library, 366 Coteau Street W, P.O. Box 2500, Moose Jaw, Saskatchewan, Canada, S6H 6Y2.

Regina — Director of Vital Statistics, Department of Public Health, 3475 Albert St., Regina...S4S 6X6.
— Saskatchewan Archives Board, 3303 Hillsdale St., Regina...S4S 0A2.
— Saskatchewan Provincial Library, 1352 Winnipeg St., Regina...S4P 3V7.
— Saskatchewan Genealogical Society Library, Box 1894, Regina...S4P 3V7.

Saskatoon — Saskatoon Public Library, 311 23rd St. E, Saskatoon...S7K 0J6.

YUKON TERRITORIES

Whitehorse — Government of Yukon Libraries and Archives Branch, 2071 Second Ave., Box 2703, Whitehorse, Yukon Territory, Canada Y1A 2C6.
— Yukon Territory Registrar of Vital Statistics, Box 2703, Whitehorse...Y1A 2C6.

BRITISH ISLES

ENGLAND

Many genealogical sources, such as parish registers, wills, marriage records, deeds, apprenticeship records, manorial records, some census returns, and nonconformist (Congregational, Presbyterian, Methodist, Quaker, Catholic, etc.) registers are located in the county record offices. An excellent reference for their locations and holdings is *In Search of Your British and Irish Roots,* by Angus Baxter (New York: William Morrow and Company, Inc., 1982).

Baptist Historical Society, 4 Southampton Row, London WC1B 4AB, England.

British Library, Great Russell St., London WC1B 3DG, England (formerly British Museum)

British Newspaper Library, Colindale Ave., London NW9 5HE, England

Catholic Record Society, 5-24 Lennox Gardens, London SW1X 0DQ, England

Congregational Library, Memorial Hall, 2 Fleet Lane, London EC4, England

General Register Office, St. Catherine's House, 10 Kingsway, London, WC2B 6JB, England. (Births, deaths, marriages after 1837, England and Wales)

Greater London Records Office, County Hall, London, SE1 7PB, England.

Guildhall, Library of the Corporation of London, Aldermanbury, London EC2P 2EJ, England.

Huguenot Society, c/o Society of Genealogists, 37 Harrington Gardens, Kensington, London SW7 4JX, England.

(The) Irish Genealogical Research Society, 82 Eaton Square, London SW1, England.

Jewish Historical Society of England, 33 Seymour Place, London W1H 5AP, England.

Jewish Museum and United Synagogue Archives, Woburn House, London, England.

Lambeth Palace Library, Lambeth, London SE1 7JU, England.

Liverpool Palace Library, William Brown St., Liverpool, L38EW, England.

Manchester Central Library, St. Peter's Square, Manchester M2 5PD, England.

Methodist Archives and Research Centre, Epworth House, 25–35 City Road, London EC1, England.

Presbyterian Historical Society of England, 86 Tavistock Place, London WC1, England.

Public Record Office, Chancery Lane, London WC2A 1LR, England. (Will not do searching for a correspondent but will provide names of qualified researchers)

Public Record Office Branch, Ruskin Avenue, Kew, Richmond, Surrey TW9 4DU, England.

Religious Society of Friends, Friends House, Euston Road, London NW1 2BJ, England.

Society of Genealogists, 37 Harrington Gardens, Kensington, London SW7 4JX, England. (Can suggest sources or course of action for a search in the U.K.)

WALES

National Library of Wales, Aberystwyth, Dyfed, SY23 3BU, Wales.

SCOTLAND

Aberdeen City Libraries, Central Library, Rosemount Viaduct, Aberdeen AB9 1GU, Scotland.

Edinburgh City Archives, City Chambers, Edinburgh EH1 1Y3, Scotland

Episcopal Church in Scotland, Theological College, Rosebery Crescent, Edinburgh, Scotland.

Glasgow City Archives and Strathclyde Regional Archives, City Chambers, Glasgow G2 1DU, Scotland.

Glasgow Public Library, Mitchell Library, North St., Glasgow G3 7DN, Scotland.

General Register Office for Scotland, New Register House, Princes St., Edinburgh EH1 3YY, Scotland. (Vital records, 19th century censuses, parish registers)

National Library of Scotland, George IV Building, Edinburgh EH1 1EW, Scotland.

Orkney Library, Laing Street, Kirkwall, Orkneys, Scotland. (Archives of the Orkney Islands)

Scots Ancestry Research Society, 3 Albany St., Edinburgh EH1 3PY, Scotland.

Scottish Catholic Archives, Columba House, 16 Drummond Place, Edinburgh, EH3 6PL, Scotland.

Scottish Historical Society, c/o Department of History, University of Aberdeen, Aberdeen AB9 2UB, Scotland.

Scottish Record Office, P.O. Box 36, H. M. General Register House, Princes St., Edinburgh EH1 3YY, Scotland.

Scottish Records Association, c/o The Archivist, The University, Glasgow G12 8QQ, Scotland.

Shetland Islands Archives, Council Offices, 93 St. Olaf St., Lerwick, Shetlands, Scotland.

West Register House, Charlotte Square, Edinburgh EH2 4DF, Scotland.

Western Isles Archives, Public Library, Stornoway, Isle of Lewis, Scotland.

NORTHERN IRELAND

Belfast Library and Society for Promoting Knowledge, 17 Donegall Square North, Belfast BT1 5GD, Northern Ireland.

General Register Office, Department of Health and Social Services, Oxford House, 49–55 Chichester St., Belfast BT1 4HL, Northern Ireland (1922 to the present)

General Register Office, Joyce House, 8–11 Lombard St. East, Dublin 2, Republic of Ireland. (Vital records before 1922)

Presbyterian Historical Society, Church House, Fisherwick Place, Belfast 1, Northern Ireland.

Public Record Office for Northern Ireland, 66 Balmoral Ave., Belfast BT9 6NY, Northern Ireland.

Society of Friends Meeting House, Railway Street, Lisburn, County Antrim, Northern Ireland.

Ulster Historical Foundation, 66 Balmoral Ave., Belfast BT9 6NY, Northern Ireland.

Ulster Historical Society, Law Courts Building, Belfast, Northern Ireland.

REPUBLIC OF IRELAND (EIRE)

General Register Office, Joyce House, 8–11 Lombard St. East, Dublin 2, Eire. (Vital records, 1845 to present for Eire, 1845–1922 for Northern Ireland)

National Library of Ireland, Kildare St., Dublin 2, Eire.

National Archives of Ireland, Kildare St., Dublin 2, Eire.

Public Record Office of Ireland, Four Courts, Dublin 7, Eire.

Registry of Deeds, Henrietta St., Dublin 1, Eire.

Religious Society of Friends, House Library, 6 Eustace St., Dublin, Eire.

Representative Church Body Library, Braemor Park, Dublin 14, Eire.

Royal Irish Academy, 19 Dawson, Dublin 2, Eire.

The Genealogical Office, Dublin Castle, Dublin 2, Eire.

Trinity College Library, College St., Dublin 2, Eire.

BARBADOS

Department of Archives, Black Rock, St. Michael, Barbados, West Indies.

Registration Office, Coleridge St., Bridgetown, Barbados, West Indies.

BAHAMAS

Bahamas Public Record Office, c/o Ministry of Education and Culture, Box N3913/14, Nassau, Bahamas.

Public Library, Rawson Square, Nassau, Bahamas.

Registrar General, General Register Office, Box 532, Nassau, Bahamas (Vital records)

NATIONAL ARCHIVES

National Archives, Pennsylvania Ave. at Eighth St. NW, Washington, DC 20408. Tel.: 202-523-3130.

The Eleven Regional Branches of the National Archives

Atlanta—National Archives, Southeast Region, 1557 St. Joseph Ave., East Point, Georgia 30344. Tel.: 404-763-7477. Serving Alabama, Florida, Georgia, Kentucky, Mississippi, North Carolina, South Carolina, Tennessee.

Boston—National Archives, New England Region, 380 Trapelo Rd., Waltham, Massachusetts 02154. Tel.: 617-647-8100. Serving Connecticut, Maine, Massachusetts, New Hampshire, Rhode Island, Vermont.

Chicago—National Archives, Great Lakes Region, 7358 South Pulaski Rd., Chicago, Illinois 60629. Tel.: 312-581-7816. Serving Illinois, Indiana, Upper Michigan, Minnesota, Wisconsin.

Denver—National Archives, Rocky Mountain Region, Building 48, Denver Federal Center, P.O. Box 25307, Denver, Colorado 80225. Tel.: 303-236-0817. Serving Colorado, Montana, North Dakota, South Dakota, Utah, Wyoming.

Fort Worth—National Archives, Southwest Region, 501 West Felix, P.O. Box 6216, Fort Worth, Texas 76115. Tel.: 817-334-5525. Serving Arkansas, Louisiana, New Mexico, Oklahoma, Texas.

Kansas City—National Archives, Central Plains Region, 2312 East Bannister Rd., Kansas City, Missouri 64131. Tel.: 816-926-6272. Serving Iowa, Kansas, Missouri, Nebraska.

Los Angeles—National Archives, Pacific Southwest Region, 24000 Avila Rd., P.O. Box 6719, Laguna Niguel, California 92677. Tel.: 714-643-4241. Serving Southern California, Arizona, and Clark County, Nevada.

New York—National Archives, Northeast Region, Building 22–MOT Bayonne, Bayonne, New Jersey 07002. Tel.: 201-823-7252. Serving Lower Michigan, New Jersey, New York, Ontario Canada east of 84°, Panama Canal Zone, Puerto Rico, Virgin Islands.

Philadelphia—National Archives, Mid-Atlantic Region, 9th and Market Sts., Philadelphia, Pennsylvania 19107. Tel.: 215-597-3000. Serving Delaware, Pennsylvania, Washington DC, Maryland, Ohio, Virginia and West Virginia.

San Francisco—National Archives, Pacific Sierra Region, 1000 Commodore Dr., San Bruno, California 04066. Tel.: 415-876-9009. Serving Hawaii, Pacific Ocean area, Nevada except for Clark County, California except for southern California.

Seattle—National Archives, Pacific Northwest Region, 6125 Sand Point Way NE, Seattle, Washington 98115. Tel.: 206-526-6500. Serving Alaska, Idaho, Oregon, Washington.

TERRITORIAL AND STATE CENSUS RECORDS

General Sources for Locating State Census Records

Brown, Mary J. (comp.), *Handy Index to the Holdings of the Genealogical Society of Utah.* Logan, UT: The Everton Publishers, Inc., 1971.

Dubester, Henry J. (comp.), *State Censuses.* Washington: Library of Congress, Census Library Project, 1948.

Greene, Evarts B. and Virginia D. Harrington, *American Population Before the Federal Census of 1790.* Reprint of 1932 edition. New York, 1966.

Guide to Genealogical Research in the National Archives. Washington, DC: National Archives and Records Service, 1983.

Stemmons, John (comp.), *United States Census Compendium.* Logan, UT: The Everton Publishers, Inc., 1973.

Stevenson, Noel, *Search and Research.* Salt Lake City: Deseret Book Co., 1959.

STATE NAME — DATE OF ENTRY INTO THE UNION — SOURCE OF CENSUS

Alabama — 1819

18th century scattered censuses — Published in *Deep South Genealogical Quarterly* of the Mobile Genealogical Society, vols 1–3, 5.

1801, 1808, 1810 — Washington County and 1819 residents of northern Alabama — Published in *Alabama Genealogical Register* of Tuscaloosa, vol. 9.

1820 territorial census — State Archives, Montgomery; published by Genealogical Publishing Co., Baltimore, 1967; published by *Alabama Historical Quarterly* of the State Archives, vol. 6.

1850, 1855, 1866 state censuses — State Archives in Montgomery.

Alaska — 1959

1871 Sitka Census — Taken by U.S. War Department, printed as 42nd Congress, 1st Session, H Ex Doc 5, p. 13–26.

Arizona — 1912

1850, 1860, 1870 federal territorial censuses included Territory of New Mexico.

1860, 1864, 1866, 1867, 1869 territorial censuses — National Archives and in Department of Library and Archives, State House, Phoenix.
1866 — Pahute, Mohave, Pima, Yuma, Yavapai counties only
1867 — Mohave, Pima, Yuma counties only
1869 — Yavapai County only
1850, 1860, 1864 — printed as 89th Congress, 1st Session, S Doc 13, Serial 12668–1.

1850–1910 federal territorial censuses — National Archives.

Arkansas — 1836

1829 Sheriff's census — Arkansas History Commission, Old State House, Little Rock.

1830 federal territorial census — National Archives.

California — 1850

1852 — Office of the Secretary of State and California State Library, Sacramento, and in the DAR Library, Washington, DC.

Colorado—1876

1860 federal territorial census included with Kansas—National Archives.

1885—State and National Archives.

Connecticut—1788

17th century residents lists—Published in the *New England Historic and Genealogical Register.*

1776 census of Newington County—Josiah Willard, *A Census of Newington, Connecticut Taken According to Household in 1776.* Hartford: Frederic B. Hartranft, 1909.

Delaware—1787

17th century residents lists—E. B. O'Callaghan (comp.), *Documents Relative to The Colonial History of New York.* Albany, 1856; also in National Genealogical Society *Quarterly,* vol. 53. Ronald Vern Jackson (ed.), *Early Delaware Census Records, 1665-1697.* North Salt Lake, UT: Accelerated Indexing Systems, 1977.

None after 1790.

Florida—1845

Early residents lists in *Territorial Papers of the United States,* vols. 22-26.

1825 territorial census—National Archives and Florida State Library.

1830, 1840 federal territorial censuses—National Archives.

1855, 1885 state censuses—National Archives.

1895, 1905, 1915, 1925—Originals destroyed.

1935, 1945—Office of the Commissioner of Agriculture, Tallahassee.

Georgia—1788

Fragmentary 1824, 1831 state censuses—Georgia Department of Archives and History.

Townsend, Brigid S. (comp.), *Indexes to Seven State Census Reports for Counties in Georgia, 1838-1845.* R. J. Taylor, Jr., Foundation, c1975.

Hawaii—1959

Idaho—1890

1870, 1880 federal territorial censuses—National Archives; 1880 census copy in Idaho Historical Society; published in 1973 by Idaho Genealogical Society.

None after statehood.

Illinois—1818

1810, 1818 territorial censuses—State Archives. Also published in Margaret Cross Norton (ed.), *Illinois Census Returns, 1810 and 1818.* Collections of the Illinois Historical Library, vol. 24, c1935.

1820, 1825, 1835, 1840, 1845, 1855, 1865—State Archives; indexed through 1845, but existing records cover only scattered counties.

Indiana — 1816

1853, 1865, 1867 — Check with the county auditor of each county; some of the returns have been preserved; some have not.

Iowa — 1846

1836 — Territorial census taken under the direction of the Wisconsin Territorial government. Index published as Ronald Vern Jackson (ed.), *1836 Territorial Census of Iowa,* North Salt Lake, UT: Accelerated Indexing Systems, 1973.

1840 federal territorial census — National Archives.

1844 census of Keokuk County — National Archives.

1846 census of Louisa, Polk, and Wapello counties — National Archives.

1847, 1849, 1851, 1852, 1854, 1859, 1885, 1895, 1905, 1915, 1925 state censuses — State Archives; 1905 census closed; 1847–1859 name only heads of households.

Kansas — 1861

1855–1859, 1865, 1875, 1885, 1895, 1905, 1915, 1925 state censuses — Kansas State Historical Society, Topeka; 1855 — Willard Heiss (comp.), *The Census of the Territory of Kansas, February, 1855.* Knightstown, IN: Eastern Indiana Publishing Co., 1968.

1860 federal territorial census — National Archives.

Kentucky — 1792

According to Beverly West Hathaway, *Kentucky Genealogical Research Sources,* West Jordan, Utah: Allstates Research Company, 1974, there are no state censuses for Kentucky. Apparently the ones listed in other sources for 1803–1891 do not list heads of household by name but are statistical only.

Louisiana — 1812

Maduell, Charles R. (comp.), *The Census Tables for the French Colony of Louisiana from 1699 through 1732.* Baltimore: The Genealogical Publishing Co., 1972. From Library of Congress, microfilm copies of manuscripts in Archives des Colonies in Paris.

Robichaux, Albert J. (comp.), *Louisiana Census and Militia Lists, 1770–1789.* Harvey, Louisiana, 1973. Originals in General Archives of the Indies, Seville, Spain.

Voohies, Jacqueline K. (comp.), *Some Late 18th Century Louisianians, Census Records, 1758–1796.* University of Southwestern Louisiana, 1973.

18th century censuses of New Orleans and other areas of Louisiana have been published in the Louisiana Historical Society *Quarterly,* vols. 1–6.

1804 list of free black residents — *Territorial Papers of the United States,* vol. 9.

1810 federal territorial census — National Archives.

Other censuses were taken between 1805 and 1858, but they reportedly do not contain genealogical information.

Maine — 1820

1790 federal territorial census — National Archives.

No record exists of state censuses taken at the direction of the state.

Maryland—1788

17th century residents lists—published by Maryland Historical Society, *Archives of Maryland*, vol. 1, 5, 7, 8, 13, 20.

1710 residents—Calendar of Maryland State Papers, vol. 1, 1943.

1776, 1778, 1783–1785, 1798, 1801–1805 censuses—Hall of Records.

Massachusetts—1788

1779 census—National Genealogical Society *Quarterly*, vol. 49–51.

1855, 1865 state censuses—State archives.

Michigan—1837

Jackson, Ronald Vern (ed.), *Early Michigan Census Records, 1799, 1806, 1827.* Salt Lake City: Accelerated Indexing Systems, 1976.

1827 territorial census, which some claim is the same as the one called the 1820 territorial census, is in the Detroit Public Library and National Archives.

1837 census—check the various county courthouses.

1894, 1904 state censuses—Michigan State Library.

Check the State Archives, county courthouses, local libraries for others taken up to 1904.

Minnesota—1858

1810 census, Michilimackinac County (Mackinac)—Detroit Public Library.

1820, 1827 censuses, several counties—National Archives, Detroit Public Library.

1830, 1850 federal territorial censuses—National Archives.

1849, 1857, 1865, 1876, 1885, 1895, 1905 censuses—State Archives. Some of these also in National Archives, State Historical Society, Genealogical Society in Salt Lake City, and Minnesota State Library.

Detroit censuses between 1750 and 1810—Detroit Public Library.

Mississippi—1817

1805, 1808, 1810, 1816, 1818, 1820, 1822, 1823, 1825, 1830, 1837, 1840, 1841, 1845, 1850, 1853, 1860, 1866, 1870, 1880 state censuses—Mississippi Archives, record group 2 and 28. Scattered counties exist for 1805–1845.

1816 state census in Norman E. Gillis, *Early Inhabitants of the Natchez District*, Baton Rouge, 1963.

1831–1832, 1837, 1839, 1855, 1856, 1926–39 federal Indian censuses—Mississippi Archives.

1907, 1925–33 enumeration of Confederate soldiers and widows—Mississippi Archives record group 29.

1792, 1837 Natchez census, 1908 Centreville census, 1920 Hattiesburg census—Mississippi Archives.

1809 Madison County census—*Territorial Papers of the United States*, vol. 5.

French, English, Spanish provincial records, groups 24, 25, 26 in the Mississippi Archives.

Missouri — 1821

1840 state census — New Madrid, Newton, Pike, Randolph, Ray, Rives (later Henry), Shelby, Stoddard, and Warren counties only. Missouri State Archives.

1844 state census — Callaway County only. Missouri State Archives.

1868 state census — Cape Girardeau County only. Missouri State Archives.

1876 state census — Benton, Calloway, Cape Girardeau, Christian, Greene, Holt, Howard, McDonald, Montgomery, Osage, Phelps, Reynolds, and St. Francis counties. Missouri State Archives.

Montana — 1889

1862–63, 1864 censuses — Montana Historical Society.

1860 federal territorial census — Eastern part of Montana included in the unorganized part of Nebraska Territory. Western part of Montana included in Washington Territory. National Archives.

1870, 1880 federal territorial censuses — National Archives.

Nebraska — 1867

1854, 1855, 1856, 1865, 1869, 1870, 1874, 1875, 1876, 1877, 1878, 1879, 1880, 1882, 1883, 1884 state censuses — Nebraska Historical Society. 1854–1856 published in Evelyn M. Cox, *1854–1856 Nebraska State Censuses,* Ellensburg, Washington, 1973.

1860 federal territorial census — National Archives.

1885 state census — National Archives.

Nevada — 1864

1860 federal territorial census included in Utah Territory — National Archives.

1872 state census — Secretary of State Office, Carson City 89701.

1875 inhabitants — Nevada State Historical Society, Reno.

New Hampshire — 1788

1786 heads of families in Peterborough — *State Papers,* vol. 10.

New Jersey — 1787

1693 census of New Sweden — *Genealogical Magazine of New Jersey,* vol. 13, Genealogical Society of New Jersey, Newark.

1855, 1865, 1885, 1895, 1905, 1915 state censuses — State Library.

New Mexico — 1912

1790, 1823, 1845 censuses — published in Virginia L. Olmsted, *Spanish and Mexican Colonial Censuses of New Mexico, 1790, 1823, 1845,* Albuquerque, 1975.

1850–1910 federal territorial censuses — National Archives.

1885 state census — National Archives.

New York — 1788

An Inventory of New York State and Federal Census Records, 1825–1925, New York State Library, 1942.

Stevenson, Noel C., *Search and Research.* Salt Lake City: Deseret Book Co., 1959. County by county listing of where the state censuses of New York are: county clerks' offices, New York State Library, public and historical libraries.

1698 census, Westchester County — *New York Genealogical and Biographical Register,* vol. 38.

1814, 1825, 1835, 1845, 1855, 1865, 1875, 1892, 1905, 1915, 1925 state censuses — New York State Library has considerable records.

North Carolina — 1789

1701 residents — *National Genealogical Society Quarterly,* vol. 53.

1741–52 colonial census — *Journal of North Carolina Genealogy,* Raleigh.

1784–87 state census — State Archives.

None after 1790.

North Dakota — 1889

1850 federal territorial census included with Minnesota (Pembina County, North Dakota) — National Archives, and has been published.

1855, 1885, 1905, 1915, 1925 state censuses — State Historical Society.

1860, 1870, 1880 federal territorial censuses — National Archives, under Dakota Territory.

1900 federal census was first to designate North Dakota and South Dakota instead of simply Dakota.

Ohio — 1803

1790 reconstructed census — Indexed in *Ohio Northwest Territory 1790,* by Ronald Vern Jackson (ed.), Accelerated Indexing Systems.

1800, 1803 Washington County only — Microfilm copy in National Archives. Indexed in Ronald Vern Jackson (ed.), *Early Ohio Census Record,* Accelerated Indexing Systems, 1974.

Oklahoma — 1907

1860 federal territorial census under Arkansas — National Archives, Oklahoma Historical Society in Oklahoma City.

1890 territorial census — Oklahoma Historical Society and microfilm copy in Stillwater Public Library. Counties available: Logan, Oklahoma, Cleveland, Canadian, Kingfisher, Payne, Beaver.

1900 federal territorial census — National Archives.

1907 Seminole County census — National Archives.

Oregon — 1859

1845, 1849, 1853, 1854, 1855, 1856, 1857, 1858, 1859, 1865, 1875, 1885, 1895, 1905 territorial and state censuses of scattered counties — State Archives.

1845, 1849 territorial census — Oregon Historical Society, Portland.

1850 federal territorial census — National Archives.

Pennsylvania—1787

1693 census along the Delaware River—*Genealogical Magazine of New Jersey,* vol. 13, of the Genealogical Society of New Jersey, Newark.

1761 census of Pittsburgh—*Pennsylvania Magazine of History and Biography,* vol. 6, of the Historical Society of Pennsylvania, Philadelphia.

1779, 1786, 1793, 1800, 1807, 1814, 1828, 1842, 1849, 1863 state censuses of scattered counties—Pennsylvania State Library.

Rhode Island—1790

Various residents lists—*New England Historical and Genealogical Register.*

1747, 1774, 1782, 1865, 1875, 1885, 1895, 1905, 1915, 1925, 1935 state censuses—Rhode Island Historical Society, Providence.

1770, 1779, 1875, 1885 state censuses—State Archives.

South Carolina—1788

1829, 1839, 1869, 1875 state censuses of scattered counties—South Carolina Department of Archives and History.

No state-wide state censuses.

South Dakota—1889

1860, 1880, 1885, 1895, 1905, 1915, 1925, 1935, 1945 state censuses—South Dakota Historical Society, Pierre.

1900 federal census was first to designate North Dakota and South Dakota instead of simply Dakota.

Tennessee—1798

1770–1790 settlers on the Cumberland River—Richard Fulcher, *1770-1790 Census of the Cumberland Settlements,* Richard Fulcher, Box 21, Brentwood, TN 37027. See also Vol. 16, *Ansearchin' News* (address below).

1798 slaves and their owners—*Ansearchin' News,* Vol. 8, No. 3. Quarterly of the Tennessee Genealogical Society, P.O. Box 111249, Memphis, TN 38111.

1800 census reconstructed from tax records—Published as *Early East Tennessee Tax Payers* by Pollyanna Creekmore (comp.), Southern Historical Press, Easley, SC, 1980.

Texas—1845

1819–1826 census—National Genealogical Society *Quarterly,* vol. 45.

1829–1836 census—Texas State Archvies; Marion Day Mullins, *The First Census of Texas 1829-1836.* Washington: National Genealogical Society, 1976.

1829 (Tenaha District), 1834–1835 censuses—National Genealogical Society *Quarterly,* vol. 40–44.

1840 Republic census—published by The Pemberton Press, 1 Pemberton Parkway, Austin, 78700.

1858 state census—Barker History Center, University of Texas, Austin, in file #993, John H. Haynes papers.

Censuses were taken in 1847, 1848, and 1851 but have not been located.

Utah—1896

1850–1880 federal territorial censuses—National Archives.

1851 territorial census for scattered counties—*Utah Genealogical and Historical Magazine,* vol. 28–29, Genealogical Society of Utah. Index for 1851 census has been published: Obert, Rowene and Helen Blumhagen (eds.), *Genealogical Researchers Record Roundup,* vol. 1–2, Salt Lake City, 1968.

Vermont—1791

censuses of scattered towns—Vermont Historical Society.

Virginia—1788

17th century residents—*William and Mary Quarterly,* vol. 24; Hotten, John Camden, *The Original Lists of Persons of Quality,* New York, 1880; *New England Historical and Genealogical Register,* vol. 31; *Virginia Magazine of History and Biography,* vol. 16, of the Virginia Historical Society.

1758 residents of some counties—Hening, William W. (ed.), *Statutes at Large,* vol. 7. New York: R & W & G Bartow, 1823.

1782–1785 heads of families, used in place of missing 1790 census—published by the Bureau of the Census, Washington, 1908.

Washington—1889

1849 census, Lewis County—Oregon State Archives.

1850 census Clark County—National Archives.

1871, 1872, 1883, 1885, 1887, 1888, 1889, 1892 state censuses—Washington State Library.

West Virginia—1863

Wisconsin—1848

1820, 1830 territorial censuses under Michigan census—National Archives.

1839 residents of Southwestern Wisconsin—National Genealogical Society *Quarterly,* vol. 58.

1836, 1838, 1842, 1846, 1847, 1855, 1865, 1875, 1885, 1895, 1905 state censuses—Wisconsin State Historical Society, Madison. (1905 state census is the only one to show names of all family members, and is also in the Office of the Secretary of State, Madison.)

Wyoming—1889

1860 federal territorial census included with Nebraska—National Archives.

1860, 1870, 1880 censuses—National Archives. 1880 original in Wyoming State Archives, Cheyenne.

1905 state census—Office of the Secretary of State, Cheyenne.

1915, 1925 censuses were taken but their whereabouts are unknown.

1890 FEDERAL CENSUS

Most of the 1890 population schedules were destroyed by fire. Fragments do exist for counties in these states:

Alabama	Illinois	New Jersey	North Carolina	Texas
Georgia	Minnesota	New York	Ohio	District of Columbia

The special census of Union veterans and their widows from 1890 is available for:

District of Columbia	Minnesota	New Jersey	Oregon	Utah
Kentucky	Mississippi	New Mexico	Pennsylvania	Vermont
Louisiana	Missouri	New York	Rhode Island	Washington
Maine	Montana	North Carolina	South Carolina	West Virginia
Maryland	Nebraska	North Dakota	South Dakota	Wisconsin
Massachusetts	Nevada	Ohio	Tennessee	Wyoming
Michigan	New Hampshire	Oklahoma	Texas	

THE FIRST FEDERAL CENSUS AVAILABLE FOR EACH STATE*

Alabama	1830	Nebraska	1860
Alaska	1870	Nevada	1860
Arizona	1850	New Hampshire	1790
Arkansas	1830	New Jersey	1830
California	1850	New Mexico	1850
Colorado	1860	New York	1790
Connecticut	1790	North Carolina	1790
Delaware	1800	North Dakota	1860
District of Columbia	1790	Ohio	1820
Florida	1830	Oklahoma	1860, then 1900
Georgia	1820		1880 for Indians only
Hawaii	1900	Oregon	1850
Idaho	1870	Pennsylvania	1790
Illinois	1810	Rhode Island	1790
Indiana	1820	South Carolina	1790
Iowa	1840	South Dakota	1860
Kansas	1860	Tennessee	1820, 1810 (fragments only)
Kentucky	1810	Texas	1850
Louisiana	1810	Utah	1850
Maine	1790	Vermont	1790
Maryland	1790	Virginia	1790
Massachusetts	1790	Washington	1860
Michigan	1820	West Virginia	1870
Minnesota	1850	(part of Virginia until 1863)	
Mississippi	1820	Wisconsin	1820
Missouri	1830	Wyoming	1860
Montana	1860		

*Censuses may be missing for several reasons:
1. State or territory not yet organized.
2. Census was taken but schedule misplaced, not turned in, ruined, or destroyed.

FIVE-GENERATION CHART #_____

Compiled by _____

Address _____

b = birth date & place
m = marriage date & place
d = death date & place

See Chart #

16
17
18
19
20
21
22
23
24
25
26
27
28
29
30
31

8 b m d
9 b d
10 b m d
11 b d
12 b m d
13 b d
14 b m d
15 b d

4 b m d
5 b d
6 b m d
7 b d

2 b m d
3 b d

1
b
m
d

Spouse _____

#1 on this chart
is the same as # _____
on Chart # _____.

FAMILY RECORD OF THE _____ FAMILY

Birth date _____

Birth place _____

Death date _____

Burial place _____

Military service:

_____

Full name of husband

Birth date _____

Birth place _____

Death date _____

Burial place _____

_____

Full name of wife with maiden name

Other spouses

Marriage date _____

Place _____

#	Sex	CHILDREN Full Name	Birth Day	Mo	Year	Death Day	Mo	Year	Marriage to	Date
1										
2										
3										
4										
5										
6										
7										
8										
9										
10										
11										
12										
13										
14										
15										
16										
17										
18										

Husband (notes)

Wife (notes)

Husband's Father _____

Wife's Father _____

Husband's Mother _____

Wife's Mother _____

FAMILY RECORD OF THE _____ FAMILY

Birth date	
Birth place	
Death date	Full name of husband _____
Burial place	
Religion	His father _____
Politics	
Occupation	His mother _____
Education	

Birth date	
Birth place	
Death date	Full name of wife _____
Burial place	
Religion	Her father _____
Politics	
Occupation	Her mother _____
Education	

Other spouses (his or hers)	
	Marriage date _____
	Place _____

CHILDREN OF THIS MARRIAGE

#	Full Name	Birth	Death	Marriage
1	_____			
2	_____			
3	_____			
4	_____			
5	_____			
6	_____			
7	_____			
8	_____			

FAMILY RECORD OF THE _____ FAMILY

Birth date	
Birth place	Full name of husband
Death date	
Burial place	
Religion	Occupation
Politics	Education

Birth date	
Birth place	Full name of wife with maiden name
Death date	
Burial place	
Religion	Occupation
Politics	Education

Other spouses (his or hers)	Marriage date _____
	Place _____

CHILDREN of this marriage

#	Full Name Nickname	Birth	Death	Marriage
1	_____			
	Religion_____	Politics	Occupation	Education
2	_____			
	Religion_____	Politics	Occupation	Education
3	_____			
	Religion_____	Politics	Occupation	Education
4	_____			
	Religion_____	Politics	Occupation	Education

Husband's Father _____, Mother _____

Wife's Father _____, Mother _____

OUTLINE OF THE LIFE OF _____
name of ancestor

Note: Fill in information on marriage(s), children, education, military service,
illnesses, religious milestones, jobs, migrations, family events, deaths, etc.

YEAR	EVENT
_____	Born at _____
_____	Death. Burial place _____

CENSUS CHECK ON _____ FAMILY

Born _____ Where _____ First Census _____

Father's Name _____ Age in First Census _____

Married _____ Spouse _____ Died _____

CENSUS YEAR	COUNTIES SEARCHED / NOTES	COUNTY WHERE FOUND / NOTES	PAGE

QUICK REFERENCE — ALPHABETICAL ANCESTORS

Surname or Maiden Name	Given Name	Birth Year	Death Year	Primary Residence	Location on 5-Gen. Chart	Family Group

PROBLEM SEARCH RECORD

THE SEARCH FOR _____
name of ancestor

PROBLEM	SOURCES TO TRY / QUESTIONS TO ANSWER

1790 CENSUS

Township or Local Community _____ County _____ State _____

Enumerator _____ Date Census Taken _____ Enumerator District # _____

Page	Name of Head of Family	Free White Males 16 years & upwards including heads of families	Free White Males under 16 years	Free White Females including heads of families	All Other Free Persons	Slaves	Dwellings / Other information

1800 or 1810 CENSUS

Local Community ——————— State ———————

Enumerator ——————— Enumerator District # ———————

County ——————— Supervisor District # ———————

Date Census Taken ———————

Written Page No.	Printed Page No.	Name of Head of Family	Free White Males					Free White Females					All other free persons except Indians not taxed	Slaves
			under 10	of 10 & under 16	of 16 & under 26 *including heads of families*	of 26 & under 45 *including heads of families*	of 45 & up *including heads of families*	under 10	of 10 & under 16	of 16 & under 26 *including heads of families*	of 26 & under 45 *including heads of families*	of 45 & up *including heads of families*		

1820 CENSUS

Local Community ———— ———— County ———— State ————

Enumerator ———— Date Census Taken ———— Enumerator District # ————

Supervisor District # ————

Written Page No.	Printed Page No.	Name of Head of Family	Free White Males including heads of families						Free White Females including heads of families						Foreigners Not Naturalized	Persons engaged in Agriculture	Persons engaged in Commerce	Persons engaged in Manufacture	Free Colored Persons Males				Free Colored Persons Females				All other persons	Slaves
			to 10	10 to 16	*16 to 18	16 to 26	26 to 45	45 & up	to 10	10 to 16	16 to 26	26 to 45	45 & up					to 14	14 to 26	26 to 45	45 & up	to 14	14 to 26	26 to 45	45 & up		

* Those males between 16 & 18 will all be repeated in the column of those between 16 and 26.

1830 or 1840 CENSUS   Part 1

Local Community _____

Enumerator _____

State _____

County _____

Date Census Taken _____

Enumerator District # _____

Supervisor District # _____

Free White Persons (including heads of families)

Written Page No.	Printed Page No.	Name of Head of Family	Males													Females												
			under 5	5–10	10–15	15–20	20–30	30–40	40–50	50–60	60–70	70–80	80–90	90–100	100 & over	under 5	5–10	10–15	15–20	20–30	30–40	40–50	50–60	60–70	70–80	80–90	90–100	100 & over

1830 CENSUS   Part 2

Local Community —————

County —————

State —————

Enumerator —————

Date Census Taken —————

Enumerator District # —————

Supervisor District # —————

Written Page No.	Printed Page No.	Name of Head of Family (from previous page)					
			Slaves	Males	under 10		
					10–24		
					24–36		
					36–55		
					55–100		
					100 & up		
				Females	under 10		
					10–24		
					24–36		
					36–55		
					55–100		
					100 & up		
			Free Colored Persons	Males	under 10		
					10–24		
					24–36		
					36–55		
					55–100		
					100 & up		
				Females	under 10		
					10–24		
					24–36		
					36–55		
					55–100		
					100 & up		
					TOTAL		
			White Persons included in the foregoing who are		deaf & dumb under 14		
					deaf & dumb 14–25		
					deaf & dumb 25 & up		
					blind		
					foreigners not naturalized		
			Slaves & Colored Persons included in the foregoing who are		deaf & dumb under 14		
					deaf & dumb 14–25		
					deaf & dumb 25 & up		
					blind		

1840 CENSUS   Part 2

State _____

County _____

Enumerator District # _____

Supervisor District # _____

Local Community _____

Enumerator _____

Date Census Taken _____

Written Page No.	Printed Page No.	Name of Head of Family (Previous Page)	Free Colored Persons — Males					Free Colored Persons — Females					Slaves — Males						Slaves — Females						T O T A L	Number of Persons employed in each family in — Mining	Agriculture	Commerce	Manufacturing & Trades	Ocean Navigation	Canal, Lake, River Navigat'n	Learned Prof'ns & Engineers	Revolutionary or Military Service Pensioners in the foregoing — Name	Age
			under 10	10–24	24–36	36–55	55–100	under 10	10–24	24–36	36–55	55–100	100 & up	under 10	10–24	24–36	36–55	55–100	100 & up	under 10	10–24	24–36	36–55	55–100	100 & up										

1850 CENSUS

Post Office or
Local Community ————————

County ————————

State ————————

Enumerator ————————

Date Census Taken ————————

Enumerator District # ————————

Supervisor District # ————————

Written Page No.	Printed Page No.	Dwelling in order of visitation	Family Number in order of visitation	Name of every person whose usual place of abode on 1 June 1850 was with this family	Description			Profession, Occupation, or Trade of each Male over 15	Value of Real Estate Owned	Place of Birth naming state, territory, or country	Married within the year	In School within the year	Persons over 20 unable to read & write	If deaf & dumb, blind, insane, idiot, pauper or convict
					Age	Sex	Color							
		1	2	3	4	5	6	7	8	9	10	11	12	13

1860 CENSUS

Post Office or
Local Community ——————

Enumerator ——————

County ——————

Date Census Taken ——————

State ——————

Enumerator District # ——————

Supervisor District # ——————

Written Page No.	Printed Page No.	Dwelling Number	Family Number	Name of every person whose usual place of abode on 1 June 1860 was with this family	Description			Profession, Occupation, or Trade of each person over 15	Value of Real Estate Owned	Value of Personal Estate Owned	Place of Birth naming state, territory or country	Married within the year	In school within the year	Persons over 20 unable to read & write	Deaf & dumb, blind, insane, idiotic, pauper, or convict
					Age	Sex	Color								
	1		2	3	4	5	6	7	8	9	10	11	12	13	14

1850 or 1860 CENSUS   Schedule 2 — Slaves

Local Community ——————   County ——————   State ——————

Enumerator ——————   Date Census Taken ——————

(1850)

Written Page No.	Printed Page No.	Names of Slave Owners (1)	Number of Slaves (2)	Age (3)	Sex (4)	Color (5)	Fugitives from the State (6)	Number Manumitted (7)	Deaf & dumb, blind, insane or idiotic (8)	Number of Slave Houses (9)
					Description					
		1								
		2								
		3								
		4								
		5								
		6								
		7								
		8								
		9								
		10								
		11								
		12								
		13								
		14								

(1860)

Written Page No.	Printed Page No.	Names of Slave Owners (1)	Number of Slaves (2)	Age (3)	Sex (4)	Color (5)	Fugitives from the State (6)	Number Manumitted (7)	Deaf & dumb, blind, insane or idiotic (8)	Number of Slave Houses (9)
					Description					
		1								
		2								
		3								
		4								
		5								
		6								
		7								
		8								
		9								
		10								
		11								
		12								
		13								
		14								

1870 CENSUS

Local Community ———— County ———— State ————

Enumerator ———— Date Census Taken ———— Enumerator District # ————

Supervisor District # ————

Written Page No.	Printed Page No.	Dwelling No.	Family No.	Name of every person whose place of abode on 1 June 1870 was in this family	Description			Profession, Occupation, or Trade	Value of		Place of Birth	Parents		Month born within the year	Month married within the year	In school within the year	Cannot read	Cannot write	Deaf & dumb, blind, insane or idiotic	Males eligible to vote	Males not eligible to vote
					Age	Sex	Color		Real Estate Owned	Personal Estate Owned		Father Foreign-born	Mother Foreign-born								
		1	2	3	4	5	6	7	8	9	10	11	12	13	14	15	16	17	18	19	20

1880 CENSUS

Local Community _____ County _____ State _____

Enumerator _____ Date Census Taken _____ Supervisor District # _____

Enumerator District # _____

Written Page No.	Printed Page No.	Street Name	House Number	Dwelling Number (1)	Family Number (2)	Name of every person whose place of abode on 1 June 1880 was in this family (3)	Color (4)	Sex (5)	Age (6)	Month born if during census year (7)	Relationship to head of this household (8)	Single (9)	Married (10)	Widowed / Divorced (11)	Married during year (12)	Profession, Occupation or Trade (13)	Months unemployed this year (14)	Currently ill? If so, specify. (15)	Blind (16)	Deaf & dumb (17)	Idiotic (18)	Insane (19)	Disabled (20)	School this year (21)	Cannot read (22)	Cannot write (23)	Birthplace (24)	Birthplace of Father (25)	Birthplace of Mother (26)

Columns 4–6 are grouped under **Description**. Columns 15–20 are grouped under **Health**.

1900 CENSUS

Local Community _____

Ward _____

Enumerator _____

County _____

Date Census Taken _____

State _____

Supervisor District # _____

Enumeration District # _____

Written Page No.	Printed Page No.	Street	House Number	Dwelling Number (1)	Family Number (2)	Name of every person whose place of abode on 1 June 1900 was in this family (3)	Relationship to head of family (4)	Color (5)	Sex (6)	Birth Date Month (7)	Birth Date Year (7)	Age (8)	Marital status (9)	# Years married (10)	Mother of how many children? (11)	# of these children living (12)	Birthplace of This Person (13)	Birthplace of This Person's Father (14)	Birthplace of This Person's Mother (15)	Year of Immigration (16)	# Years in U.S. (17)	Naturalized Citizen (18)	Occupation of every person 10 & older (19)	# months not employed (20)	# months in school (21)	Can read (22)	Can write (23)	Speaks English (24)	Owned or rented (25)	Owned free of mortgage (26)	Farm or house (27)	No. of farm schedule (28)

1910 CENSUS

Local Community ———
Ward ———
Enumerator ———

County ———
Date Census Taken ———

State ———
Supervisor's District No. ———
Enumeration District No. ———

	Page No.
	Street
	House No.
1	Dwelling No.
2	Family No.
3	Name of each person whose place of abode on 15 April 1910 was in this family
4	Relationship
5	Sex
6	Color
7	Age
8	Marital Status
9	# Years — Present Marriage
10	Mother of how many children?
11	# living children
12	Birthplace of — This Person
13	Birthplace of — Father
14	Birthplace of — Mother
15	Year of Immigration
16	Naturalized or alien?
17	Speaks English? If not, give name of language.
18	Profession or Occupation & nature of business
19	Profession or Occupation & nature of business
20	Employer or Wage Earner or Working on Own Account
21	Out of work 15 April 1910?
22	# weeks out of work in 1909
23	Can read
24	Can write
25	School since 1 September 1909
26	Owned / rented
27	Owned free of mortgage
28	Farm or house
29	No. on farm schedule
30	Civil War Veteran
31	Blind
32	Deaf & dumb

Index